Reformation Europe

Here are two of the most tantalising questions in Western history: How could the Protestant Reformation take off from a tiny town in the middle of Saxony, which contemporaries regarded as a mudhole? How could a man of humble origins who was deeply scared by the devil become a charismatic leader and convince others that the Pope was the living Antichrist? Martin Luther founded a religion which up to this day determines many people's lives in intimate ways, and so did Jean Calvin in Geneva one generation later. This is the first book which uses the approaches of the new cultural history to describe how Reformation Europe came about and what it meant. It also challenges the idea that Protestantism was a more rational religion of the Word, providing a unique and lively discussion of Protestant everyday culture across Europe.

ULINKA RUBLACK is Lecturer in History at Cambridge University and Fellow of St John's College. Her previous publications include *The Crimes of Women in Early Modern Germany* (1999) and, as editor, *Gender in Early Modern German History* (2002).

NEW APPROACHES TO EUROPEAN HISTORY

Series editors
WILLIAM BEIK *Emory University*
T. C. W. BLANNING *Sidney Sussex College, Cambridge*

New Approaches to European History is an important textbook series, which provides concise but authoritative surveys of major themes and problems in European history since the Renaissance. Written at a level and length accessible to advanced school students and undergraduates, each book in the series addresses topics or themes that students of European history encounter daily: the series embraces both some of the more 'traditional' subjects of study, and those cultural and social issues to which increasing numbers of school and college courses are devoted. A particular effort is made to consider the wider international implications of the subject under scrutiny.

To aid the student reader, scholarly apparatus and annotation is light, but each work has full supplementary bibliographies and notes for further reading: where appropriate, chronologies, maps, diagrams, and other illustrative material are also provided.

For a list of titles published in the series, please see end of book.

Reformation Europe

Ulinka Rublack

Cambridge University

PUBLISHED BY THE PRESS SYNDICATE OF THE UNIVERSITY OF CAMBRIDGE
The Pitt Building, Trumpington Street, Cambridge, United Kingdom

CAMBRIDGE UNIVERSITY PRESS
The Edinburgh Building, Cambridge, CB2 2RU, UK
40 West 20th Street, New York, NY 10011–4211, USA
477 Williamstown Road, Port Melbourne, VIC 3207, Australia
Ruiz de Alarcón 13, 28014 Madrid, Spain
Dock House, The Waterfront, Cape Town 8001, South Africa

http://www.cambridge.org

First published 2005

Printed in the United Kingdom at the University Press, Cambridge

Typeface Plantin 10/12 pt.   *System* LaTeX 2$_\varepsilon$ [TB]

A catalogue record for this book is available from the British Library

Library of Congress Cataloguing in Publication data
Rublack, Ulinka.
Reformation Europe / Ulinka Rublack.
      p.   cm. – (New approaches to European history)
Includes bibliographical references and index.
ISBN 0 521 80284 9 (alk. paper) – ISBN 0 521 00369 5 (pbk. : alk. paper)
1. Reformation.   I. Title.   II. Series.
BR305.3.R83   2005   274'.06 – dc22   2004054629

ISBN 0 521 80284 9 hardback
ISBN 0 521 00369 5 paperback

Contents

Illustrations

Cover illustration: Lukas Cranach the Elder, *The Pope-Ass*, 1545, individually coloured woodcut. Reproduced by permission of the British Library.

Figures

Map

Acknowledgements

This book has been written for Bob Scribner, who originally was meant to write it, but died of cancer before being able to do so. I have also written it *for* him as a teacher whose sheer enjoyment of history, wit, imaginativeness, clarity and boldness was so wonderful to experience. The finishing of the original German manuscript was made possible through a much appreciated additional term of leave granted by the Arts and Humanities Research Council, and a slightly different version of this book has already been published as a Fischer Taschenbuch in 2003. No one could wish for a more supportive series editor than Tim Blanning, and Elizabeth Howard and Alison Powell unfailingly provided prompt advice at Cambridge University Press. I am also extremely grateful to friends and colleagues who discussed parts of the manuscript, or helped me in other ways, in particular Hans-Christoph Rublack, Francisco Bethencourt, Daniela Hacke, Scott Dixon, Mary Laven, Jack Goody, Lyndal Roper, Philip Benedict, Robin Briggs and David Lowe. Francisco I also thank for making life so unimaginably happy while I completed and translated this book in Paris, during my leave and two pregnancies, in the middle of our ever more joyous life with João and Sophie – *afinal, a melhor maniera de viajar é sentir.*

Chronology

1378–1417	Great Schism
1402	Jan Hus begins to preach at the Bethlehem church in Prague
1415	Hus is burnt in Constance
1439	Weakening of conciliar movement and reinforcement of papal power
1456	Invention of the printing press and movable metal type in the West
1466 or 1469	Birth of Erasmus
1483	Birth of Luther
1484	Birth of Zwingli
1485	Utraquism is recognised as a legal religion in Bohemia
1509	Birth of Calvin
1512	Luther takes his doctorate and begins lecturing in Wittenberg
1512–17	Fifth Lateran Council
1516	Publication of Erasmus's New Testament in Greek and an original Latin translation, challenging the approved Vulgate version
1517	Luther's ninety-five theses
1518	Zwingli begins his ministry in Zurich
1519	Election of Emperor Charles V; Leipzig disputation between Eck, Luther and Karlstadt
1520	Luther threatened with excommunication by Pope Leo X, Luther publishes three programmatic treatises, *Address to the Christian Nobility of the German Nation, A Prelude on the Babylonian Captivity of the Church* and *The Freedom of a Christian*
1521	Luther formally excommunicated; the Sorbonne judges Luther's Leipzig arguments to be wrong; meeting of the Imperial Diet in Worms; Frederick of Saxony protects

	Luther at the Wartburg, where Luther stays until March 1522, translating the New Testament
1521–5	Wide dissemination of Reformation ideas in urban and rural areas of Germany and Switzerland
1523	*Religionsgespräche* in Zurich and consolidation of the Reformation
1524	Erasmus challenges Luther in *De Libero Arbitrio*
1524–5	Peasants' War
1526	Battle of Mohács; beginning of church and school visitations in Saxony; Balthasar Hubmaier and his supporters settle in Nikolsburg
1530	Confession of Augsburg prepared by Melanchthon and presented to the Imperial Diet
1531	Death of Zwingli in the Second Kappel War; Zwingli replaced by Bullinger
1532	Reformation in Geneva
1534	Act of Supremacy in England, acknowledging Henry VIII as supreme head of the English church; first big wave of anti-Protestant prosecution in France; first complete edition of Luther's Bible translation finished; election of Pope Paul III
1534–5	Anabaptists take over Münster
1536	Death of Erasmus; first version of Calvin's *Institutio Religionis Christianae*; Gustav Vasa confiscates church property in Sweden
1536–8	Calvin's first stay in Geneva
1537	Danish church order under Christian III; re-opening of Copenhagen's university with a curriculum similar to Wittenberg's; introduction of the Reformation in Norway; Henrician Reformation introduced in Ireland
1541	Calvin begins his Reformation in Geneva; first French edition of his *Institutio Religionis Christianae*
1542	Lutheran church order in Schleswig Holstein
1544	Second wave of anti-Protestant prosecutions in France
1545	Opening of Council of Trent
1546	Death of Luther
1545–7	Smalkaldic War; death of Henry VIII of England and Francis I of France
1548	Imperial Interim
1549	*Consensus Tigurinus*; First English Prayer Book; upper Hungarian cities declare their support of Protestantism

1552	War of the Princes in Germany; second, more reform-orientated version of the *Book of Common Prayer*
1553–8	Mary Tudor attempts to re-establish Catholicism in England
1555	Peace of Augsburg; reinforcement of prosecution of Protestants in the Netherlands
1556	Charles V ends his reign
1558	Elizabeth I queen of England
1559	Academy of Geneva founded; first national synod of French Protestants; John Knox returns to Scotland; Anglican church is given shape; Christian III of Denmark dies
1559–62	*Auto de fe* against Spanish 'Protestants' in Seville and Valladolid
1560	Philip Melanchthon dies; consolidation of Scottish Reformation
1562	Massacre of Vassy; First War of Religion in France until 1563
1563	Council of Trent ends; a Reformed catechism is formulated in Heidelberg and Frederick III establishes Calvinism
1564	Death of Ferdinand I; death of Calvin and succession of Theodore Beza as moderator of the Company of Pastors
1566	Hedge preaching and iconoclasm in the Netherlands
1567	Alba reinforces prosecution of Protestants in the Netherlands
1568	Transylvanian estate assembly recognises Catholic, Lutheran, Reformed and anti-Trinitarian churches
1570	End of Protestant reform movement in Italy
1571	First Protestant church order in Sweden; Battle of Lepanto
1572	Massacre of St Bartholomew in France; Holland and Zeeland decide to fight against Spain
1575	*Confessio Bohemica* of reformed Utraquists and Bohemian Brothers
1576	Holy League of French Catholics formed
1577	German Lutherans agree on Formula of Concord
1578	Beginning of re-Catholicisation in inner Austria
1581	Declaration of Independence of northern provinces in the Netherlands; *Second Book of Discipline* in Scotland
1585	Antwerp taken by the Spanish

1589	Accession of Henry of Navarre (converts to Catholicism in 1593)
1593	Sweden commits itself clearly to Lutheranism
1598	Edict of Nantes
1603	Death of Elizabeth I of England; accession of James VI
1607	First church order in Norway
1608	Protestant Union founded in Germany
1609	Protestant League founded
1618	The Reformed Frederick V of the Palatinate elected king of Bohemia; outbreak of the Thirty Years War
1642–6	First English Civil War
1648	Peace of Westphalia; recognition of united northern provinces in the Netherlands as autonomous from Spain; Second Civil War in England
1649	30 January execution of Charles I of England and dissolution of the monarchy on 17 March

Prologue: Prophecy

In 1523, two university professors called Martin Luther and Philipp Melanchthon delivered to their Wittenberg printer a short pamphlet about two monsters. Melanchthon had written about a monster with a long, feminine body and an ass's head, Luther about a deformed calf which stood upright (see figure 1). The corpse of the ass-monster had surfaced in the Tiber in Rome in 1496; the calf had only recently been found in Saxony. Luther stated that since he was no prophet he was unable to identify providential signs. Even so, he knew that both 'gruesome figures' had been sent by God. He hoped that the end of the world was near. There had been so many signs that something had to happen. He explained that the calf with its ragged friar's clothes showed that God wanted monks and nuns to leave their convents.

Melanchthon likewise urged readers to take the signs seriously. The Roman monster had shown that the last days of the world had begun. Just as an ass's head did not fit a human body, so the Pope could never be the spiritual head of the church. The head of the church was Christ alone. Not just the head, but all parts of the monster's body bore meaning. Its left foot was like a griffon's, because the canons grabbed all the wealth of Europe for the Pope. The female belly and breast symbolised the Papacy's belly, 'that is, cardinals, bishops, priests, monks, students and such like whorish people and pigs, because their whole life consists of nothing but gobbling food, of drinking and of sex'. The monster's skin was like that of a fish: this symbolised the princes who clung to the papal order; the old man's head on the monster's buttocks signalled the decline of papal power.[1]

The 'Pope-Ass' became an icon of Protestant propaganda. In 1545 she appeared on the first of a series of ten woodcuts entitled 'A true depiction of the Papacy', directed against the papal campaign to summon a

---

[1] Phillipus Melanchthon, Doct. Martinus Luther, *Deuttung der zwu grewlichen Figuren Bapstesels zu Rom un Munckalb zu Freyberg in Meyssen funden* (Wittenberg, 1523), reprinted in *Luthers Werke*, Weimarer Ausgabe, vol. XI (Weimar, 1900), pp. 357–85.

Der Bapſteſel zu Rom

Figure 1. Lukas Cranach the Elder, *The Pope-Ass*, 1520.

church council. The monster now sported sexy legs, pointed breasts and a firm body, a depiction which symbolically linked sexualised femininity and evil (see cover illustration). This equation of the Papacy with a hybrid monster was to touch the audience's fascination with and fear of mixed categories, and a desire for clear codes of civilised male and female behaviour. Luther commented: 'This terrible image depicts what

God thinks about the Papacy. Everybody who takes it to heart should be frightened.'[2]

Through such drastic words and images, the scholars Luther and Melanchthon and the artist Cranach changed the course of history. Their attacks on the corruption and hypocrisy of the institutions of the church showed extraordinary results. Countless monasteries and convents were dissolved. Monks, nuns and priests were released from their vows of celibacy, and exhorted to marry and start families. More Europeans than ever before refused to recognise the Pope as head of their church, and sought to give new moral and spiritual meaning to Christianity in their daily lives.

Luther's notion of Christian life, however, was surprisingly strongly linked to a sense of its end. The comments on the monsters convey the reformers' and many of their followers' idea of history, which is alien to most of us nowadays. Time was marked by divine providence. Almost everything that happened was controlled by God. Hence it was a Christian's duty to learn how to interpret signs which revealed God's will and to understand true divine doctrine. The end of the world was imminent. 'Antichrist' – Christ's eternal enemy – and Satan were wielding their power in it with unprecedented fury. The Antichrist had been thrown into hell by the archangel Michael, but was to return during the last days of the world. Shockingly, Luther revealed that the Papacy and Roman church themselves were not only mistaken in their views, but that they *were* the Antichrist![3]

This critique was radical, and it radically transformed Christianity. Luther's reform movement spread from Wittenberg throughout Germany and many parts of Europe. From the middle of the sixteenth century onwards Christians were divided into Catholics and those protesting against Catholic doctrine – so-called 'Protestants'. Lutherans and Calvinists formed the most important Protestant faiths and found strong political support. Many smaller groups of believers, such as Mennonites and Quakers, established their religion during the sixteenth and seventeenth centuries, and eventually took their creed from Europe to America and other parts of the globe.

Martin Luther initially did not intend to form a new church. Like many contemporaries and most reformers after him, Luther wanted one Reformed Christian church for all. 'Reformation' aimed at improving

[2] On this series of woodcuts see R. W. Scribner, *Popular Culture and Popular Movements in Reformation Germany* (London, 1987), pp. 277–300.
[3] This theme is best explored in R. B. Barnes, *Prophecy and Gnosis. Apocalypticism in the Wake of the Lutheran Reformation* (Stanford, 1988).

existing doctrine and institutional structures from within. In addition, Luther's Reformation was about the prospect of eternal salvation. He regarded himself as a divinely sent reformer who prepared humanity for the end of the world. Instead, unwittingly, he helped to create a faith which for a long time in Western history has determined some of the most intimate aspects of many people's lives: whom they would marry, whom they would fight, what they thought of as good or evil.

Religious world-views

Beliefs in monsters or the Antichrist seem to have little to do with the perhaps more familiar image of Luther as a 'rational', enlightened reformer. But writing Reformation history means engaging with the mindset of people whose very notions of time, space and existence were generally different from ours. Consider that before Copernicus published his main book on the heavens in 1543, and often for much longer, Europeans imagined the earth to be at the centre of the cosmos. Maps showed Jerusalem as the centre of the world. By Luther's time people were hearing about the 'New World' discovered by Columbus. The reformer Bullinger nonetheless asked: 'Who cares about Indians? Who cares about the Pope?' Christian culture continued to assert its difference from other ethnicities, and often violently so. Thus, between 1450 and 1550 Jews were increasingly accused of murdering Christian boys and desecrating hosts. They were either integrated in such a way as to show the superiority of Christians, or were converted or banished. In Spain, Muslims had been converted since the end of the fifteenth century. During the sixteenth century all their customs were forbidden and Christian churches were imposed on their settlements. Finally, they were forcibly resettled and then banished altogether. Turks were mostly imagined as slaughterers of innocent Christian children and successful ruler-warriors. Western politics continually faced the problem of how to counter Ottoman advances, which made the 'Turkish danger' manifest and the end of Christianity imaginable.

Then as now Christianity gave meaning to existence by means of a mythical narrative that connected the stories of both earth and cosmos. Building on Jewish tradition, this astonishing narrative began with God's creation of the world, the living together of man and animals, the expulsion from paradise through the fall of man, the birth of a divine son by a virgin, his life, crucifixion, ascension, and the possible prospect of a similar assumption of all dead either at the end of their lives or the end of the world.

Time was structured by the extremes of sin and salvation; past, present and future could never be experienced as fully separate. There had been important prophecies about the future in the past. The acts of the Antichrist perhaps rendered them present already. Everyday behaviour either pleased or offended God and had consequences for one's eternal life. A host of unsettling questions ensued from these views. How were sins judged? Could penalties be paid on earth? How close was the end of the world?

God revealed his truth and updated his judgements on the state of the world not just through a sole prophet and 'his church', but through the Bible, cosmic signs, such as comets, and worldly signs, such as floods, miracles and visions. These notions of divine action raised persistent debates about which human beings – Popes, cardinals, saints, learned theologians or ordinary virtuous Christians – and which institutions – such as church councils or universities – were appointed to reveal God's messages.

Early modern Christianity became even more complex through its belief in a host of mighty spiritual powers. The devil was given his power by God, but he seemed also able to counter some of God's plans. Luther, for instance, imagined their fight as a cosmic chess game, in which God failed to master some of the devil's moves or had to watch how his own moves might cause damage nonetheless. Nobody knew for sure whether certain things happened because of divine or evil intervention. Belief in demonically possessed witches rapidly spread during the sixteenth century. The persecution of witches and the learned debate about how to deal with them testify to the anxieties which ensued about the workings of evil in the world. John Dee, the English scholar and astrologer, conversely conducted conversations with angels as good spirits. The Hungarian king Stephen was intrigued. Queen Elizabeth I remained sceptical.[4]

Early modern culture and existence therefore pondered the relationship between human action and the 'macro-cosmos' with utmost intensity and urgency. To what extent was human action autonomous and to what extent was it determined by God, evil powers, angels, or even the stars, fortune, luck and destiny? Could these forces be questioned and influenced in such a way that one knew how to act to avoid misfortune and fulfil one's wishes, or God's laws, in order to gain eternal life?

Along with humanism and its interest in antiquity, printed ideas and an expanded university education, the Reformation movements helped

[4] Deborah Harkness, *John Dee's Conversations with Angels: Cabala, Alchemy, and the End of Nature* (Cambridge, 1999).

to provide yet more possible answers to these problems. Many debates had been prefigured during the Middle Ages. But now they were opened more widely, led to different conclusions and resonated with contemporary social and political change. Religion, in short, was no 'opium of the people'. It had the potential to change the order of the world.

Politics

And to many it seemed as if such a change was urgently needed. The church had appeared corrupt for a long time. The Papacy constituted an important political, military and territorial power. Monasteries and bishops owned land in all of Europe, and they and the urban clergy enjoyed extensive legal rights and privileges. These were continually contested by peasants and burghers, noble families and rulers, and even by large sections of the clergy, who themselves campaigned for a poorer and purer life. France formed a national church to assert some autonomy from papal power during the fifteenth century. Spain and Portugal similarly fought for independence from Rome, their rulers preferring to nominate their own rather than papal favourites as bishops. While the powerful French, Spanish and Portuguese monarchies had thus chosen to maintain some independence from Rome within a unified Catholic church, the many different political agents in the German-speaking lands could not agree to form a national church.

A simple reason why Luther's movement found initial political support in Germany and finally led to the formation of a new church rests in the 'polycentric' structure of that strange political entity, the 'Holy Roman Empire of the German Nation'. The make-up of this Empire can be sketched as follows. It mainly consisted of territories governed by a prince or by a bishop who simultaneously acted as secular prince, and of cities which were not ruled by princes. Around 1500, several 'free', Imperial cities of the South, like Augsburg and Nuremberg, were important centres of trade, while the northern Hanse cities, such as Hamburg and Lübeck, once more grew in importance as the North Atlantic trade took off around 1600. Representatives of free Imperial cities and territorial lords decided collectively about common concerns, while the Emperor was elected and his powers negotiated by a body of princes.[5]

Since 1440, only members of the house of Habsburg had been elected as Emperors, and they turned into a strange species of 'elected hereditary' rulers. Their hereditary lands were mainly in Austria. German

---

[5] An excellent introduction in English is Peter H. Wilson, *The Holy Roman Empire 1495–1806* (Basingstoke, 1999).

princes thus avoided electing one of their own as Emperor, who then might have been able to extend his power over other German territories. They opted for a foreign power, and, after each voting prince had been substantially bribed, for a family whose increasingly manifold possessions seemed to guarantee financial resources and a restricted interest in German politics.

Ideally then, the Imperial constitution served the interest of all major political powers in Germany by ensuring as much protection and as much autonomy from the Emperor as possible. The Reformation movements made religious choice part of these complex political attempts to secure power and liberty. The Habsburgs remained Catholics. But as soon as it became clear that a number of princes would support the Reformation, a new era of religious politics between different confessions, an era of confessional politics therefore, began in Germany. This is not to say that, here as elsewhere, German powers decided on religious matters purely on political grounds. Closer analysis shows that some decisions were motivated by deep piety and others by interest in political gains, while most decisions were based on motives which escape our neat modern distinction between religion and politics. The acknowledged objective of politics was to honour God and install a 'truly' Christian order. The question was what constituted such an order.

Thus, in 1525 common people revolted in many parts of Germany to fight for their vision of a just and godly society. But they were quickly quietened – no true reformation from below was allowed to take place – 'godly authorities', magistrates and princes were to decide. And yet they themselves violently disagreed. In 1555, after two short wars between the Emperor, supported by German Catholics and Protestant forces, the Peace of Augsburg stipulated that each ruler should determine the faith in his or her territory, a decision later summarised by the formula *cuius regio, eius religio*, whose rule it is, whose religion it is. The Swiss Confederation had already been divided into Catholic and Reformed towns and regions since 1529. How would German Catholics and Protestants cooperate to conduct Imperial politics? For it was only after 1555 that three main confessions consolidated their Reformed institutions and doctrinal hold on the population: Lutheranism, Catholicism, with its renewed fervour after the Council of Trent (1545–63), and Calvinism, which emerged as the second mainstream Protestant faith and awaited its recognition by Imperial law. As Calvinism spread, the whole of Europe was undergoing dramatic changes. In France, the Netherlands, Scotland, Hungary and Poland, Reformed preaching attracted substantial parts of the population, and in England a Protestant culture became ingrained during Elizabeth I's reign. The increasingly fragile period of cooperation among the German political powers and the further spreading of different faiths and allied power interests in Europe ended in the Thirty Years War.

The Thirty Years War (1618–48) was the longest and most extensive war over religion and power ever fought in Europe. The peace that was finally achieved affirmed much of the 1555 settlement for the German lands.[6] The Holy Roman Empire continued to have no unified confession and thus no unified imperialist military goals. Calvinism was legitimised. The rights of religious minorities in the different territories were extended. Protestant and Catholic Imperial Estates were once more prepared to seek compromises in the interest of a 'reason of state'. The principles of federal cooperation were thus strengthened within the parameters which had been agreed in the late fifteenth century. German politics needed common instruments to keep the peace and uphold justice. The political forces financed institutions such as an Imperial Chamber Court. They continued trying to maintain independence from the Habsburgs in so far as it was useful and possible. Until the rise of Prussia as an overarching Protestant power within Germany after 1740 and the final unification of Germany in 1871, all governmental problems, such as the financial poverty of small territories or the ambitions of larger territories, were handled within this political framework and – remarkably – by representatives adhering to three Christian confessions.

Interpretations

When Leopold von Ranke began modern historical writing about the Protestant Reformation in the nineteenth century, he was fired by the vision he was witnessing of the rise of Prussia. Here was the historical chance to get rid of backward Catholicism, and to create a politically unified, strong, united Protestant state. Protestant history was thus interlinked with political concerns about German nationhood. To a surprising extent it has always remained so. Later generations, of course, followed different visions. For Marxist historians in the German Democratic Republic, the Reformation marked a national loss of any critical spirit towards authority, especially during the Peasants' War and through the alleged affirmation of princely authority and traditional social hierarchies by Lutheranism. Other historians have argued that the early 1520s represented a unique opportunity for a 'republican turn' in German

---

[6] An outstanding overview and analysis available in English is Ronald Asch, *The Thirty Years' War. The Holy Roman Empire and Europe, 1618–1648* (Basingstoke, 1997).

politics.[7] Current mainstream interpretations favour the liberal idea that the Reformation furthered the federative constitution and positive pluralism which distinguish Germany today.[8] More radical historians assert that the Reformation and its contribution to a federal political structure saved Germany from the problematic consequences of the large European nation-states: absolutist power structures, aggressive warfare, empire-building and aggressive capitalism.[9]

What has changed since Ranke, too, is that Protestantism is no longer seen as a more 'modern' religion than Reformed Catholicism. It is recognised that renewed Catholicism made substantial efforts to teach people Christian doctrine, fight their 'superstitions' and discipline their behaviour.[10] In addition, there are now more attempts to integrate what we know about different national Reformations into a synthesis charting what the Reformations meant for Europe as a whole. This clearly means emphasising that both Protestant and Catholic reform movements catalysed a series of crucial historical debates that have since shaped Western thought. They involved arguments for the freedom of opinion, for more participation in religious and political decision-making and the right of resistance against authority. They could even question the superiority of Christians over New World 'savages': French Protestants living around 1557 in Guanabana Bay in Brazil, for instance, saw no difference between cannibals and those who imagined they absorbed Christ's body with the host. Arguments of such a kind were further developed during the Enlightenment to support general religious tolerance and the further separation of state and confessional politics. All early modern men and women who voiced their views in these debates, only a minority of them intellectuals, played a part in this historical process of opinion formation.[11]

In spite of these heated debates, from the sixteenth century onwards Europeans had to face the fact that Western Christianity was divided

---

[7] This viewpoint is most strongly expressed by Peter Blickle, see, for instance, his *Die Reformation im Reich*, 3rd edn (Stuttgart, 2000).

[8] Most prominently Georg Schmidt, *Geschichte des Alten Reichs. Staat und Nation in der Frühen Neuzeit 1495–1806* (Munich, 1999).

[9] Thomas A. Brady Jr., *The Politics of the Reformation in Germany: Jacob Sturm (1489–1553) of Strasbourg* (Atlantic Highlands, 1997), p. 250.

[10] For a summary see R. Po-Chia Hsia, *The World of the Catholic Renewal 1540–1770* (Cambridge, 1998).

[11] The classic overview in English on the history of ideas relating to religion and resistance is Quentin Skinner, *Foundations of Modern Political Thought*, vol. II (Cambridge, 1978); an important case study of how issues of tolerance occupied women and men in their daily lives is provided by Dagmar Freist, One Body, Two Confessions: Mixed Marriages in Germany, in Ulinka Rublack (ed.), *Gender in Early Modern German History* (Cambridge, 2002), pp. 275–304.

and that completely different notions of what constituted a true religion coexisted among them. Opposing truth claims were dissected again and again. Over the centuries, the analytical tools which thus developed critically to assess truth claims and the sheer necessity for many people of dealing with different institutionalised religions day-by-day have contributed to our contemporary familiarity with a relativist world-view which no longer assumes the priority of any particular world religion.

Reformation history thus can no longer be plausibly written from a partisan perspective. Sociological and anthropological approaches have powerfully changed recent historiography. They suggest, above all, posing anew two simple questions: how did Luther and Calvin, who seem so strange to us in many respects nowadays, manage to gain any influence at all? What did their new religious 'truths' mean for people in their everyday lives?

In answering these questions this book proposes two arguments. First, that the success of Lutheranism and Calvinism can be analysed only by restoring to Wittenberg and Geneva a sense of place and personality. Luther and Calvin were not successful because people were waiting to hear their brilliant doctrine and only needed to hear the truth. They were successful because they found themselves in specific places with specific institutions and resources, and worked together with particular people in specific ways (chs. 1 and 3). They need to be portrayed not just as towering individual figures, but as highly able team-workers, group leaders and managers of human and institutional resources. Specific psychologies attached to how they built up and maintained their charisma, and both reformers helped to prepare their mythical memory among their supporters in Wittenberg and Geneva during their lives. It was, perhaps, less the uniqueness of their ideas than the much more mundane ways in which the reformers managed their movements in and from Wittenberg and Geneva which explains their success as founders of religious cults. This is why we need to begin to *locate* their work properly (see Epilogue).

Second, Protestant identities which developed in sixteenth- and seventeenth-century Europe do not fit the image of a more 'modern' religion. These identities need to be understood in their own terms and time: as post-Reformation Protestantism (ch. 4). Protestantism in no way clearly contributed to a rationalisation of belief-systems and a 'disenchantment of the world' from 'magical-sensual' elements, as the sociologist Max Weber argued and as many people nowadays assume.[12] On the contrary, it might be historically more accurate to talk about

---

[12] Max Weber (trans. Talcott Parsons), *The Protestant Ethics and the Spirit of Capitalism* (New York, 1958), p. 105.

a Protestant 'super-enchantment' of the early modern world until *c.* 1650, because Protestantism lent such prominence to ideas about the Antichrist, devil, providence and eternity. Its focus on the 'Word' does not turn early modern Protestantism into a 'logo-centric' religion either. We need to ask what meanings were given to 'the Word' at the time, that is, which symbolic cultural practices were connected to the experience of hearing, speaking, singing or being silent, to writing and reading. Word-related practices were strongly imbued with sensual and emotional qualities. Certainly, prayer and psalm singing became more important than devotion of images, but no one would seriously maintain that this implies a more 'rational' relationship with the divine. We also need to recognise that religion is not defined by a fixed set of beliefs and ideas; it rests on their diverse social interpretation. We therefore need to know about the appropriation of ideas among noble families, artisans, and the marginal – men and women, young people and the old, town people and country folk, people in one village and another, in one region or country and another – for all these people, the records tell us, made religion work for themselves in different ways.

Early modern people perceived the senses in peculiar ways, and they also seem to differ from us nowadays so much because they experienced the world through manifestations of cosmic power and because damnation and salvation were so important for them. Hence notions of time were strongly spiritualised. In successive chapters this book engages with this part of people's mentalities by drawing attention to contemporary notions of prophecies and providence, and even to the role of clocks and calendars. It is high time, then, to turn to Martin Luther.

1   Martin Luther's truth

The story of how Martin Luther turned into a man who changed world history is as strange as it is fascinating. Luther was born in 1483.[1] His father Hans was a small upwardly mobile mine owner from a peasant background in a tiny east German town. His mother Margareta came from a wealthier peasant family. Both parents wanted their talented son to study law and to enjoy a respectable and profitable career. Martin was aged twenty-two when he rebelled against these plans. One day he escaped a lightning stroke by calling on St Anna. In gratitude, he entered the Augustine monastery in Erfurt. He detested any legal notion that there might be coexisting viewpoints which might be equally right. There had to be one truth, to be found in God. Dissatisfied with the state of the existing church and its doctrines, he decided to discover for himself what this truth might be.

Luther shared his frustrations with many contemporaries. He lived in an age in which people vigorously debated how to live a Christian life and how to define the proper rights of the church. Both lay and clerical reform initiatives had long been under way in different parts of Europe. From 1380 onwards, for instance, men and women from artisan and merchant families in the Netherlands and northern Germany had been forming hundreds of communities. These Sisters and Brethren of the Common Life tried to live simply and spiritually, outside convent walls and earning their own living. Towards eastern Europe, in the early fifteenth century, the reform preacher Jan Hus took up the idea of the Englishman John Wyclif that the king and the nobility should reform the church, returning it to a truly spiritual life, and deprive it of all secular dominion and property. Hus found much popular support from a broad social spectrum. Many monasteries were no longer given donations. Wealthy citizens spent less on elaborate funeral rites and more on gifts for the poor. The movement was highly active and articulate. In 1412, for instance, there were large

---

[1] Martin Brecht, *Martin Luther*, transl. James L. Schaaf, 3 vols. (Minneapolis, 1985–93) is the most reliable and detailed guide on the reformer's life.

street demonstrations in Prague. At one of them, a person had been dressed up as a prostitute riding a horse. Mass bells were tied to her body and papal edicts around her bare breasts.[2] Having reached the seat of the king and archbishop, the demonstrators shouted against indulgences. Hus was burnt as a heretic at the church Council of Constance in 1415 and subsequently became a martyr for those committed to radical church reforms.

Indulgences were sold by the church in order to counterbalance the weight of sins for which souls suffered in purgatory, and this to many seemed such a bluntly self-interested way of toying with religious anxiety that critics all over Europe began to discuss the issue. In 1482, Parisian scholars sarcastically commented: 'As soon as the coin in the coffer rings/ The soul from purgatory springs', and this phrase soon circulated in several languages. Around the same time, no fewer than 10,000 German peasants attacked the Prince-bishop of Speyer. They rhymed: 'If anyone asks what's going on: With these clerics the world will always be wrong.' All over Europe, critical voices multiplied. In Florence, Girolamo Savonarola could be heard preaching in 1497: 'You used to be embarrassed about vanity and voluptuousness; now, whorish church, you are no longer.' He predicted divine punishments for Rome and the whole of Italy. Many envisaged more communal power over church affairs. Thus, in 1513, the Cologne guilds demanded that clerical privileges should be abolished and priests be elected communally to teach the 'pure biblical word'. Three years later, in 1516, the leading humanist Desiderius Erasmus published a translation of the New Testament from the Greek and voiced strong concerns about the accuracy of the official Latin Bible, the Vulgate. The election of every new Pope led people to hope for institutional reforms and more thorough clerical learning.

Despite all these protests, demands and concerns, few doubted the Pope's role as head of the church and the necessity for the clergy as fundamentally as Luther did after 1517. By now he was calling for the dissolution of all monasteries and the 'priesthood' of all believers. Luther's positions had become radicalised when he had taken a public stance against the indulgence trade in 1517 and written ninety-five theses defending his arguments. A Dominican preacher called Johann Tetzel had particularly enraged him and others, because it seemed as if everyone could be absolved for everything and thus 'God was no longer God, as he had bestowed all divine power on the Pope.' 'Christians', Luther declared with characteristic force in one of his ninety-five theses, 'should be taught

---

[2] See Thomas A. Fudge, *The Magnificent Ride: The First Reformation in Hussite Bohemia* (Aldershot, 1998).

that if the Pope knew the exactions of the preachers of indulgences, he would rather have the basilica of St Peter reduced to ashes than built with the skin, flesh and bones of his sheep'.[3] But what remained of Luther's confidence in Popes soon waned. In 1518, he explained his theses to Leo X and challenged papal infallibility. Leo summoned Luther to Rome and then instructed his legate, Cardinal Cajetan, to confront Luther at Augsburg and possibly to arrest him. Luther told Cajetan upfront that only faith in the Word of Christ and his grace would prepare people for death and salvation. Faith in works instead of the Word led to nothing. As Rome demanded his release and Leo asserted the church's teaching on indulgences, Luther formed his views that the Papacy could not claim to be head of the church by divine right and that the indulgence trade proved that the Pope was the Antichrist.

Luther now saw himself in the middle of a cosmic fight between God and Satan.[4] Having left the Erfurt monastery, he had become a provincial theology professor in Wittenberg, who was presumptuously telling people what the Bible really said and denouncing the Papacy and church as 'born of the devil'. The drama was intensified by the fact that Luther, following the Augustinian tradition of his order, regarded men as completely depraved descendants of Adam and Eve. He saw no trace of a 'good' human nature. Redemption was completely dependent on God's grace and Christian belief. God had promised his grace and salvation through the crucifixion of his own son. Only through believing in this one truth – the redeeming, biblical truth which Luther had recognised through his exegesis of Paul – could one live until the longed-for end of the world.

These ideas endowed Luther and his supporters with an extraordinary sense of mission. In December 1520, for instance, Wittenberg students gathering in front of the town church read the following announcement by the Greek scholar Philip Melanchthon, who had become Luther's most important follower:

All those who support the biblical truth are hereby told to come to the Holy Cross church outside the city walls at 9 a.m. All godless papal constitutions and the writing of the scholastics will be burned following an old apostolic custom. The enemies of the Bible want to burn Luther's pious and biblical writing. Gather quickly, devout students, and take part in this sacred act which pleases God! Perhaps the time has come for the Antichrist to reveal himself.[5]

---

[3] Translated and quoted in an excellent English collection of sources: Pamela Johnston and Bob Scribner (eds.), *The Reformation in Germany and Switzerland* (Cambridge, 1993), p. 13.

[4] This aspect is well brought out in Heiko A. Oberman, *Luther: Man between God and the Devil* (New Haven and London, 1989).

[5] Quoted in Ruth Kastner, *Quellen zur Reformation 1517–1555* (Darmstadt, 1994), p. 110.

Wittenberg was a small town mostly made up of humble houses. The river Elbe connected it to Hamburg, Magdeburg, Dresden and Prague, but the trade route from Frankfurt to Poland passed it by. Luther had built up strong support within the university and radicalised the students in specifically early modern ways. Thus, immediately after the burning of the Canon law, the works of Aristotle and some scholastic writers that Melanchthon had called for, about one hundred students gathered for a carnival procession. Musicians played. Some students dressed up as professors and the Pope. The sail of their carnival float was a giant papal bull. Students piled up books by Luther's enemies and collected firewood along the way. They processed to the town centre where books were thrown into a new fire. Hymns were sung. The next morning, Luther told his lecture audience in German that it was necessary to burn the papal seat. Those unable to distance themselves from papal power would not be saved. The students, who soon were to become clerics and officials, had to risk their temporal lives – or else lose their eternal lives. These students' lecture notes let us glimpse how Luther could act as nothing less than a spiritual demagogue.

But not all of those who were interested in Luther's messages followed him without doubts. One of Luther's Lübeck students wrote that even the 'enemies of the gospel' admitted that they had heard not a man 'but a spirit' in his lectures. Luther could not 'teach such astonishing things' through his own abilities alone, but must be influenced by a good or a bad spirit. Melanchthon, several Wittenberg professors of mathematics, and Catholic astrologers all analysed the constellation of stars and planets at Luther's birth. In 1520, a Swiss organist reported that the reception of one of Luther's most successful treatises *For the Christian Nobility of the German Nation* caused great surprise: 'Some think, the devil speaks from these pages, others think the Holy Ghost.' How, then, did Luther manage to convince people that he was influenced by a good spirit and win a larger audience and enduring trust? How did Lutheranism manage to become a church rather than a sect?

In 1921, the sociologist Max Weber described the charisma of those who successfully manage to claim that a higher spirit has been revealed to them as the 'great revolutionary power' in traditional societies.[6] Luther's example bears this out. Five aspects were crucial for this process. First, Luther became an outstanding theologian, preacher, debater, speaker, writer and translator. He was in effect an early modern 'media-man', that is to say, someone who knew how to harness the possibilities opened up by the relatively new medium of print to his cause. Second, Luther identified with several role models: saints (St Martin), prophets

[6] Max Weber, *Wirtschaft und Gesellschaft* (Tübingen, 1956), pp. 181f.

(Elias, Daniel), biblical commentators (St Paul, the Apostles) and the Bohemian reformer Jan Hus. This relativised the novelty of his teaching, legitimised his actions for many of those who were already critically minded and at least implicitly served to demand similar devotion in his diverse audiences. He was adept in commenting on all major contemporary issues, most prominently indulgences and the meaning of the biblical Word, but also many social and economic issues. He offered himself as a role model for those hoping for change. Third, between 1519 and 1521, while a papal commission prepared the case against him and before his meeting with the new Emperor Charles V in Worms, on which many placed their hopes for church reforms in German lands, Luther directly addressed those involved in Imperial politics. He presented his cause as a key moment in the battle for German sovereignty against Rome, and he used all the jargon of German liberty and honour which characterised a fervent patriotic rhetoric among noblemen, knights, princes and humanists. Fourth, Luther developed a theological doctrine which integrated elements from different spiritual and intellectual traditions, such as medieval mysticism and Renaissance humanism. By doing so, he again appealed to a diversity of audiences. He integrated these elements in such a way that they led to a new, surprising and consoling religious experience for all those who would seek salvation through faith in God's grace alone. The final aspect, which, it is argued here, proved decisive for the initial success of the movement, was Luther's basis in Wittenberg. For truth depends on how ideas become true for people at specific places; it has its own social history. Hence, we need to identify how Luther worked in Wittenberg, how its local structures help to explain the success of the Lutheran movement and how he disseminated his ideas from there.[7]

The student Reformation: Wittenberg as Jerusalem

What did Wittenberg consist of? As a map drawn in 1546 shows, it was a place with about ten streets between three gates.[8] The town centre was situated between a castle in the west and an Augustinian monastery in the east. The duke resided in the castle; the monastery was Luther's home. Next to the monastery lived Melanchthon, in a house which the town council built for him in 1536. The town hall, market square and town church formed the town centre: they were the secular and spiritual

---

[7] This approach has been inspired by Steven Shapin, *A Social History of Truth. Civility and Science in Seventeenth Century England* (Chicago, 1994) and Steven Shapin and Simon Schaffer, *Leviathan and the Air-Pump. Hobbes, Boyle, and the Experimental Life* (Princeton, 1985).

[8] See in particular Helmut Junghans, *Wittenberg als Lutherstadt* (Berlin, 1979).

centres of communal life. At the South Gate, situated between the market square and the castle, the rich court artist and pharmacist Lucas Cranach had built the largest house in town in 1512 – a Renaissance building with eighty-four rooms and fourteen kitchens for his workers and visitors. There was no gate to the north of town, because the area was too swampy for a road, but a modest Franciscan monastery stood there. It added to the short list of religious buildings: the castle chapel, the town church, the Augustinian monastery, a small chapel of the order of St Anthony to the west and the All Saints Foundation. Wittenberg citizens were mostly artisans who served the local market. Art and printing became the only export businesses. Fishermen lived outside the town. Including these suburbs, Wittenberg numbered 400 houses and 2,000 inhabitants. Compared to Strasburg with its 20,000 inhabitants, or Cologne and Nuremberg each with 40,000, it really was a marginal place (figure 2).

How could the Reformation take off from this town? Its very smallness helped. Compared to other towns, far fewer civic institutions and interest groups needed to be integrated into the Reformation movement. But Wittenberg was also much more than a small orderly German burgher-town, since it had its new university. Its history reveals how early sixteenth-century Wittenberg was restructured by its duke, Frederick the Wise, an enigmatic and complex man.

In 1485, Saxony was divided between two brothers, Ernst and Albrecht. Ernestine Saxony retained the *Kurwürde*, the electoral status which conferred a voting right at Imperial Diets. But its main town, Wittenberg, was regarded as a 'poor, dirty town'. Ernst's son Frederick (1463–1525), ruled from 1486. From 1495 onwards he attended all Imperial Diets and developed his role as an influential Imperial politician. In Wittenberg he employed the best artists, Albrecht Dürer among them, to decorate his late-Gothic castle. In 1505, he attracted the up-and-coming artist Lukas Cranach to his court from Vienna, and began commissioning precious metalwork from renowned Augsburg artists and the local goldsmith Döring. He cultivated contacts with humanists and with the powerful city of Nuremberg. He collected books, and, more passionately, relics. Once a year all relics were put on show and Frederick successfully lobbied the Pope to grant indulgences to visitors. In 1502, Frederick founded the university in Wittenberg; it received its statutes in 1508. The university library was located in the castle, managed by a young humanist called Georg Spalt. The castle chapel doubled as the university church. In 1502, the Augustinians settled in Wittenberg, too, and were welcomed by Frederick as they funded professorships and offered lecture rooms. The monastery was a reform congregation; its thirty monks and twenty visitors from as far as the Netherlands studied there.

Figure 2. Hieronymus Nützel, *View of Wittenberg*, 1591. The drawing of Wittenberg's street in the 1540s is no longer extant. This engraving from the end of the century wishes to represent a grand town, attractive for students, long after Luther's death. To the left we see the castle; the town church stands in the middle, and to the right (I) we see the Augustinian monastery, which had been inhabited by Luther, his family, students and guests. Also to the right, next to the river, we see how Wittenberg catered for sixteenth-century students' leisure pursuits, such as nude swimming, bowling and walking.

All this was to make the court and town important, and to entice young noblemen, the sons of bourgeois officials, eager monks, promising academics and wealthy travellers to redirect their horses from the road to Poland to the mud-holes on the smaller track to Wittenberg. In 1521, even the town hall was completely rebuilt. Five years earlier, Cranach had designed and possibly painted a mural of the Ten Commandments for it, vividly depicting the Devil and Death. Cranach himself sat on the council, and had negotiated that only he was authorised to deal with medicines and spices in Wittenberg. The goldsmith Döring was also a councillor. The main poles of influence in this town were thus formed by the duke and those he patronised: the town council, the town church, the university and the Augustinian monastery. Strikingly, most institutions and many buildings in Wittenberg were new, rebuilt or being rebuilt. No traditions hindered innovation. Wittenberg could emerge as a place reborn. Within the first ten years of the sixteenth century, a new elite developed. Lukas Cranach was the richest man and eventually became Wittenberg's mayor. The duke's secretary, Georg Spalt, was promoted as a promising humanist. He translated all of Frederick's speeches and letters into eloquent Latin and some of Erasmus's writings from Latin into German. Finally, there was a small group of university professors who built their own town houses. This, too, was a new trend. Most medieval professors had belonged to an order.

Thus, the town soon acquired new status. Flocking to it were the pious, who wanted to see Frederick's relics, Dutch Augustinians and international academics, and students from Nuremberg, northern and eastern Germany and eastern Europe. Artisan painters, carpenters, builder journeymen and printer journeymen also swelled the flourishing trades. But clearly Frederick's fame as well as his and Wittenberg's wealth rested on the new university. It brought in fees, and money was spent on rents, furniture, servants, food, drink, music, clothes, books, bookbinders, bathhouses, brothels, smiths and candle-makers.

The culture of academic knowledge

The duke needed to attract students. Wittenberg, however, was one of an already dense web of eastern and middle European universities: Prague (founded in 1348), Erfurt (1392), Leipzig (1409) and Frankfurt an der Oder (1506). Language and confession were not yet barriers – Latin was spoken everywhere, and academics with a doctoral degree could lecture everywhere.

Thus, in 1502, a man called Andreas Meinhard, who later became Wittenberg's city-scribe, was commissioned to write a booklet advertising the advantages of studying in Wittenberg.[9] It described Frederick's art collection, most of which students presumably never saw. It described in similar detail the relic collection, which they saw once a year. All this was to demonstrate that they would study under a powerful and pious Christian prince. The collections also raised curiosity, as they included a rib of St Rupert, tissue from the blood-stained cloth in which Christ had been crucified, a bit of the stone on which Jesus had cried, and some of Mary's milk.

The fictional conversation conducted in this brochure between Meinhard, who had settled in Wittenberg from humanist Cracow, and the student Reinhard, who initially had only intended to pass through Wittenberg on his way to Cologne, described what was academically exciting about Wittenberg's divinity school before Luther arrived:

M: A Magister of a foreign university is going to talk in a disputation.
R: Is all of the university going to assemble on this occasion?
M: Everybody knows how rare this is. Few are going to be absent.
R: How many questions is the Magister going to treat?
M: Three questions and six axioms, from which he is going to draw sixty-eight conclusions.
R: That really makes for a very wide thematic range.
M: A confused and, in my opinion, very difficult one.
R: Which teaching is the Magister going to follow?
M: I am not sure.
R: Which method contains more truth, that of St Thomas, or that of that clever man Duns Scotus?
M: Both methods are equally well founded and argued for.

Even though it did not intend to criticise scholasticism, this dialogue reveals why so many academics and their patrons were ready to admit a new culture of knowing. Scholasticism cultivated sharp, logical argumentativeness, but it often seemed to lead to entangled methodological discussions for their own sake. They all turned on methods of rationally justifying religious beliefs and their systematic representation, which was based on Aristotle's philosophy. The Dominican Duns Scotus and the Franciscan Thomas Aquinas were the two exponents of this tradition and of a 'realist' dispute about how to *organise* knowledge about universals. They were confronted time and again. No convincing resolution seemed to be in sight, or even desired.

---

[9] Andreas Meinhard, *Über die Lage, die Schönheit und den Ruhm der hochberühmten, herrlichen Stadt Albioris, gemeinhin Wittenberg genannt: ein Dialog, herausgegeben für diejenigen, die ihre Lehrzeit in den edlen Wissenschaften beginnen* (Leipzig, 1986), pp. 223f.

Luther's transformation

In 1512, Luther had become a 'sworn doctor of the Bible' in Wittenberg. One year later he began lecturing in biblical studies. Until now, his career had been promising, but not brilliant. He had abandoned his law degree in an age when men of distinction often held joint degrees in law and theology. He had studied neither at the prestigious universities in northern Italy nor at the Parisian Sorbonne. Nobody thought of him as a young genius who possessed outstanding abilities and talents. He was thirty years old when he began lecturing, and still unpublished. Even so, his order valued him highly, and he had cultivated close contacts with the Augustinian monastery and university over several years.

Around 1516, Luther's intellectual values changed. He accepted humanist criticisms of Aristotle and scholastic methods, accusing scholastics and traditional theologians of simply embroiling themselves in logical thought, of being fixated on Aquinas and Scotus, of ignorance of the Bible and church fathers such as Augustine, and of inability to relate knowledge to life. Luther's own thought had been shaped since his Erfurt days by a rich 'nominalist' tradition based on Augustine that had developed during the Middle Ages. It addressed fundamental questions about the nature of salvation, grace and human sinfulness. Apart from Augustine he valued St Paul most highly. St Paul was a man of change, which is how Luther increasingly came to think of himself.

Luther, the searcher, had become a man with a mission. He sent his colleague Nikolaus von Amsdorf a bound copy of Augustine, and begged him to stop studying logicians and philosophers. Von Amsdorf soon admitted having been 'seduced' by scholasticism. Luther affirmed that theology could no longer be just about scholarly debates; man's eternal life and the true life on earth were at stake. In 1517, his colleague Andreas Karlstadt, who was three years older than Luther as well as highly ambitious and productive, was similarly convinced that scholasticism had failed to accommodate Augustine. He immediately campaigned for this insight. Other colleagues agreed to remove Aristotle almost completely from the lecture programme. Aristotle was regarded as holding the view that human beings could become virtuous only through their deeds and that they could attain knowledge and self-knowledge through reason. Luther disagreed strongly. For him, both scholasticism and humanism trusted human reason far too much.

Soon, the university reforms began.[10] Luther influenced appointments to strengthen the coherence of what he wanted to be taught in

---

[10] See Walter Friedensburg, *Geschichte der Universität Wittenberg* (Halle, 1917); Jens-Martin Kruse, *Universitätstheologie und Kirchenreform. Die Anfänge der Reformation in Wittenberg 1516–1522* (Mainz, 2002).

Wittenberg. Apart from Greek, which was in the hands of the 21-year-old Melanchthon, the teaching of Hebrew was essential. Luther and Melanchthon wanted someone who taught more than linguistic skills. Meditating on biblical passages in Hebrew or Greek was now particularly recommended, in order to be as close as possible to the original spirit of revelation. Two professors of Hebrew were dismissed within a short period of time. The next professor was a quiet man, who was already a known quantity in Wittenberg, Matthäus Goldhahn.

Such a control over university appointments was only practicable in a small, new university and owed much to the support of the ducal secretary. Biblical exegesis became the business of a small group of experts who were chosen by Luther, and whose influence he could control. Seen from outside, every member of the Wittenberg team was supposed to have studied the Bible independently and reached the same conclusions as Luther. Therefore, these insights could seem collective, scholarly and true. Appointments and dismissals, hiring and firing, nonetheless were important to manufacture consent, and to present the Wittenberg truth to students, the duke and the wider public as coherent and plausible.

The small, marginal university of Wittenberg and its few professors thus gained a unique profile through criticising traditional teaching and supporting Luther. Von Amsdorf, whose noble status mattered, announced that Luther had converted him. Karlstadt now poured out writings against lawyers and 'sophists', against free will, good works and the notion of a virtuous human nature. He was eager to discuss his theses with leading Saxon theologians. Soon, Luther sent off his own theses against the indulgence trade to the Archbishop of Mainz. They were posted at the castle church, printed, copied in manuscript, and soon available all over Germany. The ninety-five theses demonstrated the benefit of Luther's doctrine of grace to a large audience. His theology had nothing to do with purely 'academic' problems. It served a better public order and life. Whereas in 1517 the university had only numbered 200 students, the figures now rose dramatically. Biblical truth was to conquer Wittenberg. Luther boasted that the success of his theses could only be explained by divine support and regarded himself as a prophetic reformer.

Wittenberg as a model of a peaceful princely and urban Reformation

Opponents voiced their concerns clearly: was this insistence on a 'biblical truth' not likely to cause immense confusion and political instability? Could not everybody now claim to have found a different truth? How could one prove that the Holy Ghost had given a particular person or group of people the grace to find a true interpretation?

These questions remained pressing for the Reformation movement. Luther therefore needed to establish his authority as biblical translator and exegete in the early years of his fame as a Roman heretic. He also had to defend his divinely chosen status by demonstrating his ability to create some degree of social and political harmony. He had to convince the Wittenberg court, university and citizenry of his ideas and recognise and exclude those proposing a 'false' doctrine. The new truth could only become a model for other rulers and towns if a safe religious consensus were established, opponents were efficiently excluded and secular rule remained powerful.

This was no easy task. Luther had been formally excommunicated by the Pope in January 1521. He had delivered an address at the Imperial Diet in Worms in April 1521, in which he declined to recant any of his positions, since his conscience was 'taken captive by God's Word'. Charles V placed him under the ban of the Empire in May. Luther was now a heretic and outlaw, and rested hidden in Frederick the Wise's Wartburg castle.

In the meantime, students who had made their way to Wittenberg expected a prophetic revelation so much that one of them reported in the autumn: 'See, God has awakened another prophet, a monk of the same order, who can preach the gospel also with such purity and luminousness that everybody calls him a second Martin.'[11] Luther, he thought, could not possibly preach any better than this man, Gabriel Zwilling. Melanchthon, too, attended his sermons in the Augustine monastery. Luther seemed to have been replaced. In December, three men from nearby Zwickau arrived. They called themselves prophets, preached against infant baptism, called for the slaughter of all Catholic clergy and prophesied that within a few years the world was going to change to such an extent that no bad sinners would survive. One of them had been pelted with stones in Prague. They had apparently bounced off without hurting him. Such miraculous signs impressed. One of the prophets announced that Luther was often right, but not all the time, and: 'There would come another . . . with a still higher spirit.' Melanchthon and other university professors interrogated the Zwickau men, but were unable to decide whether or not they possessed the prophetic gifts of the first Christians. Clearly, Luther's charisma and authority were not yet fully secured. They needed to be asserted.

[11] Kastner, *Quellen*, p. 122.

At around the same time, moreover, some students began to act militantly. The small Franciscan community was silenced, and so were the few monks from the order of St Anthony. A church altar was attacked, and the windows of the All Saints Foundation were smashed. Next, Karlstadt started preaching in the town church. University professors inconclusively debated whether mass should be reformed. Frederick the Wise prohibited all changes. Karlstadt wrote in November that Christ had more authority than a duke or the conservative laity. He married and made his wedding a big show. By December he started to celebrate mass wearing ordinary clothes and without making the signs of the cross. Confession and fasting were no longer preconditions for receiving communion, and he gave the cup to all. In January more than a thousand people received the Eucharist in both kinds, with bread and wine. Already by February, however, the duke had ordered the abolition of most of these reforms. Different practices within Wittenberg caused disagreement; 'some do not confess to a priest but only to God', one report stated, 'some think that to confess to another layperson, to accuse oneself and to receive absolution is an important matter. Some say that confession is unnecessary.'[12] For Frederick, as for all rulers at the time, this could not possibly signal the beginning of a productive debate. Frederick saw the right way 'obscured'. This produced 'annoyance' and unrest, and meanwhile he was reminded every day that even the religious tolerance he had shown thus far had met huge pressure from Imperial politicians. Von Amsdorf was told to restore order in the town church, Karlstadt and Zwilling were accused of instigating rebelliousness. The town council decided that they needed Luther back in Wittenberg.

After ten months at the Wartburg, where he wrote incessantly, translated the New Testament and struggled with his isolation, the devil and his digestion, Luther now returned as the only person able to create unity and clarity in Wittenberg and all 'German lands'. He wanted to prove once more that his mission was divine. His return was a matter of delicate diplomacy, because it forced the duke to admit publicly that he had protected an outlawed heretic and perhaps even to face military invasion. Luther thus cleverly wrote to Frederick that he acted without any self-interest. On the contrary, he was ready to sacrifice himself in the battle against Satan. Moreover, he knew he was the only one who could prevent the rebellion of the common man.

In March 1522, this comment did not respond yet to any real popular threat. It was a tactical move, because rulers notoriously feared their subjects' protest. The cardinal of Mainz, for instance, had written before

---

[12] Johnston and Scribner, *The Reformation*, p. 34.

Emperor Charles V's election in 1519 that the Empire was exhausted and poor and the levying of higher taxes would lead to revolts. If this situation continued, cities and estates might prefer to 'turn Swiss' – that is, form a free confederation without overlord – rather than being part of the Empire. Princes and noblemen might lose their power.

Yet soon, and despite Luther's return, Reformed ideas did indeed inspire radical politics. Much of the debate centred on the question about when to implement change, an issue which Luther and Karlstadt first fought out among themselves in Wittenberg. Luther was politically attentive to his weary and pressured duke and argued that political obedience and the effects of true preaching needed to be firmly established in the community before reforms could begin. He now preached in the town church every Sunday and affirmed that he was the laity's main Shepherd. At the same time he continued his policy of trying to place loyal supporters in key positions. Gabriel Zwilling acknowledged Luther's superiority and his own mistakes, and was later rewarded with a good position. The ducal secretary Georg Spalt became court preacher, and one of Luther's most loyal followers, Justus Jonas, became head of the All Saints Foundation, which was the last Catholic bastion in town.

This political cautiousness explains why Luther celebrated communion in both kinds only in January 1523, giving the laity bread and wine, for 'the closer our Mass resembles the first Mass of all, which Christ celebrated at the Last Supper, the more Christian it will be'. Enough 'respect for the weak' had now been shown, and so Luther taught that bread and wine did not transform into the body or blood of Christ, but that they were nonetheless present in their substances and assured man of his promised salvation. Holy Communion was thus neither a miracle of transubstantiation nor a mere sign or meal of remembrance. Luther thereby retained a strong notion of the importance of Christ's presence, just as he had shown his own presence to be crucial for order and harmony in Wittenberg.

True teaching and false prophets

Only Karlstadt continued to oppose these views and left Wittenberg in 1523. His theological views were characterised by the notion that humans possessed the ability to develop good and even God-like features in themselves, and that God required man to live according to his law. Luther, by contrast, emphasised the depravity of human nature, which did not allow any steady development towards the good or divine. Karlstadt held that everybody was able to sense God internally. The experience of true faith, moreover, was not necessarily tied to reading or hearing the Bible. It expressed itself above all in a socially committed lifestyle which prized equality and help for the poor. In contrast to Luther, who tended to opt for a courtier's outfit when he wore secular dress, Karlstadt, who came from a wealthy urban family, started dressing down as a peasant. He began to plough fields and preach in a rural community in the Saxon Saale region. He abolished all church images and infant baptism, and allowed the laity greater participation in all decision-making. The Eucharist was celebrated as a meal of remembrance of Christ's death. Luther and Karlstadt, former colleagues, who had always competed to some extent, began to write against each other openly and to doubt each other's right to announce 'true' doctrine. All over the Saale region peasants began to voice their unrest, and a radical preacher called Thomas Müntzer supported them. Luther wrote that Karlstadt was on Müntzer's side. In 1524, Frederick the Wise banished Karlstadt from his territory.

Long before the great German Peasants War broke out it was therefore clear that Luther supported the princes in their quest to retain a paternalist status quo with clear social hierarchies. His theology now visibly supported a political order in which the current secular order remained intact. Luther's abhorrence of violence likewise demonstrated that the 'Holy Ghost' rested with him and his peaceful Wittenberg followers. They, too, were 'poor sinners' and did not possess the full spirit, but they had received it first. Again and again the superiority of the Wittenberg circle was thus defended to secure the legitimacy of announcing the only pure and true doctrine. That they should radically distance themselves from 'false prophets' as 'spirits of unrest', and above all from a man called Thomas Müntzer, was just as vital.

Müntzer, like Luther, was a man in his early thirties and thus part of a Reformation movement which presents itself partly as a generational anti-establishment conflict.[13] He did not lead a steady life, but tried to find work as a minister in different places without gaining any stable protection. For him, the Bible was not the essence of revelation, since revelation manifested itself in a person's behaviour. Faith became alive in a heart which had been radically taken by God's spirit and had been forced to live in the spirit of the crucifixion and to abandon selfishness. Man could thus liberate himself from sinfulness and show his election. Those who had been elected had to eliminate the Godless

---

[13] Tom Scott, *Thomas Müntzer: Theology and Revolution in the German Reformation* (Basingstoke, 1989) provides a good introduction; Peter Matheson (ed.), *The Collected Works of Thomas Müntzer* (Edinburgh, 1988) is indispensable.

and prepare the world for the second coming of Christ. Only the poor and those of a low social rank could be part of the chosen, as well as princes happy to use their swords on their behalf. For Müntzer, Luther was a servant of godless princes and a flatterer of noblemen. Diplomacy and flattery were unnecessary because the empire of Christ was so close. Luther and Müntzer therefore shared the expectation that the end of the world was imminent. In spring 1525 Müntzer led peasant troops in Thuringia into battle. He had written to the people of Allstedt, where he had preached for some time and introduced the first fully vernacular liturgy, 'If you are unwilling to suffer for the sake of God, then you will be martyrs for the devil . . . Go to it, go to it, while the fire is hot.' One year later he was executed.

What happened in the 'Peasants' War, which began in summer 1524 in the southern Black Forest, then spread to many regions by April and May 1525, the troops being almost completely defeated by Charles V in June?[14] We first of all need to note that not only peasants were involved. In upper Germany, Thuringia, Franconia, in Alsace, Swabia, Switzerland and Tyrol, the troops – which mostly acted defensively – were not just made up of peasants. A substantial number of small rural towns and some larger cities supported the rebellion. Between 70,000 and 100,000 people lost their lives. The mayor of the small German Imperial city of Ulm had sarcastically foretold such an end to an assembly of peasants. They were like 'frogs in the spring', he said. 'You come together and croak "Gwark! Gwark!", and then the stork comes along and swallows you up. You also cry "Woe! Woe!", and the lords will come along and strike you dead.'

He remained right. But meanwhile the peasants' cries were usually far more eloquent than a mere 'Woe! Woe!'. In Ulm, for instance, one man stood up and declared:

The assembly which I lead has no intention of causing disturbance or using force, of which we have little . . . This present assembly has no other complaint . . . than that they are aggrieved beyond measure by you, the lords, in body and in spirit, and it is impossible to bear this any longer. In spirit, because they are robbed of the Word of God, and so must endure the greatest danger to the salvation of their souls; in body, because the assessments and burdens are so fierce and harsh that neither can be borne by their land or soil.

Soon, active resistance and alternative forms of government were justified with recourse to Scripture. In May 1525, for example, one pamphlet announced that the Bible demanded that lords should only act 'from

---

[14] Robert W. (Bob) Scribner and Tom Scott (eds.), *The German Peasants' War: A History in Documents* (Atlantic Highlands, 1991) has a superb historiographical introduction and a extensive selection of documents.

godly law'. Any harm inflicted on poor people contradicted this law. 'Yea, they scream, curse and revile the rebellion so evilly', the anonymous writer asserted, 'and never think thereby about the cause of the disturbance, which is themselves and their godless being.' A confederation without lords, as in Switzerland, benefited common people; here it resounded again: the radical political idea to 'turn Swiss'.

Less radical rebels struck deals with their lords. One Thuringian nobleman, Count Bodo of Stolberg, was forced by peasants to sign a declaration of four articles: 'First, that you should allow the Word of God to be preached purely and without hindrance. Second that you make free what Christ has made free: wood, water, meadow, hunting, for each to use according to his need. Third, that you destroy the remaining castles . . . Fourth, that you shed your grand titles and give honour to God alone.' In return, he was promised all monastic property in his lordship, albeit without the food and wine in their cellars!

Elsewhere monasteries were stormed, and men and women vented their long-pent-up anger against the privileged lives of monks and nuns. Peasant women near Heggbach convent promised the nuns that they would scratch out their eyes, make them wear cheap clothes and endure the pains of bearing children and rape, if they did not treat their men leniently for plundering the convent's goods.

The rebels' religious demands had been prefigured in some previous protests. But now they were presented across an unprecedented broad spectrum of lists of grievances and often headed them. For the very first time in history, and extraordinarily so, a popular movement was assisted by a new generation of theologians in arguing that their demands were not just legitimised by traditional secular rights but corresponded to a true Christian understanding, were supported by the Bible and were thus legitimised by God. The notion of such a 'divine right' had likewise surfaced in some previous revolts, but was taken up widely in 1524/5.

Twelve articles from the upper Swabian town of Memmingen found the widest consent among the rebels. The local minister, who was influenced by the Zurich reformer Zwingli, had assisted in writing them. These articles were immediately copied, printed, read aloud and discussed thousands of times. 'In the first place', those gathered in protest would hear, 'the Gospel is not the cause of disturbance or rebellion, since it speaks of God as the promised Messiah, whose Word and life teach nothing but love, peace, patience, and concord, so that all who believe in this Christ become loving, peaceful, patient, and of one mind.' To what extent common people shared such a Christian ethic and deeply Protestant convictions remains impossible to decide.

As in Memmingen, articles concerning religion usually demanded that the Bible should be preached by a communally elected minister, who would be forced to reside in their parishes. Goods due to be given to him were to be reduced or abolished, or the community was to be allowed to decide about them. The rights of ecclesiastical courts were to be limited. These demands were sometimes widened to include an article demanding that Scripture should be the yardstick of all political and social life. What kind of political, social and religious order would follow from this was not (yet) spelt out. Individual rights of ownership, however, were never questioned and all revolts mainly aimed to reduce the demands made by lords. In the face of territorial state formation and the monasteries' tightening grip on the population, greater political participation was another principal aim.

The 'movement of 1525', as this remarkable protest by peasants and citizens should perhaps be called, was hence characterised by its brevity and intellectual creativity. Within a few months, parts of the movement articulated not just articles of complaint but constructive thoughts towards a more egalitarian constitution. In order to be termed a 'revolutionary' movement the demands nonetheless remained too preliminary, limited and the whole spectrum of opinion too diffuse. Those who survived were mostly imprisoned or had to pay fines, and some areas negotiated compromises in response to their demands.

Luther recommended that all rebels be killed, since they had taken up the sword without God's command. Since 1520, Luther himself had learnt to speak more cautiously about Christian liberty. Then he had announced ambiguously and appealingly: 'A Christian is a perfectly free lord of all, subject to none. A Christian is a perfectly dutiful servant of all, subject to all . . . One thing and only one thing is necessary for Christian life, righteousness and freedom. That one thing is the most holy Word of God, the Gospel of Christ.' Now he made absolutely clear that liberty was firmly based on obedience to rulers, magistrates and those learned interpreters of Scripture who were truly guided by the Holy Ghost. Luther thus affirmed conservative ideas of paternalistic power and protection within a social hierarchy.

More progressive thinking was available at the time. Europe had for decades witnessed sophisticated debates about representative or consultative forms of political organisation. Protestant groups in the Swiss Confederation even began restructuring communal life and property along egalitarian principles. But Luther's conservative commitment followed from his view of human nature. Inequality was God-given, part of his curse on man and fundamental to all life on earth after the fall, just like inequality between man and woman. No alternative life was possible.

Emotional lives

We thus need to emphasise time and again that Luther regarded life as hardship, with many more bad than good days. His hopes did not rest on a better life on earth but a speedier end of it, so that eternal life might begin. The problem of all eschatological movements, however, was that the world did *not* end, not even in 1524, the year of a widely anticipated great flood. Even so, when Luther decided to marry in 1525 he still did not expect the marriage to last long. It had become high time for him to take this step. His enemies said he led a dissolute life. After all Luther had justified breaking monastic vows because he deemed human sexuality so powerful that no one was able to live celibate. Many nuns who had left their convents came to Wittenberg. Luther forced himself to marry one of them, Katharina von Bora, who came from a poor noble family. Those, like the humanist Erasmus, who continued the culture of male celibacy and bonding, and regarded it as serving a higher spiritual and scholarly cause, responded with great excitement and ridicule. It was a huge departure. Like Luther, a whole generation of ex-monks and married scholars needed to adjust to not merely regarding life with a woman as impure or embattled, but as containing companionship and joyful moments. Even Melanchthon managed to overcome his worries that his wife would constantly disturb his work. Luther formed a deeply emotional attachment to his wife, although he still wished her to keep quiet at table. By 1540, his letters addressed her as 'dear housewife', 'Lord Kethe', 'little dear' and 'little love', and he would sign in return 'M. Luth. Your old little love.' He cherished their children.[15]

In order to understand the specific emotional dynamics which underpinned Luther's charisma within Wittenberg, however, we need to ask about Luther's relationships with men. Luther was the spiritual leader of the Wittenberg circle. Its composition was unique and decisive for its success. At its centre stood Georg Spalt, who mediated between Luther and Frederick the Wise; Lukas Cranach, who operated as his art director and publisher; and Philip Melanchthon, the respected humanist and high-ranking Greek scholar. Loyalty was crucial. How was the relationship between these men and their 'God-given reformer' experienced and expressed? Only looking at these emotional dynamics can properly anchor the reform movement in its human dimensions. For we are not dealing with 'minds' reacting in a rational way to 'ideas', but with men who were inspired and involved as whole human beings.

---

[15] Susan C. Karant-Nunn and Merry Wiesner-Hanks (eds.), *Luther on Women. A Sourcebook* (Cambridge, 2003) provides a full picture of Luther's views.

Two wider cultural contexts are important for our understanding of the emotional languages which developed between men at the beginning of the sixteenth century. Boys were taught in schools or privately tutored by men, and then further educated by and among men in monasteries, chancelleries or universities. These experiences typically created early and lasting bonds with particular teachers who became role models. Close relationships were given meaning through the concept of a 'spiritual fatherhood'. 'Sons' followed their 'father' and his teaching, his view of work and life, and he introduced them to a network of contacts and recommended them for positions. If their ideals began to diverge, as in the case of Luther and his teacher Staupitz, both sides experienced severe emotional pain.

The humanist movement opened a new way for adult men to relate. It revived classical ideas of friendship, and tried to adjust them to early modern lives. Whereas intellectual fatherhood was tied to relationships within a common institutional context, a humanist friendship could be conducted among people anywhere in the *res publica litterarum*. It was freely chosen and sustained by correspondence, gifts, messengers, acquaintances and occasional visits. Printed collections of letters, most influentially that of Erasmus (see pages 69–73), soon prefigured a whole manner of relating, which the educated discussed and absorbed.

But such correspondence also caused insecurities about whether sentiments were expressed genuinely, or just out of politeness, or to serve an elegant rhetorical form. The Reformation movement thus developed the notion of an authentic 'Christian' friendship and inspired a highly emotional language. In April 1520, for example, Philip Melanchthon wrote to the young Breslau theologian Johannes Heß: 'Greetings, my dearest brother', and

> You are wrong, Heß, if you assume that there could be anyone who might please me more than you, whom I welcomed into my heart as soon as I met you, like no one else. For I do not agree with the view that in a Christian friendship one needs to wait for a measure of salt, of which the philosophers write that one should have eaten it with him whom one calls a friend, even if some trust has already been established. A Christian heart does not play with hiding itself, so that it seems to me that just in a single meeting I got to know all of you. This is why I would like you to trust in this – for I write nothing rhetorically, but simply and truly – that you are loved by us vehemently (*vehementer amari te a nobis*).[16]

The language of intimacy, simply and truly expressed, and the notion of a wholehearted 'Christian' friendship served to strengthen the sense of a

---

[16] Georg Kretschmar (ed.), *Die Reformation in Breslau* (Leipzig, 1960), pp. 36f.

distant person's part in and loyalty to the Wittenberg 'cause'. It formed a crucial part of the psychology of the movement.

How did these different models of male emotional bonding shape the Wittenberg circle? Spalt, Frederick the Wise's secretary, provides a telling example.[17] Georg Burckhardt had been born in Spalt near Eichstätt as an illegitimate child in 1484. Before the middle of the sixteenth century, illegitimacy was relatively frequent, even among wealthier people, not least through the many relationships which clerics sought. These children probably searched for more reliable father figures or mentors later in their lives. They were also likely to leave their family early on. Georg Spalt matriculated in Erfurt when he was aged fourteen. He followed his favourite professor to the newly founded university of Wittenberg, but returned to Erfurt to study law. He joined the Erfurt humanist circle. 'Georg Spalatin', writes his biographer Irmgard Höß, was 'not a really productive and original spirit. This explains his clear need to seek connections with men who could serve as his spiritual leaders.' His admired teacher Mutian found Spalt a job as private tutor in a well-known monastery, and then recommended him to the Wittenberg court. Spalt kept writing incessantly to Mutian. He also admired Erasmus, wrote letters to him and sent him translations of his works. This was also a prestigious career move for an aspiring humanist. Spalt moreover compiled a Saxon chronicle to show the achievements of Frederick the Wise's dynasty and bolster its claims for influence.

With time, a typically early modern character-mix evolved: Spalt was distinguished by his 'great industriousness', a 'strong sense of duty', an extreme notion 'of order in everyday life', a positive attitude towards princely authority and the princes' control over political matters, a strong belief in the devil and interest in astrological matters. Spalt needed to find a permanent position and material safety, and thus depended on patronage and obedient and useful behaviour. He looked for male friends, because he had grown up with the notion that scholarliness and having a family ruled each other out. Thus, he never lived with a woman until he was in his forties. He searched intensely for theoretical and spiritual guidance, for truth and ways to find it, and accordingly revered those who seemed to open paths towards it. Luther himself guided his encounter with the Bible. In 1523, Spalt accepted Luther's view that man was fundamentally sinful. The only public conflict between Luther and Erasmus (see p. 71) revolved around this issue. When it erupted in 1524, Spalt

---

[17] See Irmgard Höss, *Georg Spalt 1484–1545. Ein Leben in der Zeit des Humanismus und der Reformation*, 2nd edn (Weimar, 1989).

sank into deep depression. He needed to choose between Erasmus and
Luther, but now no other choice but Luther seemed to be left for him.
He wanted to withdraw from court. But Luther did not allow him to go,
because he needed the man whom Frederick the Wise trusted so much.
Luther told Spalt not to act selfishly. He had to serve the cause, the
progress of Lutheran reforms, for which Spalt did so much by balancing
Luther's directness with diplomacy and prudence. After Frederick's death
in 1525, Spalt retired to the countryside. His self-esteem nonetheless
remained strongly linked to Luther's approval. When Luther criticised
him once, Spalt again got seriously depressed. Luther in turn spiritually 'comforted' him in a letter which assured Spalt of his redemption
from sin.

This exchange was characteristic of how Luther created emotional
dependence. It was taken for granted that he was the great man, clear
and robust in situations of crisis. His own fights and depressions resulted
from battling with the devil, not from human exchange and fragile emotions. His criticism hurt. Afterwards he offered protection and comfort,
which nonetheless implied an affirmation of his superiority. As time went
by, Luther saw Spalt turning into an 'old, weak' man. Every four months
he would still come up to Wittenberg and look after the university's library
matters.

Luther likewise felt himself to be stronger than Melanchthon.[18] He was
ever happy to admit that he often went over the top temperamentally, but
defended his behaviour by arguing that this was natural for anyone who
fought the Pope, church and Satan all at once. Melanchthon, by contrast,
'naturally' seemed like a university scholar who lived primarily through his
mind. He was slightly built, thin, liberally neglectful of his appearance,
and had a fine, interesting face with a prominent forehead (figure 3).
Luther and Melanchthon embodied different kinds of masculinity and
were represented as complementing each other, as the couple on which
the strength of the Wittenberg movement rested. For Luther became
physically increasingly massive with age. It was as if the weightiness of
the reformer manifested itself in flesh and blood. He exuded strength and
life. His polemics were powerful. Already in 1519 the humanist Mosellan
had had to admit that, despite the deep impression Luther had made on
him, 'one thing is criticised by everybody, that he is too forthright and
sharp in his punitive judgement, more than it suits . . . a theologian'.

Melanchthon himself was not opposed to polemics, but more sensitive
to the contexts in which it was best used. He certainly should not be

---

[18] Heinz Scheible, *Melanchthon. Eine Biographie* (Munich, 1997) provides a useful
introduction.

Figure 3. Albrecht Dürer, *Philip Melanchthon*, 1526. Depicting a man who does not care about his clothes, hair or beard, whose shoulders seem small and who has a strangely fixed gaze at nothing, Dürer might have proposed a visual rhetoric of scholarly appearances. Dürer himself, by contrast, was even teased by some friends because he cared so much about his beard. Apart from Melanchthon's mild smile there is nothing flattering in the image. For those who did not regard them as emblems of scholarly integrity, these visual signs might equally have been taken as a reference to bad, sectarian thought.

imagined only as a 'noble', withdrawn, purely academically minded man
either. His most able disciple, Johann Stigel, for instance, presented an
epigram at a Wittenberg poetry contest. It was directed against a Catholic
Frenchman called Stephanus Doletus: 'Because you write nothing other
than dirt, nothing other than awful things, because you speak nothing
but disgusting shit, you should rather be named Oletus, for your muse
knows nothing other than dirt.' Presented in Latin, this was an exer-
cise in 'humanist poetry'.[19] Melanchthon himself rhymed for satirical
broadsheets depicting the devil shitting out monks or peasants farting
in front of the Pope. Indeed, we can only understand the mentality
of people at the time if we register that distinctions between good and
bad were made through the opposition of what was clear and light with
dirty, shitty matter. Excrement was smeared at doors of opponents of
the Reformation movement. Luther's supporters urinated publicly into
incense cases. Protestant broadsheets were full of the symbols of excrement and dirt, and those who knew Latin laughed about epigrams such
as Stigel's. Melanchthon was no exception. In contrast to Luther he was
also greatly interested in astrology – another aspect which does not fit our
modern notions of 'scholarliness'.

How can we characterise the relationship between Luther and
Melanchthon? Melanchthon, as has been mentioned before, was only
in his early twenties when he came to Wittenberg. He was immediately convinced that Luther was a 'guardian against false doctrine', and
overwhelmed by his personality. Luther in turn developed protective
and tender feelings towards Melanchthon. He seemed not only young,
but slightly fragile. Soon Luther addressed his letters to him as 'my
sweet Melanchthon'. He deeply respected Melanchthon's scholarship as
'clean', deep, 'clear', even as superior to his own. But he also defined
their roles: Melanchthon was, and had to be, not just 'clean', but 'clean
and quiet', and to sow the field which Luther's strength first needed
to plough. Luther encouraged Melanchthon to lecture in theology, but
only because he trusted Melanchthon would not disagree with his views.
Melanchthon nonetheless repeatedly became deeply troubled, not least
about the progress of the Reformation movement.

He expressed this psychosomatically, by worrying himself ill. Luther
would then assert that Melanchthon had a somewhat fragile spirit, but
that he fully trusted him, the cause, and God's protection. Melanchthon
knew that he ultimately stood or fell with this vision while Luther was
alive. He tried to avoid any direct confrontation. Only during the proceedings of an Imperial Diet meeting in Augsburg, in 1530, did he come

---

[19] Bärbel Schäfer, Johann Stigels antirömischen Epigramme, in Heinz Scheible (ed.),
Melanchthon in seinen Schülern (Wiesbaden, 1997), pp. 60f.

close to risking a serious conflict. He reported hardly any news to Luther and continued to seek compromises with Catholics. When his policy ran into difficulties, he was in pain. Luther interpreted Melanchthon's tactics as anxiety, a sign of his tender spirit, and lack of faith. Luther saw the devil as his real counterpart, and was ever ready to confront him. To seek compromises in principles of faith was weakness. Luther threatened that he would not speak or write to Melanchthon any more. Only when Melanchthon admitted that the Reformation's cause completely depended on him ('apart from you no one can comfort us') did Luther reply. He again dismissed efforts to mediate with Catholics. There was only one biblical truth. Melanchthon's desire to compromise was a personal weakness and a weakness in faith, caused by the devil's attacks. God would direct the Lutheran cause, as long as he and his followers believed in him. Melanchthon meanwhile saw full well the political consequences of such a view. It meant either persecution or fighting an armed battle against the Emperor and Catholic powers, a war among Christians.

One final scene which defined the relationship between Luther and Melanchthon took place in 1539. It came in the aftermath of a bigamous marriage by the Protestant Duke Philip of Hesse, which Luther had approved of and now caused a huge scandal. Melanchthon reacted against the mistake and its possible consequences by developing high fever and was away from Wittenberg. Luther once more reacted fraternally, paternally and as LUTHER for his fragile Melanchthon. He asked students to pray for him during lectures, travelled to see him, and saved him through the power of his prayer. Luther pressurised God: Since the Bible promised that the just would be listened to, either Melanchthon would be saved, or everything was a lie. Luther once more demonstrated the power of his presence and determination: Melanchthon was not to die. Both of them followed a divine mission. Instantly, Melanchthon's fever went down. Luther retained Melanchthon's loyalty through these emotional techniques. Only after Luther's death were differences laid open which destroyed the coherence of the one Wittenberg truth.

Networks: disseminating the doctrine from Wittenberg

All of this shows that from 1522 Luther largely controlled Wittenberg affairs. Only much later did he become frustrated that his sermons seemed not to affect people's way of life; but he still likened Wittenberg to a New Jerusalem in 1545. There was not even popular protest in 1525. In the same year, Frederick the Wise's son, Johann Frederick, took over rule. He was a steady Lutheran.

Creating facts: the religious conversation

But how was the new, Lutheran truth disseminated outside Wittenberg and the Ernestine territory? How could it be proved that the new truth was the only truth? How could religious change be legitimised in an orderly fashion, controlled by princes and magistrates instead of by peasants and unruly folk? Which conventions could generate facts which supported Luther against the tradition of finding religious truth through church councils? Luther always stressed his status as a learned doctor to generate trust in his teaching. He was Dr Martinus Luther. And he and his supporters had chosen to transform the academic debate in such a way that it publicly confirmed Luther's views as the only legitimate conclusion. These debates were called 'religious conversations', *Religionsgespräche*.[20]

The first conversation had taken place back in 1519. On 24 June, two hundred students and two carts arrived in Leipzig. One cart was taken by Karlstadt and his many books. Finally a wheel broke, the cart tumbled, and the professor lost balance. Luther, Melanchthon and the rector of the University of Wittenberg followed in the second cart and managed to enter the town in a more dignified way. They had all come to Leipzig to defend Wittenberg views on indulgences and other theological questions against the Dominican Johann Eck. Eck had arrived two days earlier with a servant. Wittenberg students rallied at night in front of his house. The Leipzig debate took place in the ducal Pleissenburg and was guarded by armed citizens, to contain unrest. Eck and Luther debated for twelve days, Eck and Karlstadt for five days. The *Religionsgespräch* was recorded by a notary and the dossier sent to the universities of Erfurt and Paris. Their scholars were to decide who was right.

This procedure was a complete novelty. Was it not solely up to the Pope to decide what constituted true or heretical teaching? Duke Georg of Albertine Saxony oversaw Leipzig University. A devoted Catholic, he nonetheless demanded that the church should answer all his questions concerning indulgences and purgatory, and found that it did not. Other reform-minded voices demanded a church council meeting on German soil to deal with widespread doubts about church practices and doctrines. This, however, necessitated papal consent and raised all the usual doubts about the independence of conciliar decision-making. Frederick the Wise and his brother Georg had thus come to support a decision-making process by universities in order to seek wisdom and reconciliation.

---

[20] Thomas Fuchs, *Konfession und Gespräch. Typologie und Funktion der Religionsgespräche in der Frühen Neuzeit* (Cologne, 1995) is crucial reading.

Traditionally, academic debates had asserted that seemingly contradictory arguments, i.e. about scholastic method, still affirmed one divine truth. At the start of the Leipzig conversation, the humanist Mosellanus therefore warned that since divine truth could never be wholly understood through human reason, one should find unity through a conversation. The whole assembly kneeled while the Leipzig Thomaner boys sang 'Come Holy Ghost' three times, ritually asking for divine wisdom. Leipzig nonetheless showed that debates between 'Lutherans' and their opponents could no longer maintain the aura of a sacral academic procedure serving to break through to one divine truth. Erfurt scholars declined to judge the Leipzig disputation. The matter was too delicate and they did not believe their theological competence sufficed. A commission of twenty-four Paris scholars decided against the Wittenberg doctrine. Luther and his followers refused to accept the judgement. They thus claimed for the first time, and before an international audience, that the divine spirit of truth did not rest with cardinals in Rome, with scholars at the Sorbonne or even possibly with church councils who could veto the Pope. It rested in Wittenberg, with Luther and his followers, who could formally show how to interpret the Bible in the only legitimate way.

Reports about the Leipzig debate, and a printed account of it produced in Wittenberg, turned it into a model for Protestant supporters. Luther had demonstrated in a simple manner which parts of Augustine and the Bible could be taken as proof that Christ was head of the church, rather than the Pope, who was never mentioned in the Bible. Luther insisted on God's sole immanence in biblical Scripture, which he revealed. He would announce, for instance: 'Finally we hear the Lord himself who speaks in Luke 22 . . . ', turning himself into a mediator of God's word. Luther affirmed that a single person who properly understood Scripture could be superior to all church councils. Eck, by contrast, had memorised arguments from church fathers who concurred in proving a different truth.

The debate was therefore caught in hermeneutic circles. Eck maintained that the primacy of Rome and the Papacy could not be questioned. Luther and his sympathisers held that the Pope was the Antichrist, and that no rich and powerful church leaders could ever claim to read the Bible in the right way. Contradictory decisions by past church councils showed that the Holy Ghost had never inspired those bodies. Luther had to admit that the Bible itself contained contradictory statements. In such cases he was confident that a consensus could be found 'through grace'. He maintained that the Bible exposed a unified divine truth which revealed itself to the privileged.

Leipzig thus demonstrated how the new truth could be verified. Religious conversations could now be replicated in towns and cities and could legitimate the implementation of reforms. The success of the Protestant movement thus rested on developing a practice of truth finding which appeared academically sound and reaffirmed one divine truth, firmly based on the Bible. Only thereby could Lutheranism present itself as a way to end doctrinal confusion and install a better religious, social and political order.

Breslau

The case of Breslau shows how the religious conservation was adapted from a university and court setting to an urban setting, and thus to far more complex institutional and social circumstances than in Wittenberg. Before the movement of 1525 erupted, towns were pace-makers of the Reformation. Here, the religious conversation was crucial to containing religious heterogeneity and social unrest.

Around 1520, Breslau was one of the most important east central European cities. Trade routes from Kiev and Cracow crossed in Breslau. They merged with a network of routes leading on to Vienna and Venice, or to Prague and Nuremberg, to Leipzig and Frankfurt-on-Main. Breslau was centrally positioned for the expanding east European trade. The river Oder moreover connected the city with Frankfurt an der Oder and Berlin, and through Stettin with the Baltic Sea.[21]

Early sixteenth-century Breslau possessed one cathedral, thirty-one churches and many chapels. As in most cities, the Breslau town council had sought to reduce the bishop's authority for some time, in order to establish itself as the principal 'Christian authority' whose laws alone should order urban life. Typically, the council thus found itself sympathetic to the Lutheran movement, but was anxious to avoid public unrest by establishing a unified doctrine. In 1523, it appointed Johannes Heß, who has already been mentioned as a recipient of Melanchthon's letter, as minister of a main church. Heß was the son of a local merchant who had completed his degree in Wittenberg and then served the Bishop of Breslau. The council asked him to resolve the divisions in faith. Heß himself asserted that without there being 'clear, unified preaching', no Christian behaviour was possible in Breslau. Indeed, anticlericalism abounded in the town. A goldsmith, for instance, was said to have cursed the bishop and clergy in a public bath. He had said that the town council

---

[21] Kretschmar, *Die Reformation in Breslau*, pp. 36f.

and citizens' representatives had ordered strangling the clergy on the island where the cathedral was located. Everybody had applauded him!

Heß soon organised a religious conversation at a safe place and without any popular participation to 'search for the truth and calm our consciousness'. He presented twenty-two theses on three topics. Based on Karlstadt's and Luther's Leipzig model, they mainly argued that the Bible was more authoritative than all human decisions, including those of the Roman church. Everybody should be entitled to study the Bible and hear its words preached without any additions. Heß expounded his theses for three days, first in Latin and then in German. Finally, he opened them for discussion. A select audience had assembled in the Augustinian church, and every single session was introduced by a sung 'Come Holy Ghost' and ended by a 'Praise the Lord'. Heß himself chaired the disputation, and it was part of his chairmanship to 'resolve' problematic issues or to promise a written answer at a later stage. Heß, in other words, managed the outcome of a consensus which was to secure spiritual harmony. As in Leipzig, two notaries took down an exact protocol, a procedure signalling formal correctness and lending additional weight to the occasion. Town councillors witnessing the event presumably were theologically untrained. Among the urban clergymen only a few were fit to engage in a formal theological argument based on a biblical truth. Big foliovolumes of the Hebrew Old Testament and the Greek New Testament were propped up on Heß's table. Two language experts had been ordered to attend.

The Dominicans were the dominant order in town and naturally opposed reforms. Their position had nonetheless been crucially weakened because a member of the clergy at the cathedral had been found in bed with an unmarried woman shortly before the religious conversation was held. This incident tapped into long-standing anticlerical sentiments that all clergymen were corrupt and endangered female virtue. Even so, some argumentative efforts were made. A key objection, once more, was that not everybody could interpret the Bible according to his or her understanding of it and because he or she felt privileged to do so. Unity would be lost forever. One had to follow the understanding of many in church councils and in God's church. For Heß, however, the Breslau community was the church, and the understanding of many was present in the religious conversation. He and the councillors represented it.

Heß made sure that the German, more accessible part of his talk commented on socially relevant issues which concerned this audience, particularly on the much debated attitude of the church towards marriage and clerical marriage. Then he declared 'evangelical' doctrine as biblically proven and substantive arguments against it as lacking. All those assembled had to sign a protocol containing this conclusion. Soon after, the town council announced that the Breslau clergy were now bound to teach in an 'evangelical' way.

The town council also confiscated all church property. Heß now wrote to Luther in a state of shock. He asked him to intervene against such selfishness and greed. Luther replied: 'Nothing is surprising about the fact that lords take the evangelical message to look for their own advantage and that new robbers follow the old robbers. The light of the world has risen so that we can see what the world really is, the Empire of Satan.' Luther believed not just that Satan was rampant, but that he brought to bear his mighty influence on humans fully only now, as the biblical truth was strengthened. Luther, the prophet, was particularly endangered. He therefore offered little help to Heß and closed with the words: 'Fare well to you and pray for me.'

The new truth

In Breslau, Zurich and many other towns and cities during the following years, councillors and ministers used the conventions of the religious conversation to demonstrate that a Christian magistrate and a renewed church were able to establish a consensus, which was necessary if the community wanted to retain its hope for salvation and divine grace in precarious times. Disputes, as opposed to the 'conversation', were now deemed to be 'quarrelsome and vainglorious'. A 'fraternal and Christian conversation', however, was already based on the premise that biblical truth surpassed the wisdom of church councils. Its framework was predetermined, and its rules constrained any free discussion and silenced dissonance. Ordinary citizens were usually excluded from all proceedings. Even so, it was argued that a public and impartial conversation had taken place, at which the divine spirit had been present. This was to make the new truth appear coherent and to legitimate social and religious reforms.

The religious conversation, in other words, provided magistrates with a way to solve problems of order. It secured social hierarchies within the community by morally privileging some groups and excluding others, such as 'undeserving poor', prostitutes, and nuns, monks or priests, all of whom were now depicted as leading lazy, sinful lives and disturbing the moral economy of a society based on 'holy households', which ideally consisted of an artisan and his wife, legitimate children, god-fearing, industrious journeymen and servants. These ideas redefined the 'common good' and essence of a 'Christian order' according to reform proposals which in most aspects had been voiced in civic police ordinances for some time. The success of the Protestant movement thus substantially rested on a mode of religious truth finding which enabled its alliance with important communal interest groups, magistrates, patricians and artisans to take up reform concerns.

Commenting on the proofs underpinning the new truth, Thomas More sarcastically remarked in his 1524 *Response to Luther*:

Q: How do you know that God has seized you?
L: Because I am certain . . . that my teaching is from God.
Q: How do you know that?
L: Because I am certain.
Q: How are you certain?
L: Because I know.
Q: But how do you know?
L: Because I am certain.[22]

Networks

How was the new truth disseminated outside Wittenberg apart from the religious conversation? Personal networks were important, an aspect which is easily overlooked if one assumes that the Reformation was mainly disseminated through print. Personal encounters usually created a far stronger bond between people than merely reading or hearing about someone's ideas. The example of the Breslau reformer Heß already showed how Luther and Melanchthon cultivated personal relationships and thus influenced the implementation of Lutheran policies elsewhere. Countless Wittenberg students and temporary visitors from different parts of Germany and Europe came into similar personal contact with the reformers, even if more or less intensely. Some students (such as the 'Hungarian Luther', Matthias Dévai, from 1529 to 1531) lived or ate with them as boarders. This naturally created stronger ties than the view from the back of lecture rooms.

The most important example of how a student turned into a loyal reformer is provided by Johannes Bugenhagen. Bugenhagen came from a far northern region of Germany, where he was in charge of biblical exegesis at a monastery and a member of a theological reading group in a nearby town. After reading Luther, he wrote to him, received several of his writings as a gift and decided to study in Wittenberg as a mature student.

[22] See Susan Brigden, *New Worlds, Lost Worlds. The Rule of the Tudors 1485–1603* (London, 2000), p. 96.

In his first days at Wittenberg he still harboured some doubts.[23] But soon he felt sure that all divine truth rested with Luther. Luther encouraged him to lecture, and he first did so in front of other Pomeranian students at home. Luther needed loyal supporters from different regions, who spoke local dialects and had good regional connections. During the following years, Bugenhagen turned into *the* diplomat of the Lutheran Reformation in northern Germany and Scandinavia – that is to say, areas in which Lutheranism was lastingly implemented. He tirelessly travelled to religious conversations in cities, towns and territories which were looking for a new church order based on the Wittenberg model, and mediated conflicts. He helped to translate Lutheran writings into Low German, maintained particularly close contacts with the Danish ruler Christian III and even helped to celebrate his coronation in a Lutheran style. Bugenhagen worked from Wittenberg, preached to its community, never questioned Luther's teaching, and made the new truth an organisational practicality elsewhere.

The Wittenberg circle also played a key role in placing a new generation of ministers, teachers and secretaries. Luther received a flow of letters from parishes, councils and noble families asking him to recommend his graduates. He and Melanchthon invested much time in writing letters of recommendation. Placing people enabled Luther to preserve, as far as possible, the coherence of what was preached or otherwise exposed as 'evangelical' doctrine. Numerous foreign students began to work for the Reformation in their home countries after graduating in Wittenberg. From among the hundred Polish students who matriculated between 1523 and 1546 in Wittenberg despite their country's royal legislation, Abraham Kulwieć, Stanislaw Rafajowicz, Lutomirski, Stanislaw Murzynowsky (who in 1551/2 translated Luther's New Testament version into Polish), Martin Krowicki and many others themselves became reformers.[24] By 1527, most parishes in Danish-ruled Schleswig-Holstein had Protestant ministers who had mostly been educated in Wittenberg. Johann Wenth, another Wittenberg man, co-authored the Danish-Lutheran church order and the Schleswig-Holstein church order under Bugenhagen's general supervision. He created the first academy for Scandinavian Lutheran clergy in Haderslev. The Swedish reformer Olaus Petri matriculated in Wittenberg in 1516 and

---

[23] Hans-Günter Leder and Norbert Buske, *Reform und Ordnung aus dem Wort. Johannes Bugenhagen und die Reformation im Herzogtum Pommern* (Berlin, 1985).

[24] Hans J. Hillerbrand (ed.), *The Oxford Encyclopedia of the Reformation*, 4 vols. (New York, 1996), provides useful summary biographies for many of those involved in reformer movements in different countries.

listened to Luther's early lectures. Three years later he obtained a position as secretary of the bishop in Strägnäs. His younger brother Laurentius likewise studied in Wittenberg and became Archbishop of Uppsala. The Finnish reformer Michael Agricola was born the son of a fisherman in 1510 and got in touch with Lutheran ideas through a Finnish student who had already been in Wittenberg. Michael received his MA from Wittenberg University, and Luther's and Melanchthon's recommendation helped him to become head of an important school immediately after his return to Finland. He translated the New Testament into Finnish and became Bishop of Turku. Other Wittenberg students became private ministers for noble families, especially in Austria, which was under Habsburg rule but witnessed significant noble dissent.

These were the ways in which the Lutheran Reformation became an international movement, and it is interesting to note that 16 per cent of Luther's works were published in Latin, while only 4 per cent – a total of 155 editions – were translated into other European languages.[25] Often his students were responsible for these translations and for finding printers and publishers. The works appeared in ten languages, particularly in Dutch, Danish, Czech and English; there were three Polish editions, but only one in Swedish. Programmatic reform manifestos were hardly represented; most works were part of his popular spiritual writing. A European audience therefore could only follow Luther's thought selectively and usually only a long time after a text had been written.[26] His ideas, that is, would often still travel faster through people who had been in Wittenberg than through print. Moreover, many of Luther's works in Europe appeared anonymously or under a pseudonym to pass through censorship. Also, translations were rarely accurate. They altered the text in ways which Luther was unable to control. All the same, Luther was translated more frequently than any other reformer, and he was the first author ever to have German texts translated into languages other than Latin. The Wittenberg formation of personal networks which helped to disseminate Luther's ideas across national boundaries thus had a limited effect, which was nonetheless considerable in relative terms.

[25] Bernd Moeller, Luther in Europe. His Works in Translation, 1517–46, in E. I. Kouri and Tom Scott (eds.), *Politics and Society in Reformation Europe* (London, 1987), pp. 235–51.
[26] This situation did not change after Luther's death. A good example is the attempt of the Styrian nobleman Hans Ungnad von Sonneck and the Carniolan printer Primus Truber to translate the Bible and Luther's writings for the Slovenian and Croat population in inner Austria and Dalmatia, which lasted several years. From 1556 onwards Ungnad attracted several patrons for his project, which operated from the Swabian town Urach. But the initiative ended with Truber's death in 1564.

Speech, image, print: communicating the Reformation

How important was print anyway in disseminating the Reformation? For a long time historians thought that there was no question about the new technology's overwhelming importance in spreading the Reformation. Luther seemed to have become Europe's first media-star almost overnight. A careful estimate calculates that 3.1 million of his works were sold between 1516 and 1546, excluding his Bible translation. Sometimes a whole edition would sell within weeks or months. Between 1518 and 1529 80 per cent of all editions of Luther's works were published in German. Luther figured as author of 20 per cent of the 7,500 cheap broadsheets printed between 1520 and 1526. Many other broadsheets supported Luther and his teaching. Pedlars disseminated them widely, and their price roughly equalled that of a chicken or a pound of wax. Catholic writers, by contrast, were no competitors in a popular market yet, as they published little and mainly in Latin.[27]

Despite these extremely impressive facts, the question about how important print was for Luther's cause has become more difficult to answer. Only 30 per cent of the male urban population could read; 90 per cent of the German population lived in the countryside. Even with the best will in the world, few villagers could make sense of printed letters, even though reading (rather than writing) skills were to improve impressively later in the century. Do we need to conclude that even Luther's German writings would mainly have reached disaffected clerics, monks, nuns, educated men and women and well-off urban artisans? Did the readership moreover concentrate in areas within reach of the important Protestant printing presses, in Saxony, the south and a few cities elsewhere? How many of the approximately ten million German inhabitants really ever saw a Luther-print? One needs to reflect, moreover, on the example of the north German city of Bremen. No printing press operated here before the Reformation, and no 'trace of a humanist spirit' or of Luther's influence through print can be discerned. Bremen nonetheless accepted the Reformation very fast, and soon after 1522, through the sermons of a Dutch Augustinian monk who had been in Wittenberg for several years before coming to Bremen.

Objections of this kind usefully remind us that a history of the printed word needs to be linked to the history of reading. Rather than merely

---

[27] See Mark Edwards Jr., *Printing, Propaganda and Martin Luther* (Berkeley, 1994), ch. 1, for figures and Holger Flachmann, *Martin Luther und das Buch. Eine historische Studie zur Bedeutung des Buches im Handeln und Denken des Reformators* (Tübingen, 1996) for a wider discussion of Luther's attitudes. See Karin Maag (ed.), *The Reformation and the Book* (Aldershot, 1998) on Germany and other European countries.

counting how many editions a book had and how many books people owned, historians need to ask whether, how, by whom, what, when and where the printed word was read. We need to understand to what extent Reformation texts were in fact 'read'; or were they mainly read aloud to others and commented upon at the same time; or were parts left out or dismissed straight away? For ideas, it is important to stress, are not contained entities which are transmitted into people's minds; they travel and change course on the way. This is true for any period, but perhaps even more so for the early modern period, in which print could only truly reach out through the practice of reading aloud. This in turn means that reading was not a one-dimensional process in which an intended message was absorbed, but a basis for discussion and interpretation. Moreover we need to ask whether printed images were not often much more telling and memorable for most people? How did texts, images and songs influence specific communities of listeners and readers? And did sermons, after all, not remain the most efficient mass medium?

Finally, we need to consider that literary production was not just a matter of writing and getting published. It demanded hard work and reflection. For a start, printers and publishers had to be persuaded to invest their capital. They had to produce for safe markets, and to avoid the obstacles of censorship. They needed to produce cost-efficiently, but Luther wanted high-quality printing for his major works, and depended on workshops using good paper, typefaces, artisans and correctors, all of which were expensive and hard to find. Last but not least, seventy years after its introduction, print was still regarded as a 'new' medium and enjoyed an ambiguous status in Europe.[28] These cultural attitudes towards language, print and the spoken word unexpectedly reveal where a man like Luther saw his priorities.

The spoken word

For Luther, the immediate reflection of the divine spirit remained supremely alive in the spoken word. Even by 1520 – the year in which Luther published his three most important programmatic tracts *The Freedom of a Christian*, *Address to the Christian Nobility* and *A Prelude on the Babylonian Captivity of the Church* – Luther maintained that the dissemination of 'living books', of preachers, was far more important than of his writings. This attitude, however, was not primarily motivated by the fact that Luther was living in a barely literate society and knew that he could never rely on print as a true mass medium. It needs to be explained

[28] Adrian Johns, *The Nature of the Book: Print and Knowledge in the Making* (Chicago, 1998).

in terms of contemporary attitudes towards orality which surprise us nowadays. In 1519, for instance, Luther decided against preparing a new edition of his commentary on psalms because speech added so much 'light and grace' for listeners, which the 'chaos of letters' could never contain. Humanists shared this view. 'Writing', Erasmus declared in his famous collection of proverbs and sayings, commenting on the entry *Viva Vox*, 'is a kind of voice, but somehow it imitates the real voice. Gestures and movement are lacking; in one word: life.'[29] Erasmus thus believed that the 'true' spirit was demonstrated through 'natural' speech. Any learned display of rhetoric and gestures had to be abandoned.

Given such views and his radical ideas, it was essential for Luther to appear authentically as if the 'spirit of truth' became alive in him. A 'naturally' prophetic style thus clearly remained in part a studied style, for Luther's appearances had a social and political dimension. He did not want to appear as self-important and a trouble-maker. He wanted to show princes, noblemen and the estates that they could trust him, that he was a man of unity and peace despite being radical. He ideally needed to appear as modest, honest and steadfast. And since virtue was symbolised through rhetorical and visual devices, a prophet's way of speaking and appearing were just as important to create trust in the truth of what he said as what was said. Form and content were inseparable.

A testimony to this is that before the Leipzig debate the humanist Mosellan had warned that one should speak without any 'witty brilliance, false accusations, shouting, artfully crafted conclusions'. Instead, the debaters should prove the argument of the other person wrong in a clear and modest way. Luther himself dismissed a free 'Italian' manner of disputing, which in his view presented 'airy' arguments. All his arguments, he claimed, were soundly based on biblical passages and he wanted them to be minuted by notaries with 'German honesty', so that they could be verified. Luther belonged to the Italo-sceptics of his time. Everything Italian, *welsch*, was likely to be false, simulated and effeminate. This had sexual implications, since one word for male homosexuality was *welschen* and Italians were commonly defamed as 'arse-fuckers'.[30] German men praised themselves for their simplicity, courage, honesty, clarity and a straight-up-and-down heterosexual masculinity which distanced itself from anything feminine or 'sodomite'. Luther's way of conducting the Leipzig debate thus intended to show his patriotic, eloquent manly conduct. This gendered representation strengthened the superiority of

---

[29] *Collected Works of Erasmus* (Toronto, 1982), vol. XXXI, p. 161.
[30] See Helmut Puff, *Sodomy in Reformation Germany and Switzerland 1400–1600* (Chicago, 2003), Part II.

Reformed arguments. 'I am suggesting this [manner of debating]', Luther wrote to Karlstadt, 'so that we do not witness this awful boasting . . . which we can see in Eck's Vienna disputation, and so that the shouting and displeasing gestures are reduced, with which debaters behave in our time and destroy the truth.' And this explains why Luther held a small flower in his hand at Leipzig. This was a graceful gesture of modesty open to men at the time, and it helped to avoid gesticulating.

In order further to understand the mindset which informed such attitudes we need to note that Luther followed an Augustinian epistemology of the senses, which placed hearing above seeing. This attitude again was widely shared by humanists. Many, for instance, believed that music mediated truth. For Luther, too, music was the highest art after theology. God had created her harmonies, and she immediately took over listeners. Luther thus did not contribute to a rationalisation of the senses, but shifted the notion of how the divine could best be apprehended decidedly from seeing to hearing – believing followed from hearing. Such views also explain why sermons in the early years of the Reformation movement could suggest that, by hearing the Lutheran message, Christ literally 'fell' into the heart of those listening. As hearing became believing it was linked to salvation; and implicit or explicit promises of this kind help us to understand why the early Reformation sermon drew such crowds and why this was a movement primarily based on preaching.

The anticipated depth of this spiritual experience and the sensuality associated with it becomes even clearer if we note how the reformers' notions of the senses connected with medieval mysticism. Mysticism closely linked speaking with a sense of taste and eating. The divine word was to be tasted sweetly, it melted on the tongue or had to be chewed on meditatively to comprehend and absorb it fully. Through such a process of absorption, of 'internal' listening and repetition, it truly became part of a person, of his or her body and soul. The reformer Heß thus advised in his Breslau thesis that the Word of God should be meditated on, just as food was gnawed between teeth, in order to 'imprint it fully in one's heart and consciousness, so that everything shall implant itself internally and become part of nature'.[31] To apprehend truth, according to this understanding, required not just a rational, but a physical and emotional, a spiritual process. The spoken word was linked to sensual and material qualities, such as sweetness or toughness, structuring its expression and meaning. This explains why hearing could involve such intensity and emotive experiences which were later lost.

---

[31] Kretschmar, *Reformation in Breslau*, p. 107.

Such views of the tone and timbre of the spoken word furthermore resulted in a particular attitude towards the voice. Everybody listened carefully to it in order to assess the authority of what was said. The humanist Mosellan's description of the Leipzig debaters bears this out. Karlstadt, whom he disliked somewhat, had not a 'very clear and pleasant voice'; Eck was strongly built and had a 'full and rather German voice', rough rather than clear, like an actor in a tragedy, or a herald. Mosellan was more favourably disposed towards Luther, whom he perceived as mostly polite and friendly, vivacious in company, and of cheerful demeanour. He praised his voice as clear and audible. Other observers likewise described Luther's voice as 'clear', or even as 'sweet'.[32]

But once more we need to question whether this was always 'naturally' so. Luther clearly experimented with his voice as much as with rhetorical strategies to appear modest and not like an actor. Historians have always wondered why Luther muttered so quietly at the first day of the Diet of Worms, when he spoke in front of Imperial delegates to defend his cause. Was he nervous, and aware of his low status? It seems far more plausible that he consciously deployed this manner of speaking in order to seem theologically trustworthy and to display humility. After all, Paul had taught that one was to speak of God's Word with trembling anxiety. In Worms, however, Luther's technique failed. Nobody could understand much of what he said, and everybody was surprised that this was supposed to be the great challenger of the Pope. The next day, Luther appeared to be completely different. At least this contrast heightened the impression he now made – at last his 'truth' sounded solid and clear.

This is not meant to imply that Luther was always a cool strategist, who rationally controlled every aspect of a 'self-fashioning' process in order to attain his goals. Luther remained a highly emotional and spontaneous man. This was part of his charm and larger-than-life quality for some, and his gravest failing for others. But we also need to register that Luther had already learnt as a novice how to control his facial features in order to show humility. He grew up in a culture highly aware of rhetorical repertoires and writing skills. These attitudes could not but shape his behaviour; and thus it comes as no surprise that Luther carefully considered how appearances and modes of speaking might help to convey his message in different contexts.

Hence, rather than displaying spiritual modesty, Luther was often strongly polemical or admonitory when he preached and talked to lay audiences. One of his sermons on the psalms in Wittenberg, for example, commented on the verse 'for the arms of the godless shall be broken, but

[32] Brecht, *Luther*, p. 107.

God enlightens the just'. 'Wealth and power had never, or hardly ever', he declared, 'been on the side of the just.' The 'papal arm' of the godless was made up of kings, princes, bishops, priests and monks. These verdicts reveal the contradictory nature of some of Luther's views towards powerful people and, more generally, that his sermons by no means revealed the 'pure' word of the Bible, as the laity demanded and the doctrine of *sola scriptura* suggested. Luther and others revealed the Word through their interpretations of it.

Luther nonetheless told the Wittenberg laity that he had done nothing other than to bring God's pure Word into the world. It had worked effortlessly through its own strength, and had still harmed the Papacy more than any power: 'I have simply told, preached and written God's Word, otherwise I have done nothing. While I slept and while I drank Wittenberg beer with my Phillip and Amsdorf, this achieved so much that the Papacy became weak',[33] he boasted in Wittenberg in 1522 and was fond of repeating at table in later years. However, as has been shown in regard to his communication strategies, little came to Luther during his sleep. He reflected carefully on how he and his Wittenberg companions should behave in particular contexts. Considerable cultural work was required to use different modes of communication and make Luther appear a plausible prophet of divine truths.

Visual strategies

Apart from the spoken word, visual media were most important to the construction of Luther's charisma. This should come as no surprise, since early modern urban culture was awash with images, produced by a whole army of artisan and itinerant water-colourists who illustrated chronicles and manuscripts or painted images on cloth and on interior or exterior walls for everyday viewing. They would also colour printed woodcuts on single sheets or in books.

Nuremberg council edicts let us glimpse how vibrantly Reformed propaganda took off. In 1524, for instance, they prohibited selling 'shameful images, and also Luther's image'.[34] Shortly afterwards, they mentioned a stranger who sold 'small cloths with shameful images of the Pope' in the courtyard of the humanist Willibald Pirckheimer. The wife of a 'painter of letters' sold small books which called bishops a 'lake of animal excrement'; presumably she sold images as well. During the same year, one citizen had a wall of his house painted with a

---

[33] *Martin Luthers Werke*, Weimar edition, vol. IX, p. 679.
[34] Kastner, *Quellen*, pp. 93f.

fox with a papal crown and had to be told to alter it. Reform-minded Nuremberg councillors clearly responded nervously to an anarchic visual culture which was integral to public opinion. Woodcuts in particular were widely used as wallpaper in houses and inns, to protect inhabitants, to be seen by visitors and start discussions. The papal delegate Aleander thus frowned upon woodcuts which were sold en masse in Worms in 1521, depicting Luther's head, the dove symbolising the Holy Ghost, and a halo. Nuremberg town council minutes likewise noted in 1522: 'Prohibit the images of Luther with the Holy Ghost from being sold publicly.' These early portraits of Luther, as Bob Scribner writes, identified him as a saintly prophet acting within the context of divine history, so that he could be seen to 'break legitimately with the established order in the church'. At the same time, visual satires sought to 'destroy the charisma of the Papacy and the Catholic hierarchy'.[35]

Cranach the Elder and his workshop produced much of this propaganda directly in Wittenberg and began disseminating it in 1519. It needs to be noted at once that such cooperation of a court artist with a religious reform movement to produce art for a popular market is unique in history. Cranach was highly skilled, imaginative and fully exploited the visual vocabulary of an articulate popular culture which had built up a language of its own for centuries. One of Cranach's earliest and most important propaganda series for the Lutheran movement was twenty-six woodcuts contrasting the life and suffering of Christ with the life of the Pope as Antichrist, the *Passional Christ and Antichrist* (figure 4). This theme had been elaborated by heretical movements since the fourteenth century. Hussite artists, for instance, depicted Christ washing his disciples' feet and monks kissing the Pope's feet, and we know that a couple of English students in Prague chose to have their sitting-room walls painted with exactly the same theme. Similar representations were also used as posters in street demonstrations. By the early sixteenth century, common people across Europe were so familiar with this contrast of Christ's and the Pope's life that they would occasionally drum up actors and stage it during carnival processions to expose a 'normal' world turned upside down. Cranach developed this iconography in a specifically Lutheran way. He wanted to demonstrate that the Papacy was not just corrupt, but a beast and the living Antichrist. Melanchthon commented on each image. The *Passional* was printed from 1521 onwards in several editions in Latin and in German. Such woodcuts were often sent out with pamphlets and

---

[35] R. W. Scribner, *For the Sake of the Simple Folk. Popular Propaganda for the German Reformation* (Oxford, 1981), pp. 36 and 94.

Antichrist.

Es ist gewislich die Bestia vnd vnie yr es falsch prophet der durch sie geydon ist an hat do mit er vos fundt hat, die sie seynt bey de von yrin genommen / vnd sein slabt angericht seynt versenckt yn die tieffe des feures vnd schwessel vnd seyn grobe mit dem schwerck des der do reyt vssin weyssen pferde, das auf seynem maul gehet. Apocal i 19. Danne wirde vssin sebter werden der schalck yn istige dem wirde der herr Jesus totten mit dem atem seynes mundes vnd wirde yn sturgen durch die glosi seyns su- kunsse. 2. ad Tessa. 2.

Passional Christi vnd

It yezt ansehen ist er auffgehaben vnd die wolcken haben ynn hinwegt genommen vos yren augen. Dieser Jesu der vos euch yn himmel auffgenommen ist / wirde also wyder kommen wie yr yn gesehen habt zu himmel sharen. Act. 1. Seyn reych hat keyn ende. Luce. 1. Wer do mir diene der wirde mir nach volgen vnd wo ich bin do wirt meyn diener auch seyn Joha. 12.

Figure 4. Lukas Cranach the Elder, *Passional Christ and Antichrist*, 1521. In this final scene of the booklet, Christ ascends to heaven and pious folk watch him. The papal Antichrist, who has deceived so many, descends into hell, surrounded by beasts and greeted by false prophets, as the text from the book of Revelation suggests.

letters to important figures within the European reform movement, and their message was powerful.

Cranach and the Wittenberg circle also invested much in turning Luther into an icon of the new reform movement. In 1520, Spalt thus sent a selection of Luther's writing to Albrecht Dürer, who was widely recognised as the best German portraitist, presumably to hint that they would like his portrait of Luther.[36] In thanking Spalt, Dürer wrote that Luther had liberated him from much spiritual anxiety. He enclosed a copy of his first printed portrait based on a copper engraving, and politely promised that he would execute such a likeness of Luther should he see him. Spalt immediately saw the potential of this new technique which allowed for printing far more naturalistic portraits than woodcuts did. He told Cranach to execute a copper engraving of Luther. Cranach studied Dürer's method carefully and engraved one of the best-known images of Luther. It depicts Luther as a youthful monk, with deep-seated eyes, a decisive look and a bony face (figure 5).

Spalt, however, did not like what he saw. Was he aware that the papal legate Cajetan had described Luther as a man whose deep-seated eyes showed that he had 'strange fantasies'? Later descriptions of Luther similarly reveal that eyes signalled a person's character. They were 'just like his books', the Polish diplomat Dantiscus von Hofen reported in 1523, 'sharp and glittering strangely, as in the case of possessed people'. Did Cranach's first portrait suggest obsessiveness and thus 'false prophecy'? Clearly, Cranach had depicted a man who seemed far too striking. He was told to start again.

His second engraving portrayed Luther as a much heavier figure with a mild gaze. He was placed in an alcove, like a saint, held a Bible in his right hand and lifted his left hand, as if he was pointing to some higher truth. His head was slightly raised, and he looked his age. This man undeniably seemed to be inspired by a good spirit, like a divine and reliable man, not a youthful, unconventional rebel. One year later, Cranach engraved another print, which showed Luther once more respectable and pious, as a doctor (figure 6). In these ways, the Wittenberg 'Luther myth' ended up being 'no more than a refurbished, Protestant version of the traditional saint's life'.[37] The new medium was not used innovatively, but to disseminate a traditional image type. Cranach's inscription below his engravings modestly asserted that a portrait depicted only a perishable likeness: only Luther's writings created 'eternal imprints of his mind'.

---

[36] Martin Warnke, *Cranachs Luther. Entwürfe für ein Image* (Frankfurt-on-Main, 1984).
[37] Scribner, *For the Sake*, p. 249.

Figure 5. Lukas Cranach the Elder, *Martin Luther*, 1520.

'Bad paper, bad letters': print and the Reformation

It is an insufficiently recognised fact that between 1516 and 1546 most editions of Luther's works were printed in Wittenberg – a total of 1,057 editions, a majority of them in German. Augsburg published 490 editions and Basle merely 131 editions. How can we explain this surprising statistic

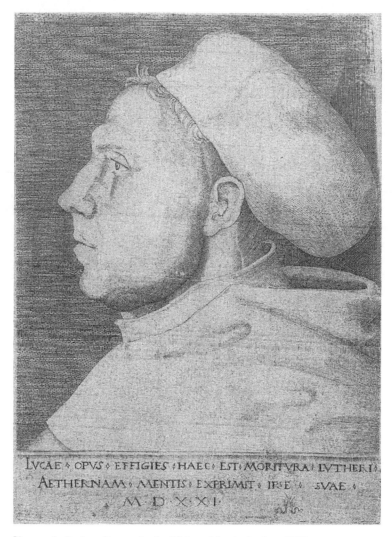

LVCAE ◦ OPVS ◦ EFFIGIES ◦ HAEC ◦ EST ◦ MORITVRA ◦ LVTHERI ◦
AETHERNAM ◦ MENTIS ◦ EXPRIMIT ◦ IPSE ◦ SVAE ◦
◦ M ◦ D ◦ X ◦ X ◦ I ◦

Figure 6. Lukas Cranach the Elder, *Martin Luther*, 1521.

and what does it mean?[38] Luther immediately saw the importance of
'proper' printing for his cause and of securing the necessary infrastructure
locally. Right at the beginning of the movement in 1519, and despite his
preference in principle for the spoken word, Luther and other professors
had successfully campaigned for the son of the highly regarded Leipzig

[38] Maag, *Reformation and the Book*, tables 3 and 4.

printer Melchior Lotter to set up his workshop in Wittenberg. He worked with Hebrew, Greek and Latin letters, which had previously been used by the famous humanist printer Froben in Basle. For an educated public, the Froben letter-type immediately increased the authority of what had been written. The Wittenberg goldsmith Döring acted as a publisher and started a bookshop; Lotter printed in Cranach's house until he was forced to move out after some disagreement in 1523. Döring and Cranach now founded a joint printing and publishing house, which operated until Cranach's withdrawal in 1525.

This means that during the phase of the Reformation movement's greatest popularity, between 1520 and 1525, Cranach acted not only as illustrator, but as printer and publisher for Luther. He and Döring provided capital for high print runs, good paper, good printing and advances for booksellers. Only this infrastructure made it possible for a key part of the dissemination of Lutheran ideas through print to be controlled locally and by Wittenberg, despite being a marginal newcomer in the printing trade. Between 1521 and 1525, 300 editions of Luther's works were published – and it is usually calculated that each of them had a print run of a 1,000 copies. This means that for Luther's works alone, 300 title pages needed to be designed in Wittenberg during these years, and that paper had to be supplied of sufficient quality and sufficient quantity – a difficult task in this period. Skilled printers and journeymen had to be found, too, as well as expert copy-editors to support the proofreading by Luther and his team; also 300,000 copies of pamphlets and books needed to be disseminated. It was not least due to this local effort that Luther became the most frequently printed Reformation author and theologian in Germany: up to his death, a third of all his works poured out from Wittenberg. Their profile and effectiveness was raised by the quality control that could be ensured through tight local supervision of the production process.

In Augsburg, the south German hub of publishing, print production also changed dramatically. Between 1518 and 1530, 1,318 editions, most of them vernacular Reformation broadsheets and pamphlets, were produced. Between 1518 and 1525, Luther wrote 425 of these Augsburg editions.[39] Luther thus had become a leading voice in a nonetheless polyvocal movement across Germany.

All the same, Luther cannot be described as a man who effortlessly controlled the new media of the printed word and image or became a 'print media-star' over night. The pamphlet about the Pope-ass and monk-calf,

---

[39] Hans-Jörg Künast, *'Getruckt zu Augsburg'. Buchdruck uns Buchhandel in Augsburg zwischen 1468 und 1555* (Tübingen, 1997).

referred to at the beginning of this book, serves as an example. The monk-calf had been found in December 1522 near Wittenberg, and was sent to Frederick of Saxony. Soon, printed reports about it circulated widely: learned people sent them to each other and common people put them on their walls. Everybody tried to understand what the monster meant.[40] One month later, Luther received an alarming letter from the Margrave of Brandenburg. He was currently in Prague and had asked an astrologer to explain the monstrous calf to him. The astrologer had published an explanation without Georg's knowledge, according to which the monster demonstrated how dangerous Luther's doctrine was. Although all copies were burnt, this interpretation rapidly spread in verse, reaching as far as Paris. Luther needed to respond and hence provided his own interpretation of the strange monk-calf. Melanchthon added his comments on the Pope-ass, and Cranach made the woodcuts accompanying the texts.

This example of the Wittenberg 'production process' illustrates several points: Luther, Melanchthon and Cranach quickly took up themes which had already aroused interest. Luther nonetheless was not free to write what he liked, but he had to react to defend his reputation. The market for prints about prodigies was lively and competitive. Once more it was only the unique teamwork of Cranach, who contributed his artistic talents, publishing know-how and connections; Melanchthon, who contributed his gift of writing and was always there to help defend Luther's reputation; and Luther's extraordinary productivity which made it possible to quickly publish a counter-attack, which was then reprinted in several other places, and was therefore likely to become the dominant interpretation.

But the example shows as well that Luther lived at a time in which he had no choice but to face the new media, and to publish or perish. This again demanded much effort and strategic thinking. Eberlein von Günzburg was one of the numerous early modern sceptics who thought that print had mainly served to circulate false views. He and Luther agreed that the booksellers' greed for profit overheated the market and confused people. The 'printers use bad paper, bad writing', von Günzburg sighed, 'I praise a printer who . . . corrects well and uses pretty letters on good paper.' Titles such as 'The Papal Pit' or 'Luther's Field Battle' were a testimony to 'loose forms'.[41] The care that went into the production of a publication, the 'serious' presentation and the reputation of the publishing house thus were of key importance to lend respectability

---

[40] Ottavia Niccoli, *Prophecy and People in Renaissance Italy* (Princeton, 1990), pp. 122–6.
[41] Kastner, *Quellen*, pp. 74f.

to Reformation writing. This was uniquely achieved in Wittenberg, but difficult to ensure elsewhere.

Apart from presentation and 'packaging' skills, other print strategies came in useful. One of Luther's most successful strategies was to address a key political pressure group during a time of political change. He did so in 1520, by publishing an *Address to the German Nobility* after Charles V had been elected as Emperor and before the first Imperial Diet meeting in his presence was to take place. The *Address* numbered fifty pages in a quarto format and was not cheap. Even so, according to one report, the first edition had a print run of 4,000 pamphlets and was sold out within two weeks. It was later translated into Dutch and Italian. Another print strategy was to edit opponents' writings and to disqualify their positions. Luther thus even fearlessly edited the Koran. He also forced opponents within the reform movement to withdraw their criticism publicly in print. An important example is Luther's former colleague and supporter Karlstadt, who ranked second as the most productive and frequently published German reformer. Luther forced Karlstadt to publish a treatise with a preface by Luther in which he explained that Karlstadt's view of the sacraments was entirely personal and by no means 'true'. This control of print publications thus once more served to suggest a consensus among Wittenberg authors, or at least to demonstrate their respect for Luther's superior theological authority. A further and more conventional communication strategy was to preface a work with a long dedication to a person of high standing whom one wanted to honour or whose support one wanted to win. Finally, as we have seen in the cases of Bugenhagen and Dürer, the Wittenberg circle freely sent out Luther's writings to a large network of potential sympathisers and 'the right kinds of people', who would then, it was hoped, become supporters or at least further recommend the piece.

In sum, the reception of all writing substantially relied on these networking strategies and a considerable cultural and material effort to create respectability and credit. A 'print media-star' did not emerge. He was made. In this sense, printing involved a far more laborious process than one might first assume if one thinks of a new mass medium that could easily be taken under control and ensure a 'fixity' of ideas in many people's minds. Print was regarded with much scepticism. There were many competitors. Plagiarism abounded. The whole enterprise was costly, which is why catchy titles sought out a wider audience. Censorship had to be fought. After the phenomenal interest in Luther's ideas waned in 1525, Cranach, presumably for these and other reasons, immediately withdrew from publishing. From now on, safe and safe-guarded publications such as hymn-books and, above all, Luther's Bible translation became Wittenberg's key publishing products.

Luther had translated the New Testament speedily by 1522, but a full edition of the Bible was only completed in 1534. The translation was vital for Luther to defend his claim that he had precise and privileged knowledge of God's Word (figure 7). In 1530, Luther thus wrote a treatise on translation emphasising the effort of his work and of his home expert team, chief among them Melanchthon and Matthäus Goldhahn: 'I have exerted myself on this translation so that I would render everything in pure and clear German. And we often had to search for a single word for two or even three or four weeks . . . Job was so difficult that Magister Philip, Aurogallus and I could hardly finish three lines in four days.'[42] This effort and expertise was to distinguish him from the 'false prophets' and Catholics and emphasised the exclusivity of the true translation, which was accomplished through profound scholarliness and the Wittenberg prophetic spirit. Luther ensured the appeal of his Bible translation by favouring the clear and yet imaginative language spoken by ordinary people, an attitude backed by his patriotism and by his wish to represent himself as a new St Paul, for Paul had also expressed himself in popular Greek to reach a wide audience.[43] It would be a mistake to assume, however, that Luther simply translated the Bible. He prefaced every part of it and included his comments on the margins of many pages. These for him were 'truthful additions', which by no means distracted from the purity of the translation and from Scripture itself. They nonetheless propagated Luther's political, religious and prophetic worldview, as in his sermons, and so did Cranach's impressive illustrations in the final biblical book of Revelation, which showed the corrupt Pope as apocalyptical Antichrist.

The 'Luther-Bible' was an immediate and lasting success. Luther's personal symbol, a rose, became the trade-mark printed on each Wittenberg copy of the Bible to testify its authenticity. Even so, copies of unauthorised translations circulated more widely. Other sections of the reform movement published their own translations. Opponents of the movement once more argued that making the Bible available to the laity had only caused 'great confusion'. Soon, even reformers began to steer the laity away from the Bible and towards straight pedagogical catechisms, which taught them one truth. After 1525, the tide of cheap prints for a mass public, which would be read aloud and inspire socio-religious discussions, had anyway

---

[42] *Martin Luthers Werke*, Weimar edition, vol. XXX. 2, p. 633.
[43] Jane O. Newman, The Word made Print: Luther's 1522 New Testament in an Age of Mechanical Reproduction, *Representations* 11 (1985), pp. 95–133. I am grateful to Sachiko Kusukawa for providing me with this article.

Figure 7. The typographically elegant title page of Luther's monumental translation of the New Testament, the *Septembertestament*, 1522.

subsided. Up to 1525, however, Luther and the Wittenberg team had been more successful than any cultural movement before and long after them in dominating the print market through an ingenious use of a new medium. Luther nonetheless did not cause a uniform, broad change of opinion in his support. He merely intensified a process of opinion formation in regard to questions about religious reforms in which his positions had become central.

Luther's Reformation: a summary

History happens accidentally and through the power of specific places and people. Wittenberg was marginal, a dot on the map. Even so, and because of its smallness, an intellectual and prophetic community developed. It disseminated its new truth so efficiently that many existing attempts to reform church and society were catalysed. Luther worked within a team whose core was accidentally formed, Melanchthon – Spalt – Cranach. This constellation was perfect to attain influence in the five central institutions: the town, the principality, the court, the university and the town council, and to undertake the further dissemination of Luther's ideas and the crafting of his image. Added to this was a small circle of loyal and active supporters, above all the diplomat of Lutheranism, Johannes Bugenhagen, who was crucial in adjusting Wittenberg teaching to church, state and urban politics in a practical way. The conventions which characterised the emotional relationship between these men were mainly based on the acceptance of charismatic leadership. They agreed with Luther's final authority and thus created a consensus among Wittenberg men which was additionally secured through a corresponding recruitment and dismissal policy at the university and in town, and through strict procedures against 'false prophets'. In regard to these latter aspects, Luther's success was anything but accidental. It was based on specific techniques of power policies and self-presentation and, moreover, on the development of the 'religious conversation' as a method of truth finding which could be used everywhere and seemed to prove as a matter of fact and thus legitimately the evangelical as opposed to the Catholic truth. This truth was part of a whole political world-view. It promised a new social order, in which theologians rehabilitated their standing. They praised their expertise which made them useful public servants. Wittenberg stood as a model of this new order and the 'Christian peace' governing among Protestants. It moreover signalled the ability of Lutherans to submit to the clear authority of one leader, one church, one prince and one magistrate. Secular power over the church was extended. Social reforms were implemented which helped to secure an orderly civic world. Random gifts for vagrants and beggars, for instance, were replaced by a 'responsible' system of almsgiving for the local, manifestly needy, pious and obedient poor.

Last but not least, the Reformation also needs to be characterised as a student reformation. The international dissemination of the movement was substantially facilitated by the 'Wittenberg' experience and the emotional bonds which Luther and Melanchthon formed with their students (see also pp. 161–5). In sum, only the unique local character of the Wittenberg context – the human, institutional and economic resources which could be mobilised there, the forms of teamwork, the psychology which structured the reformers' relationships, and the decisiveness of the political and cultural work to disseminate the new truth – explains how Martin Luther accidentally became a man who changed history.

At the same time, we need to chart the limits of his achievements. Luther thought mainly in German terms. Many opportunities to disseminate his ideas in Europe remained unexplored. Luther was sometimes able to act diplomatically, but mostly did not. He was a man of strong convictions and feelings, and they showed. The loyalty he knew how to ensure among his closest followers suppressed disagreement, which exploded after his death. Luther's belief in the imminent end of the world hindered long-term strategic thought, and as a consequence, even Reformation propaganda was 'too preoccupied with proclaiming the end of the world to show men how to live pious lives within it'.[44] In disseminating his views in print, Luther only partly gained control of the publishing market. Popular preachers and pamphleteers often propagated their own views. And of course Luther's success cannot be termed accidental within a larger historical framework. It was part and parcel of long-term reform movements since the Middle Ages.

In September 1524, Luther summarised the progress of his Reformation thus far: Protestants preached in four Magdeburg churches; the Imperial Cities had opposed the Edict of Worms at their Speyer meeting; the banishment of a Protestant minister in Augsburg had failed; the Strasburg bishop had been told to leave the city; Bugenhagen was about to implement the Reformation in Hamburg; Philip of Hesse had ordered the preaching of Scripture alone in his principality; Protestants were not persecuted in the Palatinate.

This list can be extended: Ernestine Saxony was firmly on Luther's side. At the Speyer Diet of 1526 the Imperial Estates decided that they

---

[44] Scribner, *For the Sake*, p. 249.

Figure 8. Lukas Cranach the Elder, *The Origins of Monks*, 1545, from the series *Depiction of the Papacy*. According to popular belief, gallows were haunted by evil spirits, and here Cranach depicted devils sitting on the gallows, one of them relieving himself of monks.

needed to retain control over the Reformation movement and that each of them had to justify before God and the Emperor which church policy they would chose. In powerful cities, such as Nuremberg, the council had implemented measured reforms. These served to avoid a religious and political radicalisation of urban protest and met the council's long-standing concerns, such as diminishing the influence of church courts. Luther, as we have seen, had become a publishing success, and Reformed writings, image propaganda and sermons reached a mass audience. All of this was remarkable and could easily be seen as the beginning of God's victory over the papal Antichrist.

Even so, the year 1524 also marked the break with the humanist movement around Erasmus, deeper divisions with Zwinglians (see pp. 73–9), the clearer positioning of the Catholic territories and the onset of political protest resulting in the movement of 1525, followed by the decline of Luther's publishing success and a further multiplication of reform positions, in which people from all backgrounds now found proofs for their truth by quoting German Bibles. Luther had managed to convince several princes and magistrates personally and politically of his truth. His struggle with other truth claims continued (figure 8).

2 The age of heterodoxy

Why did Luther fail to sway most of Europe? Which ideas underpinned truths other than his? This chapter introduces the dramatic life stories of five people who played an important public role in the age of the Lutheran Reformation, but whose views differed from those of Luther. It also sketches where and how the Reformation movement in Europe expanded.

Charles V

The most important representative of a different truth was Emperor Charles V. From his election in 1519 until his resignation in 1555, he was the most powerful man of the early modern period and one of the greatest rulers of all time. His Empire included Spain and its 'New World' colonies, as well as Luxembourg, Belgium, the Netherlands, Austria, the Holy Roman Empire, Lorraine, Alsace and parts of Italy.[1]

Charles was born in 1500 in Ghent, and grew up at the court of Burgundy, a place of outstanding cultural sophistication. His father died early in 1506; his mother had become mentally ill. Charles's aunt, Margaret of Austria, took care of his education. He grew to be a quiet, serious and shy man, lost nearly all his teeth and suffered from a slack jaw. German court fools despaired over him. Charles mostly wore black, was plagued by gout, and was hardly able to ride. His arranged marriage to Isabella of Portugal was nonetheless happy; several sons and daughters were born. Even so, Charles's visits to Spain were short, for he was the last Emperor who continuously travelled throughout his domains. With age, he became quieter still, and often seemed troubled. Observers were quick to wonder whether Charles had inherited some of his mother's insanity. But Charles suffered because he was unable to implement the

---

[1] Hugo Soly (ed.), *Charles V. 1500–1558 and his Time* (Antwerp, 2000) provides the best recent overview. Alfred Kohler (ed.), *Quellen zur Geschichte Karl V.* (Darmstadt, 1990) is a valuable source collection.

great projects of his rule: to defend his possessions, gain further Italian domains in order to fight off the Ottomans, and not only defeat French claims in Italy but create an encompassing European Empire, a *monarchia universalis*, which was to include France. His councillor Gattinara had instilled in him early on the vision of his becoming a great Christian Emperor like Augustus. Spanish late scholastic scholars questioned this idea, but Charles clung to it. His personal motto was *Plus Ultra*, 'Even Further', although the very size of his Empire was his greatest weakness: troops were rarely positioned where they were needed; Charles was permanently close to financial ruin; family members governed different parts of the Habsburg Empire; much and sometimes too much was delegated. Because he had entrusted his brother Ferdinand with matters relating to the Holy Roman Empire, Charles realised too late that a confessional divide had become thinkable. Nor was Charles's understanding of German matters helped by the fact that he principally understood French. Even so, his rule cannot straightforwardly be dismissed as a failure, especially if judged by the standards of the time. Charles's possessions increased during his reign of forty years; he intelligently mobilised trade capital to finance his policies and an impressive amount of administrative communication was conducted in six languages. And Charles certainly celebrated some extraordinary victories, such as the imprisonment of his great rival, the French king Francis I. He faced formidable challenges all over his Empire, and tackled them determinedly.

How can we characterise Charles's religious attitudes? During his youth, Charles was influenced by the simple piety of the modern devotion movement and the order of the Golden Fleece. The latter practised Marian devotion, but favoured worship of Christ above all. It is thus one of the ironies of history that the Emperor was a far less traditional Catholic than Luther's protector, Frederick the Wise. Charles did not collect relics, and rarely performed good works in public. He sometimes attended rituals at which bishops washed the (pre-washed) feet of poor people. But on the whole, he expressed his belief through penitence, prayers, his esteem for religious music, a virtuous life (that is, once more, by the standards of the time: he only fathered two bastards, for instance, and none while he was married) and his mission to counter the destruction of Western Christendom by Muslims, Christian heretics and the Antichrist. Charles was one of the last crusaders and regarded himself as a *Katechon*, a militant Emperor of Peace. He wished the whole of Europe to be ruled by a devout Pope without imperial pretension and a robust Christian Emperor like himself.

Even so, he was flexible in some of his views and willing to compromise, for instance in regard to the so-called 'Interim' measures in Germany after the first Smalkaldic War between Lutherans and Catholics. These allowed priests to marry and to celebrate communion in both kinds until such time as a General Church Council could decide on a permanent religious settlement. Having lost the second Smalkaldic War against the Lutherans and been compelled to make far more substantial concessions, however, Charles no longer wished to be Emperor. He retired to a small mansion in Andalusia close to a monastery obeying Augustine orders. There he led a deeply spiritual life. Bernard of Clairvaux was read aloud to him; he asked Inquisition officials for permission to use a specific French translation of the Bible, and frequently talked to his confessors. Charles's faith thus had much in common with Luther's: Bernard's teaching, the Pauline doctrine of salvation and the spirituality of psalms were important to both of them. Luther respected him as a pious man.

Charles's death further demonstrates this surprising closeness of enemies. Charles clutched the same cross that his beloved wife, Isabella of Portugal, had held on her deathbed; the Archbishop of Toledo told Charles to place all his hope in Jesus Christ, who had died for him, paid for man's sins and would defend good Catholics before God. Another cleric watching the scene thought that Charles had now been heretically tainted by a Lutheran understanding of salvation, and immediately reminded him of the great power of the saints' compassion and their intercessions. The Archbishop of Toledo was summoned before the Inquisition.

Charles's attitude towards a good Christian death differed markedly from that of his grandfather. Maximilian wished to be castigated as a penitent human sinner; all the hair on his body was shaved off, his teeth were taken out, and the corpse was covered with a coarse linen cloth, ash and chalk, placed in a simple oak coffin and buried. Charles lived within a different world of belief, which had developed during the late Middle Ages and rendered such rituals unnecessary. Christ had suffered for man on the Cross, and human sinners could trust in his grace: saints and penitential works were less important. Piety rested on a simple, devout life, reading, reflection and pastoral conversations. Tellingly, the *disciplinas* in Charles's post-mortem inventory were merely listed as decorative objects and not used for self-flagellation.

Nonetheless, Charles could not but bitterly fight Luther's radical critique of Rome, which seemed to provoke a division of Western Christendom and make it more vulnerable to Ottoman attacks. He had no time either for Luther's wholesale dismissal of convent life and distrust of patterns of Reformed Christian life, which in Charles's native Netherlands had developed for more than a century. At the height of his power in Italy Charles had himself presented as a new King David; in Burgundy he celebrated feasts in the style of popular Christian chivalric novels,

Figure 9. Titian, *Charles V at the Battle of Mühlberg*, 1548. An extraordinary depiction of Charles V as a traditional, triumphant Christian knight defeating Protestant heresy.

claiming to be a new St George. He read Caesar and books on Charles the Bold. Among the very small number of books he left after his death we find two copies of *El caballero determinado*. This poem by the fifteenth-century Burgundian court poet Olivier de la Marche had been written to marshal aristocratic sponsorship for crusades by praising the life of the Christian knight. Charles himself had translated it into Castilian. He remained deeply rooted in its mental world, aspiring to be the greatest Christian ruler of early modern Europe and its one church. He pursued his goal with a sense of mission rivalling Luther's, a limited intellect, and arrogance. The fine details of theological argument did not interest him. He wanted order, historical continuity, traditional greatness and yet greater things – *Plus Ultra!* (figure 9).

All of this may explain why Charles was so fascinated by clockwork – a pioneering technology at the time. Sixteenth-century clocks were anything but accurate. They nonetheless were commonly taken to be divine, miraculous mechanisms, which enabled diverse components to perform a common task effortlessly, calculably and with perfection. They inspired the fantasy that society should function like a clock and hence became the most important political metaphor of the age. Charles collected clocks. When he suffered a nervous breakdown after his defeat by Protestants in 1552, he woke his servants up every night; they would light the candles, and Charles would go to his clock collection continuously to dismantle and reassemble some of the clocks. It was as if he sought desperately to understand how all the elements working against each other in his Empire could be made to perform a common task. After his retirement, his much-reduced entourage continued to feature a clock-maker, which almost seems like a therapeutic measure. Every morning the clock-maker would make sure all the clocks displayed the correct time before Charles entered his rooms.

Erasmus

Desiderius Erasmus (*c.* 1466–1536) was the most famous European scholar of Luther's time and a Christian humanist.[2] For him, too, good and penitent works, rituals and even the mass were of little importance. He was born the son of a priest in Rotterdam. From 1487 he lived in a convent; in 1493 he became secretary of the Bishop of Cambrai. Two years later he started studying in Paris and soon began to travel extensively. Later, the Swiss city of Basle became his base, where he received visitors from all over Europe, built up an enormous network of correspondents and published his many writings. Erasmus dedicated his life to independent scholarship and to male friendships, and thus avoided belonging to a court, the curia, a university or a city, because he rightly feared that any such position and patronage would have forced him to defend his patrons' positions. Erasmus tried to live as a writer, either

---

[2] The best introductions are James Tracy, *Erasmus of the Low Countries* (Berkeley, 1996) and Lisa Jardine, *Erasmus. Man of Letters* (Princeton, 1993).

(a)

Figure 10a. Quentin Matsys, *Desiderius Erasmus*, medal, 1519. Erasmus not only commissioned likenesses from superior artists, he also gave permission to reproduce this medal extensively in copper, lead or bell metal. The Greek part of the inscriptions states that his writings will present a better image, a routine sentence of Renaissance artistic humility, but also a great way for Erasmus to advertise his work.

by taking on commissioned work or by working freelance – an unusual decision at the time for someone without independent wealth. He therefore needed to create effective marketing strategies. Thus, for example, he worked together closely with the prestigious Basle publisher Froben, edited his own correspondence and pressured the famous artist Dürer into engraving his portrait, so that it could be multiplied in print. The print reinforced Erasmus's cult status by depicting him sitting in his study surrounded by books and letters in the manner of depictions of St Jerome, whom the educated public particularly revered at the time (figure 10). Erasmus also tried to obtain a no-strings pension from Charles V, for whom he had written a guide for governing. As in later letters, he had advised Charles to avoid war. What, apart from destruction, could be gained through it? He opted for diplomacy, wisdom and the rejection of Imperial ambitions. In the age of Ottoman advances and the conflict between Christian confessions his attitude seemed increasingly naïve. A Christian ruler prided himself on having the courage to fight at the right time, at least to protect confessional unity. Even so, and despite the fact that the Council of Trent posthumously placed all of Erasmus's works on the index of forbidden books, the *Education*

(b)

Figure 10b. This reverse side of the medal depicts the God Terminus. Erasmus thus showed himself as a man strong enough to face that the ending of time could not be humanly controlled. The Greek legend reads 'Consider the end of a Long life – death is the ultimate limit of things'; the Latin motto, thought of as spoken by the God, is 'I yield to no one.'

of a Christian Prince was still translated into Spanish for Charles's son Philip II.

Erasmus's religious beliefs were close to the modern devotion movement, focused on the New Testament, and put a true Christian life and Christian scholarship above all narrow interpretative debates. He wrote sarcastically against degenerated mendicant orders, uneducated priests and indulgences. In voicing such criticisms he, like so many contemporaries, agreed with Luther. In contrast to Luther, however, he did not question papal legitimacy, even though he was well aware of some of the Popes' interests and abilities. Neither was he a particularly strong defender of the idea of assembling a Church Council to settle religious disputes. How then did he imagine reforms should take effect? Erasmus found himself more and more in the position of a sceptical intellectual whose views could be attacked as either indecisive or ambiguous. He simply did not think that the time was right for divisive decisions. Erasmus, over fifty in 1521 and thus an old man compared to Luther or Charles V, increasingly seemed like a man unable to adjust to the political climate of the time. He believed that education would slowly disseminate the right knowledge of Christ's words and had the power to move even ordinary people to lead a more virtuous life. He believed in mildness and the work of reform bishops. Erasmus's patience also resulted from his view that God ruled over all time – and thus over the course of world events and reforms. In contrast to Luther he did not think he lived during the Last Days. The devil and Antichrist were alien powers to him and did not motivate his thought. Early modern people inhabited diverse mental worlds – many of them were never gripped by doom-laden visions of a Judgement Day.

Erasmus's attitudes chimed with his humanist conception of man's nature, which fundamentally differed from Luther's. Erasmus discussed this issue in his only public writing against Luther in 1524, *De Libero Arbitrio Diatribe*, whose topic was the freedom of will. Erasmus disputed Luther's view that man was and remained a sinner, completely dependent on God's grace, which had been granted through the death of His Son. Luther formulated the paradox that man was *simul iustus et peccator*, just and a sinner at the same time, since even the most devout person again and again had to act in sinful ways. This, to Erasmus, seemed a dangerous conviction. Did this not imply that everybody could excuse him- or herself easily and nonetheless feel saved? Why should people be unable to decide to commit themselves fully to a pious life? Erasmus believed that the Bible gave clear directives on how to live a Christian life, and that man was able to unfold virtue from within himself and his belief to follow them. For Luther these were nice thoughts, but remote from the realities of life. They seemed part of a modern devotion movement that had become outdated and of an overly optimistic humanism. Erasmus, for his part, witnessed one year later in Basle the pouring rain mix with the blood of hundreds of defeated peasants, who had taken up their swords in the name of divine justice and grace. He felt his calls for caution had been bitterly justified.

As a theologian, Erasmus enjoyed the greatest admiration in England. In 1535, Anne Boleyn's father asked him to write a treatise on how to prepare for death. Along with his commentary on proverbial sayings, the *Adages*, which had earlier made him famous, as well as his best-selling *Handbook of a Christian Soldier* and his *Praise of Folly*, this new treatise, *De Praeparatione ad Mortem*, became one of his most popular works; it demonstrates the success of Erasmus's distinctively Christian humanist spirituality. The popularity of the treatise moreover testifies to the urgent need, which so many medieval and early modern laypeople felt, for spiritual assurance and comfort in their search for an eternal life.

The starting point of Erasmus's considerations in *De Praeparatione ad Mortem* was Plato's verdict that philosophy was nothing but a contemplation of death.[3] To understand this in a Christian way, Erasmus explained, meant realising that contemplation of Platonic formulae could not prepare one for dying. Such a preparation could only begin by reflecting on issues transcending human reason, such as God's promise of His Son to mankind, or the evil with which He threatened non-Christians. Belief had to be nurtured throughout one's life as a practice of preparing for death through prayer and a virtuous life, marked by love, hope and fearlessness. Even if traces of man's battle against sin remained within human nature, God had given everyone the means to overcome them. 'Believe in Scripture and put all your trust in Christ', Erasmus told readers. Even so, he thought that anxiety was a further gift from the Holy Ghost: only Christians who were anxious about the final judgement and about God truly believed in Him. Anyone who bought indulgences and masses for the soul was misled. While they were dying, Christians were to be comforted with the example of all those who had regretted their sins and had been redeemed to meet an eternity free from all worldly desire and elevated to a true spirit of love, belief and hope in heaven.

Erasmus died a good Christian death himself soon after completing this work, uttering psalm words and *Lieve God* until his end. He remained a cult figure: Rotterdam built a monument commemorating him in 1622, and Basle seems to have had similar plans. This, his vanity notwithstanding, he surely would have rejected. After all, he had left Basle when it became Protestant.

Zwingli

Years before the Reformation succeeded in Basle, the Zurich council had ordered in 1523 that all preaching in the town should be based on the Bible. Ulrich Zwingli was Zurich's reformer, who had preached in its *Großmünster* church since 1519. Zurich witnessed the first large urban Reformation in Europe, and Zwinglianism particularly influenced Switzerland and southern Germany; it also prefigured several Calvinist beliefs.

Zwingli was born shortly after Luther, in January 1484, the son of a local official (figure 11).[4] Ulrich was a talented pupil and at the age of ten was sent to be educated in the Swiss cities of Basle and Berne; afterwards he studied in Vienna. Aged twenty-two, Magister Zwingli became

---

[3] *Collected Works of Erasmus*, vol. LXX (Toronto, 1989), pp. 389–450.
[4] George Richard Potter, *Zwingli* (Cambridge, 1976) and Berndt Hamm, *Zwinglis Reformation der Freiheit* (Neukirchen, 1988) are important introductions to his life and thought. For a more general treatment see the excellent book by Bruce Gordon, *The Swiss Reformation* (Manchester, 2002).

Figure 11. Hans Asper, *Ulrich Zwingli*, 1531. Few portraits of Zwingli exist – towns had no court artists like Cranach; Zwingli did not have the means to commission a portrait from a superior artist and did not use his own likeness for propaganda purposes. Sentimental cultic images depicting Zwingli, for instance, as a shepherd boy, date from the nineteenth century.

a preacher at Glarus, a post he held for ten years. He twice accompanied mercenary soldiers to Italy. By the end of this period, in 1516, Erasmus's New Testament edition had been published and opened Zwingli's eyes to a faith based on the Bible. He learned Greek and Hebrew and began passionately reading the 'true books of Christendom', which he had not even held in his hands while studying. By now he was a priest at a famous Marian pilgrimage shrine in Einsiedeln, but felt increasingly alienated from Marian devotion and saint worship. Aged thirty-five, in January 1519 Zwingli moved to Zurich. He and the Basle humanist Beatus Rhenanus organised the dissemination of Luther's early writings in Zurich and even supported a network of vagrants who peddled them in the countryside. Zwingli also began to publish himself. Erasmus soon withdrew from correspondence with him and attacked the 'absolute non-sense' of a new, anonymous pamphlet against the Pope, which had been published in Zurich. He knew that Zwingli had written it. 'If everyone who is on Luther's side is like this, I wash my hands of all of them. I have never seen anything crazier than this mad stuff' Erasmus wrote indignantly. After 1521, Zwingli cleverly insisted that nobody should ask him whether he belonged to the heretics Luther or Hus. He belonged to those who regarded the Bible as a wellspring of heavenly doctrine. Truth could emerge only from true scholarship and proper divine inspiration. Zwingli, too, had thus begun to defend his charisma and claimed to be a privileged exegete of the Word.

How can we comprehend Zwingli's rapid success in Zurich, a middle-sized town of just under 6,000 inhabitants? Political and religious factors played their part, and can be sketched as follows. Switzerland had nominally succeeded in gaining independence from the Habsburgs and the Holy Roman Empire in 1499. It now constituted a confederation of cities and cantons independent of any superior overlord. A small region such as this could easily be threatened by major forces and thus had to form protective alliances. Within Switzerland, Zurich was suspected of wanting to expand its territory. Basle and Berne were consistently cautious about alliances, determined as they were to secure their autonomy in dangerous times. Foreign powers gave money to influential people and so-called 'pensions' to city councillors to buy their loyalty.

Such payments were a normal form of early modern alliance-seeking and not necessarily regarded as 'corruption'. After Charles V's election, 'pension' payments to prince electors were officially recorded. In Switzerland, however, everybody began to suspect that various parties made secret payments to different councillors simultaneously. The possible utility of an anti-Habsburg alliance with France was already openly discussed. But this would have implied some kind of tribute and an end to Swiss 'liberty'. Also, mercenary soldiers were possibly the most profitable export business of the country. This, too, caused unease. Swiss mercenaries serving different foreign rulers now sometimes even fought against each other. Their plundering and trade brought money to the poor Swiss cantons. It was not a virtuous way of conducting an economy.

Zwingli hence had been appointed to Zurich partly because he stood for a clear moral programme: he was firmly against any trade with mercenary soldiers, against 'pensions' and against alliances with foreign powers. Like Luther, he was a patriotic reformer, who unfolded a vision of Swiss self-reflection and moral purification at the right time. Foreign money, he preached, only fed a sinful desire for luxury, especially among women, and spread sinful manners. Swiss liberty was central to Zwingli's political thought. He proposed an autonomous foreign policy, and frugality, rather than selfish spending, in the interest of the common good. This change, he argued, would be facilitated if the power of the Holy Ghost were allowed to enter Swiss hearts. Its password was the message of salvation. God did not demand penitence and good works. Man, the sinner, was accepted by God, as His Son had taken all guilt upon Himself by His death. Zwingli and Luther therefore shared a common view of salvation; Zwingli moreover decisively applied it to communal life. God's law was a sign of grace. It led people to an eternal life, and believers were to open themselves to it through Scripture. A life in accordance with God's law meant joy, an opening up to God's love and engagement in communal life. Only such belief would enable citizens to endorse the kind of communal order and discipline that pleased God. Towns and cities would turn into God's 'temples', if Scripture was preached in the right way and structures of order were put into place. Secular authorities, too, needed to embrace this understanding and show urban communities the ways of law and Scripture. Zwingli had thus developed a positive vision of spiritual and political change based on his reform theology, a vision that aimed to guarantee order.

The surprising support of the majority of councillors for Zwingli is therefore best explained through his anti-pension politics, which restored an image of purity to the council, and a convincing theology, which placed the council *ex iure divino* and allowed him many more rights over the church. The Zurich church and city council were soon thoroughly interlinked. As early as January 1523 the council affirmed that it endorsed Zwingli's teaching alone and wished to avoid any further 'trouble' resulting from other theological positions. It summoned a 'religious conversation', in which all clerics of the Zurich territory and the Bishop of Constance were supposed to participate. This was supposed to be a forum for voicing 'opposing' views. The council and learned theologians were to verify whether these were supported by Scripture. Six hundred people, most of them clerics, appeared in front of the town hall. Zwingli had summarised his views in sixty-seven short theses. Among other arguments, these defended clerical marriage and denied that purgatory existed. At the end of his speech, Zwingli declared that he trusted that this had been the true voice of Scripture and that God had wanted him to speak by giving him His spirit. He then told his opponents: 'Here I am.' Thick Hebrew and Greek folio editions of the Bible were propped up in front of him. Only a few clerics attacked the man who presented himself as a godly prophet, who was supported by an impressive group of local scholars and clearly fought an easy game, for which he and the council had set the rules. He told his main opponent scathingly that he wanted to give him a *Hasenkäse*, a 'rabbit-cheese', if he were able to show that Zwingli's theology did not accord with Scripture. He told this man that his subsequent argument was ridiculous, and that he merely created trouble among ordinary folk. As in Wittenberg, diverse ideas were thus denounced as a negative plurality of viewpoints, contributing to a superfluous, 'annoying' discussion. The truth was clear, and Zwingli knew it. The council decided that Zwingli should continue preaching according to Scripture and that the clerics should stop denouncing each other as heretics. Once more the religious conversation served as a means to formalise a consensus that had already been politically decided upon.

Zwingli now quickly developed urban policies that implemented his idea of a communal church. The tithe began to be used for poor relief and schooling. Christ's image was to be worshipped through the poor rather than saints. In 1525, even priestly robes were given to the poor; they became a living image of the change the city had undergone. Selfishness, privilege and vanity, which clerics had embodied, were supposed to be a thing of the past. The resident and pious poor symbolised a new Christianity in the interest of the common good; they received wooden sculptures of saints to use as firewood. Elaborate gravestones, which were not reclaimed by families, were removed from churches and used as building material. This was how iconoclasm made social sense.[5]

During the following years, Zwingli's Zurich Reformation implemented further measures that clearly set it apart from Lutheranism.

[5] Lee Palmer Wandel, *Voracious Idols and Violent Hands. Iconoclasm in the Reformation. Zurich, Strasbourg and Basel* (Cambridge, 1995) provides an excellent comparative analysis.

Zwingli began claiming the Pope was the Antichrist, but his views were far less eschatological than Luther's. He justified resistance against non-Protestant rulers. His notion of the Eucharist also differed from Luther's. Communion was not celebrated as a meal in which Christ's blood and flesh became present; it was a ritual remembering His death for humankind, while bread and wine were regarded as merely symbolic. This in itself was a revolution in terms of how the materials of religion could be perceived. Next a 'marriage court', staffed by clerics and councillors, was introduced; this dealt with a broad range of moral misbehaviour, but did not threaten to excommunicate sinners. No church music was allowed, and all images were removed to avoid further spontaneous iconoclastic attacks by the population. Nobody suffered from 'visual anorexia', though; pious woodcuts were still disseminated on pamphlets, which Johann Froschauer produced in large numbers. Froschauer guaranteed the Zurich Reformation that crucial infrastructure of a reliable and able local Protestant printer, who had some capital and international connections. (Zwingli nonetheless never became a Reformation bestseller; his most successful book only reached six editions.) Apart from Froschauer, Zwingli's work was supported by a small, loyal team of scholars, like Leo Jud, who were experts in Hebrew, Greek or Latin and had considerable diplomatic and networking skills. Zwingli built on his expert team by creating a group that met several times a week to translate the Bible. Their collective and seemingly consensual work resulted in a distinct Zurich Bible edition, called *Prophezei* – Prophecy.

   All these measures secured Zwingli's position as chosen prophet. Even so, people whose opinions differed needed to be confronted. For the new teaching was not simply accepted by the population, but questioned and reflected on. Many people asked, for instance, whether they should continue to pay the tithe to the church, whether pastors were to be trusted at all and which rituals were adequate.[6] One Catholic chronicler stated that by 1525 many men and women in Zurich still wanted to receive communion in the traditional way. In 1526, frail old clerics preferred to leave the city rather than follow the new law and get married. From 1524 on, conflicts with Anabaptists, led by the Zurich patrician's son Conrad Grebel, and other 'radicals' abounded. These 'radicals' were united in opposing infant baptism, and divided on the centrality of Scripture for life. Fundamentalist evangelical views confronted a spiritualised stance. They also disagreed on whether secular offices and military service were

---

[6] These incidents are documented in Emil Egli, *Actensammlung zur Geschichte der Zuricher Reformation in den Jahren 1519–1533* (Zurich, 1879).

acceptable, as well as on issues relating to the role of violence, power and possession in a Christian's life. This plurality of 'truths' could not be ignored. Neither could it be eliminated by drowning opponents in Lake Zurich, the fate that befell Felix Manz in 1527. It could only be controlled.

Within Switzerland, Basle and Berne also became Protestant. Five inner Swiss areas remained strongly influenced by Catholicism, were economically dependent on the mercenary trade and wanted to retain their autonomy from Zurich. This led Zwingli and Zurich to fear that Charles V might make them allies and turn Switzerland into a Habsburg possession. Zwingli, moreover, wanted a united Protestant country. In 1529, the first Kappel War was fought. It ended with a remarkable peace agreement, decreeing tolerance between Catholic and Protestant territories: the confederation's continuity as political unity was clearly privileged over confessional unity. Zwingli, however, did not share this emphasis. After having previously dedicated religious writings to Francis I, he now tried to make an alliance with France – the Habsburg enemy. Zwingli's condition was that the true gospel be preached in France and Francis prove himself a pious regent. The alliance failed.

Soon afterwards, in 1531, rumours abounded that the inner Swiss opponents were about to attack Zurich. The response was fast, and the battle between mostly untrained Zurich citizens and Catholic mercenary soldiers lost just as fast. Zwingli, who fought himself, died. Switzerland nonetheless remained a country of mixed confessions.

Margaret of Angoulême and Navarre

Zwingli's hopes in negotiating with the French Crown focused on the influence of the king's sister, Margaret of Navarre. Margaret was born in 1492. Her brother Francis was two years younger and ruled from 1515. His whole reign was dominated by the struggle for European supremacy between his Valois line and the Habsburgs. Margaret and her brother were close and supported each other: when Francis was Charles V's prisoner in Madrid and mortally ill, Margaret rushed to his aid, nursed him and attempted to organise his escape. Francis in turn immediately protested when her *Mirror of the Penitent Soul* appeared on the Sorbonne's index of forbidden books in 1531. Margaret was an unusual woman, and Francis never tried to restrain her independent mind. Her religious poems and meditations were published during her lifetime and translated into several languages. The *Heptameron*, a collection of amusing and erudite stories about women, men and love, was posthumously ascribed to Margaret and is considered an early modern classic to this day. Like her mother, she actively intervened in politics and court life. Here, too, she retained her own voice.[7]

Why did the French Crown not welcome the Reformation? After all, the English monarchy had broken with Rome in 1529 without suffering a rebellion. Given that England was part of an island, however, it was less vulnerable to attack by either the Habsburgs or the Pope than France. France was also less centrally governed than England: a fragmentation of the country into a Protestant and Catholic part was all too easy to imagine. In Paris, Francis had to struggle with a *parlement* and a university which defended their own policies and feared any infiltration by Lutheranism. Francis was therefore the first French king who repeatedly tried to legitimate his power as 'absolute'. He represented himself as 'most Christian king', that is to say, as installed by God. His political self-representation included daily attendance at mass. A Christian king had vigorously to fight heresy and any confessional division of France: 'One king, one law, one faith' became the lasting slogan of a Gallican monarchy determined to maintain its power. Francis claimed to be interested in church reforms, but principally wished to strengthen his own influence over the appointment of bishops. Episcopal seats were important rewards for loyal supporters and thus central to holding power, for, like all early modern rulers, Francis was unable to secure loyalty through his own wealth. He thus nominated above all the French nobility of the sword and increasingly Italians for high clerical office. These men lacked theological training and had not even studied; few of them resided in their dioceses.

Calls for a spiritual renewal turned on demands for reform bishops. But the kind of reforms envisaged was left unclear or disputed. Moreover, many became cautious after 1525 – not least Margaret of Navarre. Between 1521 and 1525, a bishop called Guillaume Briçonnet, a lawyer from a high-ranking family, tried an experiment in the town of Meaux. He invited several reform-minded clerics to preach in Meaux's parishes. This upset Franciscan monks, who regarded mendicant preaching as their source of income and influence and did not want to see these threatened by learned Parisians. Briçonnet was put on trial in 1525, while Francis was a captive in Madrid. His mother was not alone in thinking that Francis's imprisonment was divine punishment for his failure to repress Lutheran

---

[7] The most inspiring work remains Lucien Febvre, *Amour sacré, amour profane. Autour de l'Heptameron* (Paris, 1944). For some general context see in particular Robert Knecht, *Renaissance Warrior and Patron. The Reign of Francis I.* (Cambridge, 1994) and Denis Crouzet, *La Genèse de la Réforme Française 1520–1562* (Paris, 1996).

doctrine sufficiently. News about the German Peasants' War fed further fears about the effects of heretical teaching.

Were Briçonnet and his circle heretical? At bottom no, for we are once again dealing with a group that was essentially influenced by the modern devotion movement as well as mystical and Pauline teaching. This, however, implied a low regard for good works to lessen one's time in purgatory as well as a faith centred on the Bible rather than the adoration of Mary or the saints. The people of Meaux were therefore called *bibliens*. The oldest 'Meaux-man' was Jacques Lefèvre d'Etaples (1450–1537), who was old enough to have met great Florentine Renaissance men like Ficino and Pico della Mirandola. Lefèvre followed some of their spiritual and esoteric Christian humanist ideas, opposed the scholastic adherence to formal logic and a fixed scholarly canon and wanted to use scholarship to understand the workings of God and His spirits. In contrast to Erasmus, he was also happy to write in the vernacular. In 1509, he published a commentary on the Psalms and a commentary on St Paul, which deeply influenced the reform movement, and in 1530 a translation of the Bible. Briçonnet corresponded with Margaret for four years, and his letters drew extensively on the importance of St Paul. Despite man's sins, grace and salvation had been granted to humans through Christ's death. Clearly, these views were close to Luther's. Luther, though, developed these insights further and politicised them, and this distinguished him from Briçonnet, Lefèvre and Margaret. Translations of Luther's works, which one printer under the king's protection continued to print even after this was prohibited, omitted such political aspects. They thus fed into the huge contemporary movement of 'Pauline enthusiasm' (L. Febvre), which nonetheless posed fundamental questions threatening Catholic doctrine, such as whether purgatory existed, or only hell.

Alas, the Sorbonne allowed little room to explore questions of this kind. After the Leipzig debate and again in 1523, most scholars had condemned Luther as a heretic. Censorship prohibited circulation of Lutheran works. For many, the term 'Lutheran' itself had become a label for reform-minded troublemakers, or for all Germans. The papal official Aleander fearfully (over)estimated them as numbering around 30,000 in Paris alone. Briçonnet distanced himself several times from accusations of Lutheranism. But by the time he was put on trial in 1525 his supporters already knew that they had to leave Meaux and seek protection. Heretics were burned at the stake now, and martyrologies began to be written.

How did Margaret respond to these events? 'Just like herself', as Lucien Febvre has dryly summarised the confusing evidence. She did not turn into a public fighter for reform, but supported important people

in the reform movement and remained theologically open in her reading.
Contrary to this image of openness we should note that she did not
exchange any further letters with Briçonnet after 1525. If we trust her
recorded correspondence, she neither responded to careful requests for
support from German reformers like Melanchthon or Bucer, nor to two
letters from Erasmus. Moreover, she later intended to marry her daughter
Jeanne to Charles V's son Philip II – a Reformed Catholic. On the other
hand there are indications that she advised Francis to support German
Protestants during the Princes' Wars. What is clear above all, though, is
that she seems never to have modified the Meaux programme, designed
to strengthen the role of bishops and encourage preaching in the Pauline
tradition. Like Erasmus, she never publicly doubted papal authority. Her
faith drew on a Pauline assurance and mystical spirituality, rather than
pure scholarship. Truth would emanate in the heart of the faithful through
a sense of the freedom endowed by God's grace and love. She was uninter-
ested in theological and political quarrels and patiently trusted in God's
revelation and the true practice of piety. She felt free to translate Luther's
1518 prayer to Our Lord in the troubled year of 1525.

The reception of reform ideas in France

Margaret's case exemplifies how selectively ideas were usually taken up
and that such reception processes were influenced by specific networks
of people forming 'interpretative communities'. The group at Meaux, for
instance, had formed an impression of Erasmus that led them to attribute
to him a rational approach to the Bible; they thus sought no connection
with him, even though we can see that intellectual links existed. Moreover, Lefèvre, Briçonnet and Margaret helped to shape a Pauline faith
that in turn led to a selective reception of Luther and influenced the
translation of his works. This example also demonstrates that innovative ideas are often implemented not solely by individuals, but by small
groups, which may then change or become static in their views. The flexible reception of ideas, moreover, depended on a person's social milieu
and on age. Whereas it is hard to see how Margaret's or Briçonnet's
reform ideas developed after 1525, several young reformers (such as Guillaume Farel, whose views were closer to Zwingli and Karlstadt) left for
Strasburg. Here a Protestant circle of men and women had formed, and
the French exile community was growing. As in Zurich, the reform movement was orientated towards changing communal politics. Farel belonged
to a circle of younger people who wanted to carry out reforms and implement new ideas in an urban environment. Margaret, by contrast, continued to operate on the level of court politics. After the Placard disaster

in 1534, during which a small group of Zwinglians put up placards all over Paris violently attacking the mass and thus causing a new wave of panic about heresy, she withdrew more frequently to her possessions in Nérac. During her brother's lifetime she continued to try to influence politics, but, it would appear, not church politics. In Nérac she surrounded herself with artists and theologians, wrote the *Heptameron*, poetry, and conscientiously ruled over her subjects. She wanted to live up to the ideal of a virtuous and cultured Renaissance court, which nonetheless endorsed Christian piety through a culture of worship. She never challenged social hierarchies. Did reform beliefs have any social meaning for her (figure 12)?

This mixture of openness and secretiveness reflects an attitude widely held among reform-minded French people after 1520; the historian of the early French Reformation David Nicholls talks about the 'shapelessness' of its formative period.[8] Until the middle of the 1530s, no leading reformer emerged. This was not just a result of state repression, but had also to do with the fact that few identified with the most prominent European reformer thus far, Martin Luther. Many of his writings were known and translated – a total of twenty-two by the year 1550. But clear sympathies for his true doctrine and its consequences for church and society were rarely voiced. In many towns, people first of all read the work of other authors and, above all, the Bible. The small groups formed by these people resembled 'theological debating societies'. In private, people mainly resorted to reading prayer books. Moreover, France lacked a university like Wittenberg, which trained new pastors and sent them out into parishes. Finally, people were only too aware of those who had perished during the Peasants' War, the fate of the Münster Anabaptists (see p. 86) and of the millers at Meaux, all of whom had quickly been silenced. Margaret herself had been attacked in a satirical play by Sorbonne students in 1533. She was keenly aware that by supporting a reform preacher like Roussel, who spoke before an audience of 5,000 in Paris that same year, she was already sailing close to the wind.

This situation changed due to a young Frenchman who had escaped to Geneva after the Placard affair and begun to formulate a third Protestant Reformed tradition. Jean Calvin (1509–64) still dedicated his *Institutions of Christian Religion*, which first appeared in Latin in 1536 and in 1542 in French, to Francis I. He and his supporters, including Farel, implemented reforms that were neither purely Lutheran nor Zwinglian. Geneva became the new Wittenberg and trained pastors for French parishes. The

---

[8] David Nicholls, France, in Andrew Pettegree, *The Early Reformation in Europe* (Cambridge, 1992), pp. 120–41.

Figure 12. Margaret of Navarre, *La Couche ou le Débat de l'Amour*. This manuscript illustration depicting Margaret of Navarre reflects a courtly, utterly romantic vision of encounters with peasant folk.

history of the Huguenot movement, the real Protestant movement in France, began after 1550. Margaret died in December 1549.

Martin Bucer

The year 1549 was also the year in which an important German reformer sought refuge in England under Edward VI. Nowadays only Reformation experts are familiar with the name of Martin Bucer, but a brief look at his dramatic biography enables us to sketch important aspects of the course of the German Reformation between 1525 and 1550 and to assess how reformers built up European networks. It also delineates the events within the Reformation movements that led from Strasburg to Geneva.

Bucer was born in 1491, in the Alsatian town of Schlettstadt. His family was too poor to support him at university, and so he entered a Dominican convent and became familiar with monastic reform ideas. Erasmus fascinated him – as he did many of his superiors. Bucer came to believe in a faith centred on Christ, the Bible and devotion to the needy. He then began to be influenced by Luther's early teaching, left his order in 1520 and became Ulrich von Hutten's private secretary. He married and planned to study in Wittenberg, but first found a position as preacher in the small Alsatian town of Weissenburg, a position that became untenable in 1523. Bucer escaped to Strasburg, where he stated in print that his preaching had brought God's kingdom closer to the people of Weissenburg and harmed the Antichrist. He predicted that the force of the enemies of the Bible would last for five months during the Apocalypse for all those guided by their five senses rather than by God's law. Bucer thus initially shared Luther's eschatological thought. A man in his early thirties with no formal training, he arrived in Strasburg a married and penniless ex-monk. His connections to the rebellious knights around von Hutten, moreover, had given him a dubious reputation.[9]

Strasburg was an early modern centre of trade and communication; printing was particularly important. It lacked a university of its own, and the journey to the nearest important university, in Basle, took more than ten hours by boat. The city nonetheless featured many orders, convents, foundations, churches, great preachers and the enormous Münster cathedral, and its inhabitants took pride in Strasburg's Germanness and the

[9] Martin Greschat and Martin Bucer. *Ein Reformator und seine Zeit 1491–1551* (Munich, 1990) and Christian Krieger and Marc Lienhard, *Martin Bucer and Sixteenth-Century Europe*, 2 vols. (Leiden, 1993) provide the most important perspectives.

absence of Jews, a pride nurtured by patriotic humanists such as Jacob Wimpheling. The city opened itself to foreign merchants and even possessed an English diplomat among its citizens. Refugees soon arrived from all quarters. The French exile community, to which Calvin belonged, jostled alongside exiles from the Netherlands, Italy, Silesia and Poland. One pastor's wife and Reformation writer, Katharina Schütz Zell, helped to make outsiders feel particularly welcome by always making room at her table for people of different convictions, feeding them soup and providing other types of support. Strasburg became one of the most heterodox cities in Europe for several decades.

Bucer himself came to insist on some clear dividing lines, particularly in regard to the Anabaptist and other 'sectarians' proliferating in Strasburg. He supported council decisions that led to the slow death of the Franconian 'seeker' Melchior Hoffmann in a Strasburg prison, and went out of his way to heal divisions between Lutherans and Zwinglians on the Eucharist debate and other prominent issues, in an effort to strengthen the unity of mainstream Protestants and Anabaptists who could be persuaded to get back into line. He believed that it was crucial to cooperate with civic and territorial authorities. This realism gradually superseded his earlier apocalyptic world-view.

These mental shifts become easier to understand if we realise that, like many other Europeans, the extraordinary events of 1534–5 had given Bucer much to think about. In the course of these two years, Dutch and German Anabaptists managed to create a 'kingdom of the Last Days' in the Westphalian city of Münster. Catholics and Protestants joined forces, and the Fugger merchants provided capital to crush the sectarian coup. Münster had been an episcopal seat until its Reformation in 1533; by 1534, Melchior Hoffmann's apocalyptical teachings had reached the city. He had found many supporters in the Netherlands, and one of them, Jan Matthijz, now prophesied that the world would end in Münster. Many moved to the city and claimed that all Christians who wanted eternal life should be baptised again. Matthijz announced that it was equally important to expel all 'unbelievers' from Münster. Anabaptists soon dominated the city and its council. In June, a Frisian woman, Hille Feiken, went to meet the troops besieging Münster. She wanted to rescue her city like the biblical figure Judith, and to kill the bishop. Matthijz soon died, and his successor Jan van Leiden dissolved the civic council and was crowned king of the New Jerusalem in September 1534. All women were told to marry; since there were more women than men in town, polygamous unions were formed. The goods of citizens who had fled were shared out among the refugees. It took until June 1535 for troops to triumph over the Münster experiment.

For Bucer and all 'orthodox' Christians, the Münster example showed that many people, longing for eternal life, could quickly be led to accept radical beliefs. Between 1534 and 1539 Bucer thus travelled almost 12,000 kilometres between Strasburg, Switzerland, south Germany, Hesse and Saxony, to mediate between Zwinglians and Lutherans and spread the true faith. After Zwingli's death, leadership of the Zurich Reformation was taken up by his loyal follower Heinrich Bullinger. Bullinger and the Basle reformer Grynaeus had become the most important diplomats of the Swiss Reformation. Unity among mainstream Protestants also seemed vital because Pope Paul III (1534–49) was now seriously planning to hold a Catholic Church Council, which would decide about reforms. It opened in December 1545 in Trent. Two months later, Luther died. Four months later Charles V began to mobilise Spanish and papal troops to fight the union of German Protestants. As early as March 1547 Charles was able to celebrate his victory at the battle of Mühlberg and visit Luther's grave. In all German lands, only the cities of Constance, Magdeburg and Bremen refused to accept Charles's victory, and these he planned to conquer. But even Catholic forces among the Imperial Estates now sought to limit the influence of an Emperor who seemed too powerful. A national council was to resolve all religious matters. Until it had reached its conclusion, so-called 'Interim' measures were announced, defining religious practice for formerly Protestant areas.

For Protestants, and thus for Bucer, the years after Luther's death and Charles's victory were the darkest of their lives. Should one obey the Emperor and reintroduce the mass? Was a right of resistance justified in the name of the Lord? If one abstained from Protestant practices, would not the threat of the Imperial sword be small compared to God's wrath? In the free Imperial city of Constance, two Zwinglian reformers, Blarer and Zwick, pressured the town council to enforce strict moral discipline among the population. Constance would thus finally become a true temple of God and be assured of His support against the Imperial troops. Citizens were again told to report all immoral behaviour, which the council would then investigate. When Charles's Spanish troops marched into Constance, however, the city fell immediately. It was re-Catholicised, and became a provincial town of Habsburg Austria.

Bucer had pressed for some time for similar policies of moral policing to be implemented in Strasburg, not least to make Anabaptists realise that orthodox Protestants were sufficiently pious in their everyday life. But he had lost trust in magistrates' ability adequately to support the disciplinary process. Instead, he favoured the independence of church institutions in policing moral behaviour; these would act with the help of communally elected 'elders'. He wanted to revive the church court, but the council forbade this. After all, one of the main reasons for introducing the Reformation in Strasburg, as elsewhere, had been the council's wish to dominate jurisdiction. Bucer's views had made him increasingly unpopular among councillors since the mid 1530s. How differently the two sides still felt about what constituted 'proper' Christian morals can be gleaned from the council's discussion about whether or not to enlarge Strasburg's brothel, at a time when most Protestant towns had already closed theirs. 'One needs to let the world remain a bit the world', the city-scribe commented in his protocol. After 1547, the population was reminded of fifteenth-century moral legislation. Bucer felt this was not enough. One could only expect God's reward and resist the Interim if the population repented its sins thoroughly. Jacob Sturm (1489–1553) now emerged as a key politician, and opposed Bucer. Sturm's Strasburg roots stretched back for generations; he looked after its relations with the Emperor and Empire.[10] He convinced the civic Schöffen to support the Interim measures and trust that some negotiation with the Emperor was still possible. Only French help would have enabled Strasburg to resist Charles V. Such help, Sturm believed, would have implied concessions of a different kind, and potentially a full-scale war in Alsace. Sturm further argued that a right to resist the Emperor legitimately only existed if God showed a clear way forward accessible to human reason. This, he decided, was not the case, and no miracle was on the cards. The Schöffen initially wanted all citizens to vote on their city's and religion's fate. Sturm convinced them that the town was full of people from all sorts of places who were not deeply rooted in Strasburg: their loyalty and sense of the common good could not be trusted. The Schöffen agreed. Many committed Protestants had already left. Others decided to live a secret Protestant life. Bucer was forced to leave. Katharina Schütz Zell, who stayed, soon wrote him one of the most desperate letters of her life.[11]

Building European networks

Bucer, meanwhile, arrived in England full of optimism. Edward VI seemed to be a young king who shared his vision of the world as the kingdom of Christ. Several noblewomen, noblemen and church officials sought to establish contact with him and he began teaching theology at Cambridge; he helped to rework the Book of Common Prayer and wrote

---

[10] Thomas A. Brady Jr., *The Politics of the Reformation in Germany. Jacob Sturm (1489–1553) of Straßburg* (Atlantic Highlands, 1997), esp. pp. 222–30.

[11] Elsie Anne McKee, *Katharina Schütz Zell*, 2 vols. (Leiden, 1999) is also an edition of many letters and writings of this prolific Reformation woman writer.

advice on church reforms. All of this seems to point to the remarkably smooth integration of a German reformer in a foreign land; Bucer had certainly laid the groundwork for this through some advance corresponding. But Bucer's case, and that of some Swiss reformers, in fact demonstrates how laborious these processes really were and the talent for networking they required. These wider contexts go some way to explaining the limits of pan-European Protestant cooperation, and we need to look at them in some detail.

Bucer had first become interested in forging links with England between 1535 and 1536. He and his colleagues thus made sure that a Latin treatise by one of the leading English Protestants, Stephen Gardiner's *De Vera Obedientia*, was printed in Strasburg and prefaced with praise for English church reformers, especially for Thomas Cranmer, the Archbishop of Canterbury. Bucer next dedicated the first volume of his important commentary on Paul to Cranmer. He spelt out his belief in the utility of a German–English Protestant alliance to fight the Pope and 'sectarians'. He then dedicated a treatise on the Eucharist to another important bishop, Edward Foxe.[12]

Next, the Zurich reformer Heinrich Bullinger sought a dialogue with Cranmer. During his long life (1504–74) Bullinger used correspondence more extensively than any other reformer to maintain and extend his influence; 15,000 letters to or by him remain. Luther, by comparison, left 3,500 letters, and by 1529 already complained of being 'flooded with letters' to such an extent 'that tables, benches, chairs, desks, windows, boxes, shelves and everything' were crowded with them. To correspond with someone important moreover did not simply entail sending a letter. As the example of Margaret of Navarre and Erasmus showed, the most likely result of 'simply' sending a letter was that the addressee failed to answer. Connections had to be sought concurrently through different means to ensure that the letter was received. Letter writing and receiving were embedded in a rich personal social context. Bullinger thus had to search for someone who had already corresponded with Cranmer and could 'introduce' him. The identity of the messenger one used was also of significance. A letter must be sent not just safely, but in an honourable way. Bullinger used the Zurich publisher Froschauer, who in turn met a Strasburg printer at the Frankfurt fair with a London outlet. Reliable and worthy messengers were a must, and long-distance letters often required a long time to reach the addressee. In the meantime, diplomatic circumstances might change. The contact between Zurich

---

[12] On this and the following see Diarmaid McCulloch, *Thomas Cranmer. A Life* (New Haven, 1996), esp. pp. 174–88.

and England was, however, strengthened through a group of six young Englishmen undertaking an educational tour, who were closely attended to by Bullinger and his team. Bullinger meanwhile told the St Gallen reformer Vadianus that he should also write to Cranmer and send him his book on the Eucharist. In 1537 – two years after the first initiative – Cranmer and Foxe both signalled that they preferred distance. They did not support the Zwinglian understanding of the Eucharist; neither were they interested in any political alliances. Gifts were viewed as expressions of self-interest, and politely rejected. One full year after Bucer had sent his book to Foxe, he received a lame letter of thanks, in which Foxe made clear that he had read none of it. Cranmer likewise took a whole year to reply to Vadianus and stated that he had read his book and found it 'altogether displeasing'. When the Strasburg preacher Capito sent a book for Henry VIII, of which Cranmer did approve, he constantly needed to remind the king to read it. Once again, its final reception turned out to be negative. It was 'displeasing'.

This brief case study clarifies why European reformers corresponded only to a limited extent. Ideas were often more effectively exchanged through personal encounters. The hardships of contemporary travel – which made Melanchthon, for instance, paranoid about crossing the channel – and of finding native translators limited the extent of such encounters. Bucer, for his part, persisted in corresponding with Cranmer. They finally met after eighteen years.

Despite all the welcome and initial help he received, Bucer soon realised that opinion about church reform was just as divided in England as elsewhere, in short, the extent to which the world here, too, remained rooted in its customary politics. He wrote to his longstanding colleague Calvin that the clergy were mostly badly trained, that they did not preach sermons and that a new generation of pastors had to be educated. Cambridge students did not much take to Bucer and colleagues wrote against his views. He remained an outsider, if for no other reason than that Cambridge scholars at the time lived a celibate life in convent-like colleges, whereas Bucer was married to the energetic Wibrandis Rosenblatt, who had previously been married to two other leading reformers and had to look after various children from these marriages. He had to run a household; yet he never learned English (and conversing with servants in Latin must have been difficult even in early modern Cambridge). He also fell ill several times. The climate, he noted, was cold and wet, and imported wine already expensive. Bucer was aged and homesick. He wrote in another letter to Calvin that he felt disowned by his fatherland and his beloved church. Two years after entering England, Bucer died, and was buried in the university church. Five years later, the

Catholic Queen Mary prosecuted him in a posthumous heresy trial. His coffin was dug up and burnt at Cambridge market together with all his writings. Four years later, the Protestant Queen Elizabeth I rehabilitated him. The rituals and anti-rituals thus performed with Bucer's remains impressively staged the divergent religious truths that England embraced during these years (figure 13).

The determination to live a pure civic life that we witness in Bucer was characteristic of a new reform movement of refugees.[13] This movement insisted on the importance of church as opposed to full secular control of church matters, and thus distinguished itself from Zwinglianism. Another spiritual leader of this movement was a Polish nobleman, Johann à Lasco, whom Edward VI appointed as superintendent of the Dutch and French Exile Church in London. A Lasco institutionalised strict moral discipline within these small communities. The determination to extend such disciplinary regimes, however, naturally could only rarely be maintained once refugees took over a town, as in Calvin's Geneva and the east Frisian city of Emden (see pp. 115–36).

Between 1571 and 1574 the natural philosopher Conrad Dasypodius renovated the clock of the Strasburg Münster church. Dasypodius was ambitious: his idea of finding modes of representing time went beyond linear time and embraced all sacred and secular descriptions of time. He showed, for example, the movement of the planets, expected eclipses and the cycle of the sun. Time and death reigned over eternity, which could be conceived as either linear or cyclical. Other displays represented the four ages of man, the four kingdoms according to Daniel's biblical prophecies, and the five markers of Christian time: creation, fall, redemption, ascension and the Last Judgement. A pelican symbolised Christ, the Redeemer, as ruler of all eternity.[14]

Artisans worked for years to build these automata and emblems. People admired the Münster clockwork then as they do now. What did it mean to create this clock in a city so deeply marked by confessional conflict, a city that had lost much of its weight within the Empire? Who turned the wheel of time? Were biblical prophecies still to become real? Thus the people of Strasburg puzzled as time passed before returning to the routine of daily life. But in contrast to Charles V's understanding of clocks, the Strasburg clockwork no longer symbolised an encompassing truth and a unified vision of order. Rather, it symbolised divergent historical ideas and possibilities.

---

[13] Heiko A. Oberman, Eine Epoche – drei Reformatoren, in Peter Blickle *et al.* (eds.), *Zwingli und Europa* (Göttingen, 1985) provides an important discussion of this theme.

[14] See Anthony Grafton, *Joseph Scaliger. A Study in the History of Classical Scholarship*, vol. II (Oxford, 1993), pp. 1f.

The Burning of M.Bucer and P.Phagius Bones.

A Solemn Procession of the University of Cambridge to St Mary's Ch...

Figure 13. Anon., Martin Bucer's Funeral Procession, a seventeenth-century broadsheet depicting the funeral procession accompanied by wailing beggars (a Catholic custom!) in a fairy-tale Cambridge, and the burning of the coffins by Mary.

The Reformation and Europe

Contrasting these five influential individuals active during the early years of the Reformation movement brings out several important points. It first of all relativises Luther's centrality for Europe. The first large city Reformation was initiated by Zwingli in Zurich; Zwinglianism enjoyed immense influence in Switzerland and southern Germany. Its rigorous implementation of Christian ideals in communal life and hostility towards the cultic use of images link Zwinglianism to the emergence of Calvinism as a third type of Protestant belief, which gained influence from the last years of Luther's life onwards. Calvinism was to become particularly dominant in east-middle Europe, the Netherlands, France, Switzerland, England, Scotland and some parts of Germany (see chapter 3).

Within Europe, a Lutheran orthodox country like Denmark therefore remained an exception.[15] Here, German migrants and merchants were the first to disseminate Lutheran ideas, and the Crown soon sympathised with Luther. Bugenhagen facilitated a Reformation following the Wittenberg model, and this was reinforced by the fact that many Danish preachers had studied in Wittenberg. So close were the links between the Danish Crown, church and Wittenberg that Christian II lodged in Cranach's house during his exile, and the first Danish New Testament was printed there. The dependence on Wittenberg imports persisted since no printing house managed to establish itself in Denmark between 1523 and 1528, and no professional bookseller or publisher set up shop until as late as 1551. Most Danish Reformation literature was translated from German, and Cranach's religious artwork was frequently imitated. Even Copenhagen's university curriculum was restructured in 1537 following the Wittenberg model. Denmark also followed a tough policy of keeping 'sectarians' out of the country early on and implemented a state Reformation which made the king head of the church in Denmark as well as Norway and Iceland, both of which belonged to the Danish Crown. The Danish Reformation remained culturally tied to German Lutheranism in an exceptionally close way.

'Shapelessness', by contrast, typified the early Reformation movements of, for example, France or the Netherlands, though Luther's influence was greater in the Netherlands than in France. Thanks to the Inquisition, however, Lutheranism was virtually non-existent in the Netherlands by

---

[15] On Scandinavia see especially Ole Peter Grell (ed.), *The Scandinavian Reformation: From Evangelical Movement to Institutionalisation of Reform* (Cambridge, 1994). Volume II of the *Cambridge History of Scandinavia* (forthcoming) will doubtless enrich our knowledge much further.

the middle of the century, while Anabaptist and other sectarian beliefs lingered longer. Both countries nonetheless saw a huge expansion of the reform movement and particularly of Calvinism in the 1560s (see pp. 122–38).

England under Henry VIII and Sweden under Gustav Vasa exemplify another path to Protestantism. Both monarchs introduced the Reformation mainly to gain resources and power, without implementing a decidedly Protestant programme. Henry VIII thus still insisted that clerics should be celibate by 1539, and his response to the people's extraordinary enthusiasm for Bible-reading was a decree in 1543 that the lower classes and all but elite women were forbidden to glance at the Sacred Book, which they were too stupid to understand.[16] In Sweden, Gustav Vasa remained head of the church until 1560. His sons were educated by Calvinist teachers, and developed Reformed or Catholic convictions. Only in 1571 was a church ordinance agreed on by church and Crown, which nonetheless remained vague in its theological principles. The church adhered to an orthodox Lutheran position and fought for its autonomy from the Crown. But the political situation changed slowly, and Sweden remained a heterodox country until a renewed, Lutheran church ordinance was decided upon in 1593. By then, England had been governed by Elizabeth I for over three decades and a popular Protestantism had finally formed (see pp. 151–3).

Since 1537, English monarchs had also declared themselves head of the Irish church, though the number of English settlers was relatively small. As a consequence, the battle between Catholics and Protestants turned into a permanent idiom of Imperial conflict that has lasted up to the present day and confronts us with the troublesome legacy of this alternate, unique path towards Protestantism: through a religion imposed on an Empire.

In Scotland, by contrast, Protestant sympathies were manifest within the court and among the nobility during the first half of the sixteenth century. From 1555 onwards, Calvinism spread through preaching campaigns by John Willock and John Knox, who had returned from Geneva. Noble Protestants remained crucial to the institutionalisation of reforms. In 1560, parliament accepted a Reformed confessional order, and in 1564 Knox and others wrote a Reformed order of worship. Reformed pastors spread throughout the highlands and islands. By the end of the century, a lively and well-organised Reformed culture had taken shape (see p. 190).

---

[16] Susan Brigden, *New Worlds, Lost Worlds. The Rule of the Tudors 1485–1603* (London, 2000) provides a full and stimulating account.

The south

In southern Europe, that is to say Portugal, Spain, Italy and Greece, the Protestant Reformation made relatively few inroads. Portugal was almost culturally immune to Protestantism. The Inquisition was introduced in 1536 and only prosecuted 200 cases against 'luteranismo' during the sixteenth century; it mainly targeted foreigners in Lisbon: the cook of the French embassy, artisans from Flanders, merchants, clerics and military personnel. In a small country with few printing workshops and bookshops, publications could easily be controlled. Ports were likewise surveyed by Inquisition officials. Indeed, no Portuguese edition of Luther's or Calvin's works appeared until the nineteenth century. Coimbra was the only large university in the country and when four professors of its Collegium Artium were suspected of Lutheranism, they were quickly silenced.[17]

In Spain and Italy interest in Reformed ideas was much greater, and controlling it was made much more difficult by the size of these countries and the density of their cities. Spain's intellectuals, court officials and clerics had been strongly influenced by conciliar debates about the need to limit papal power and Erasmian beliefs.[18] The Crown had secured far-reaching independence from Rome in church matters, such as the right to nominate bishops. This benefited the elites, and hence a major incentive for breaking with Rome was lacking. Even though Lutheran writings were circulating in Spain early on, the Spanish on the whole agreed with Erasmus and declined to support the full extent of Luther's criticism. Anxieties about the spread of Protestantism mostly affected those following a Christo-centric piety. 'Protestant' heretics detained by the Inquisition, in fact, hardly ever followed Luther or had read anything by him. Their dissent included support for the Illuminists, a group inspired by mysticism, criticism of the Pope, non-belief in saints, purgatory, confessing before a priest, the reward of good works and image worship, criticism of the celebration of the mass and discussion of reform ideas. But there was no strong affinity to Protestantism, and no Lutheran underground leader emerged. The Spanish situation thus resembles the 'shapelessness' of debating groups in French cities. The Inquisition meant that even this level of discussion carried a high-risk. Between 1558 and 1562, a large number of people were executed, following exposure in

---

[17] Francisco Bethencourt, Os Homems Que Querem Crer: Religiosidade, poder e sociedade, in Carlos Morerira Ayevedo (ed.), *História Religiosia de Portugal*, vol. II (Lisbon, 2000), pp. 68–73.

[18] See esp. Henry Kamen, Spain, in Robert (Bob) Scribner, Roy Porter and Mikuláš Teich (eds.), *The Reformation in National Context* (Cambridge, 1994), pp. 202–14.

Seville of a circle of high-standing clerics who had imported heretical prints and could count on a network of 1,000 sympathisers in other cities. During the second half of the sixteenth century the Spanish Inquisition continued to operate much more efficiently than the French. A sense of urgency in these matters was fuelled by the experience of living with a large population of converted Muslims and Jews, who, it was thought, needed to be presented with a unified Christian church to maintain credibility. The political elites' scant interest in Protestantism, steep repression and the spread of the Catholic reform movement after the Council of Trent explain why Protestantism made little headway. A stubbornly heterodox underground remained, mostly made up of foreigners, in particular French Huguenots, and was prosecuted relentlessly. Thus, between 1540 and 1614, the Inquisition of Castile and Aragon punished a total of 2,091 'Protestants'.[19] The best-known Spanish reformer, Juan de Valdes, developed a spiritualised Christo-centric faith and lived in Italy.

For Italy reliable estimates propose that Protestant ideas reached about 2 per cent of the population and that 0.5 per cent supported them.[20] Again, several of Luther's writings were available early on. But they were published anonymously, usually in a translation adjusted to fit a Christo-centric piety, and were mostly read by clerics. Around 1540, the reception widened. Groups of officials and artisans of northern and central Italian cities showed interest in Protestant ideas: devotion to saints, fasting, the belief in purgatory and the celebration of the mass were all discussed critically. In contrast to Spain, Anabaptist and Calvinist ideas also played a role.

Calvinism typically found strong support among a section of noble women, and Renée, Duchess of Ferrara, exemplifies this trend. She was raised at the court of Francis I and under the influence of Margaret of Navarre, and received her first letter from Calvin in 1541. She turned him into her spiritual adviser and her court into a refuge for 'heretics'. As in Spain, the phase of severe repression by the Inquisition began in 1550. By 1554, the Duke of Ferrara thus simply decided to imprison his wife at home to bring her to 'reason' and avoid a heresy trial. Reformed convictions began to be disguised by 'Nicodemism' – that is, hidden within the private sphere, just as the biblical figure Nicodemus

---

[19] Jaime Contreras and Gustav Henningsen, Forty-four Thousand Cases of the Spanish Inquisition (1540–1700). Analysis of a historical data bank, in Gustav Henningsen and John Tedeschi (eds.), *The Inquisition in Early Modern Europe. Studies on Sources and Methods* (Illinois, 1986), pp. 118f.

[20] Salvatore Caponetto, *The Protestant Reformation in Sixteenth-Century Italy* (Kirksville, 1999) provides a detailed discussion.

had visited Jesus only at night. Genevan Calvinists nonetheless kept sending letters and preachers to try to retain a Reformed tradition of committed martyrs.

Massive persecution campaigns made this an impossible task. In 1561, substantial Waldensian communities, which had survived through the tolerance of Calabrian landlords since the Middle Ages, were destroyed. The spirit of the Catholic Renewal was militant: from 1570 onwards we can speak of an almost complete extinction of Protestant ideas. Even Renée attended the Catholic mass for several years, before moving back to France after her husband had died and she had secured her inheritance. For the preceding years we nonetheless still occasionally find records such as one reporting a woman called Franceschina who lived in the Venetian district of San Pantalon. She told her neighbours that it was bad to attend mass. The raised host had become the golden calf of Catholics. Franceschina concluded that 'we have to worship Christ . . . not this piece of dough. He is our purgatory, and when we die, we either enter Heaven or Hell.' These voices, which can be found even among common people and, surprisingly, in all parts of Italy, including the Corsican town of Bastia, were soon silenced. As in Spain, there remained a core of committed supporters who went into exile. Most of them moved to Geneva.

Among Lutheran exiles, the biography of the Marquis Bonifacio D'Oria (1517–97) is particularly intriguing, as it demonstrates how some of these exiles could influence the European Reformation through their trans-national contacts, idiosyncrasy and geographical flexibility.[21] D'Oria came from Naples and took part in Neapolitan reform-minded discussion circles. He built up a substantial library, which he carried with him by water and land in his exile years after 1557, accompanied by two Berber slave women. He met Melanchthon, lived in Basle for many years, and visited Constantinople, Poland, Germany, Austria, France, London, Sweden and Denmark. He identified with Lutheranism, but pleaded for religious tolerance. In 1591, towards the end of his life, he founded the city library of Gdansk, then a Royal Prussian possession and called Danzig. The city supported tolerant Lutheranism and the value of education. D'Oria, who had meanwhile gone blind, gave 1,100 of his books to Danzig and died there six years later.

D'Oria's itinerary also reveals the extent to which east-central Europe formed part of the horizon of the early modern educated elites. Polish elites in particular had invested in cultural exchanges with Italy since the

---

[21] Caponetto, *Protestant Reformation*, p. 377.

Renaissance. How then did the Reformation movements influence these eastern parts of Europe?

East-central Europe

The Reformation process in the east-central European countries was crucially determined by landholding elites and ethnic motives.[22] The Hungarian case provides a good example of the nobility's influence. Around 1570, *c.* 80 per cent of the population are said to have followed Protestant beliefs, without Protestantism ever having been encouraged by the state. After the victory of the Ottomans at Móhacs in 1526, Hungary was divided into three parts. Its central part, between Belgrade in the south and Budapest in the north, was controlled by the Ottomans. The western parts bordering Austria, Bohemia and Poland were now called Royal Hungary and belonged to the Habsburgs. An eastern chunk, Transylvania, bordered Poland, Moldavia and the Ottoman Empire. The largest ethnic groups were the Magyars, Slavs and Germans. The Reformation first began to influence German-speaking towns of Royal Hungary and Transylvania; Lutheran itinerant preachers gained popularity and convinced several town councils to implement reforms. Hundreds of Hungarian students matriculated in Wittenberg.

The biography of the 'Hungarian Luther', Matthias Dévai (1500–45), provides a good example of the precarious position in which these Protestants found themselves before 1540, and illuminates why they depended so much on the support of noble families and town councils. Dévai was born in eastern Hungary, studied in Wittenberg and lived in Luther's house between 1529 and 1531. He then worked for one year each in two Hungarian towns, before being deported to Vienna by the Habsburg government. He escaped to Buda, was again imprisoned for several years, and travelled back to Germany after his release. A recommendation by Melanchthon helped Dévai to secure a position working for a reform-minded noble landlord as head of his school. He went on to work for several other noblemen, was once again forced to flee, and travelled to Wittenberg and Basle before being employed by several towns during his last years.

The influence of noblemen during the sixteenth century was substantial, since both Crown and church had been weakened substantially

[22] See Winfried Eberhard, Reformation and Counterreformation in East Central Europe, in Thomas A. Brady Jr., Heiko Oberman and James Tracy (eds.), *Handbook of European History 1400–1600*, vol. II (Leiden, 1995), pp. 551–84 and Graeme Murdoch, Eastern Europe, in Andrew Pettegree, *The Reformation World* (London, 2000), pp. 190–210 provide excellent introductions.

by the defeat of Móhacs. The nobility voiced its opinions through estate assemblies and provided provincial governors. Magnates appointed Reformed preachers and teachers in the areas they owned, but never forced their belief on the population. Protestantism thus clearly reached rural folk, but it was never supported by a broad popular movement, as in Scotland or France. Noble and urban elites organised synods, funded bursaries for students to study abroad, and regarded Protestantism mainly as an efficient means to distance themselves from Habsburg control. Fears about further Ottoman advances strengthened eschatological elements of their faith. From 1550 onwards, the Saxon population of Transylvania still identified with 'German' Lutheranism, while Magyars turned to Calvinism, which was seen as a more international faith. Ethnic motives thus shaped patterns of religious adherence, without determining them completely: some Slovaks and Hungarians formed Lutheran convictions, and some Hungarians remained Catholic.

In Poland, Jagellonian kings tried to prevent Protestant ideas from spreading during the first half of the sixteenth century. Anti-Lutheran feeling was coupled with anti-German sentiment; Lutheranism found support chiefly among the German-speaking population in Royal Prussian towns, namely Elbing, Danzig and Thorn. Protestant ideas and print literature also circulated in the universities of Krakow and Königsberg. Once again, the nobility became crucial for disseminating Protestant thought: Protestantism served as a vehicle for its criticisms of the substantial landholding power and legal privileges of clerics. In Little Poland the nobility thus demanded the secularisation of church property, the abolition of the tithe and of clerical legal immunity. Sigismund II enabled the formation of Protestant communities from 1548 onwards, and the nobility gained religious toleration in 1555. Calvinist – and thus 'non-German' – attitudes began to dominate in Little Poland, Ruthenia and Lithuania. As in Transylvania, Unitarian ideas and the influence of the Bohemian Brethren also spread. Protestant attempts to unify their confession, most prominently by Johann à Lasco, who had returned to Krakow in 1556, came to nothing. The political interests of magnates and nobles diverged and the population was reluctant to accept Protestant beliefs. Very few peasants, it seems, were converted. Even so, around 1,000 Polish Protestant communities are said to have existed between 1570 and 1580. Half of them were Calvinist. Poland-Lithuania therefore became highly heterodox, and this was reflected in its print culture. Between 1520 and 1598, ninety-eight print workshops published religious works: 40 of them supported Catholic convictions, 19 Lutheran ideas, 10 Calvinism,

8 Anabaptist thought, 10 Orthodox beliefs and 6 Judaism.[23] After 1580, Jesuit missions gained force and Catholicism triumphed over Protestantism.

In Bohemia, Lutheranism was strongly supported in northern areas bordering Catholic Saxony during the first half of the sixteenth century. Here, too, noble families and town magistrates began to appoint Lutheran preachers and headmasters. The most influential of them was Johannes Mathesius, a rector of the Joachimstal Latin School between 1545 and 1565, who had been one of Luther's late table-companions and furthered his cultic remembrance immediately after his death. In the rest of Bohemia, two religious groupings had evolved from fifteenth-century Husitism, namely Utraquists and the Bohemian Brethren. Utraquists questioned the Pope's absolute authority and jurisdictional power. They accepted the Catholic understanding of the mass, but insisted on giving the laity both the host and the chalice. Estate assemblies turned Utraquism into a recognised church. In the course of the sixteenth century, Utraquism split into a conservative and a reform-orientated camp; the latter showed an interest in Lutheran ideas. Until the 1540s, Utraquists maintained their distance towards the Bohemian Brethren, who (just like Neo-Utraquists) opposed the Catholic doctrine of the sacraments and transubstantiation. They propagated biblicism and the importance of leading a moral life. Despite these influential trends, Ferdinand of Austria still convinced a majority of the estates to support the Habsburgs against the Protestants in the Princes' War. The Bohemian Brethren fled to Poland and Moravia. They nonetheless quickly managed to recover in Bohemia. In the second half of the sixteenth century they were officially recognised by Neo-Utraquists, whose orientation by now was clearly Lutheran. The Brethren's understanding of the Eucharist and their notions of moral discipline meanwhile became influenced by Calvinism, whereas the conservative followers of Utraquism sympathised with the Catholic renewal. The first Jesuit seminary was founded in Ölmütz in 1566. But by the late sixteenth century, 1,400 of a total of 1,600 Bohemian parishes were still characterised as Protestant, and only 200 of them were led by conservative Utraquists.

The Moravian nobility maintained its right of free religious expression until 1617. Several noble families even supported Anabaptist exiles and Bohemian Brethren, shielding them as far as possible from Habsburg prosecution. Between 1553 and 1591, 4,000 men, women and

[23] Christop Schmidt, *Auf Felsen gesät. Die Reformation in Polen und Livland* (Göttingen, 2000), p. 225.

children even created large 'sectarian' settlements, calling themselves Hutterites, after the Reformation 'radical' Hans Hut. They worked and lived together, and shared all resources and profits, modelling themselves on the first Christian communities. Noble patrons welcomed the tax money, craft expertise and capital that Hutterites were able to generate in deserted areas. Hierarchies of power between the sexes, the old and the young and the administrators nonetheless remained. Those joining these communities regarded themselves as chosen Christians and joyfully expected the Last Days of mankind.[24]

Tolerance and confrontation

The privileges of east European elites remind us of ways of thinking which are easily forgotten about in accounts of the Reformation world. To label them 'tolerant' is problematic, for tolerance as a rationalised concept was sometimes practised among specific Christian groups, but usually excluded 'sectarians', Jews and Muslims.[25] Nonetheless, several developments outside eastern Europe were remarkable, such as the absence of any civil war in the Swiss Confederation after 1531 and in the Empire for some decades after 1555, for these were political entities in which more than one Christian faith was practised. Several German cities had to allow both Catholic and Lutheran worship, and in the Swiss Confederation there even remained some areas in which each parish was allowed to decide autonomously which faith it wanted to follow. Naturally, conflicts arose. But in contrast to a country like France during the Wars of Religion (see pp. 122–33) it needs to be emphasised that the German and Swiss populations and their authorities showed an enormous capacity for solving religious conflicts at least among Catholics and Lutherans, Zwinglians and later Calvinists through pragmatism instead of civil aggression. Only this ability to accept a pragmatic consensus made it possible to establish two coexisting confessions within Germany at the cost of only two brief wars, while, of course, religious unity was insisted upon within each of the Empire's territorial states and no one imagined or wished for coexistence to be the status quo for the rest of Germany's history. Most impressively, the Dutch Republic diverged from this policy and allowed several beliefs to be practised in its provinces, though their adherents did not enjoy similar rights (see pp. 136–8).

---

[24] Robert W. Scribner and Lyndal Roper (eds.), *Religion and Culture in Germany (1400–1800)* (Leiden, 2001).
[25] Ole Peter Grell and Bob (Robert) Scribner (eds.), *Tolerance and Intolerance in the European Reformation* (Cambridge, 1996) provides a good introduction.

A further development of note is the importance of so-called 'Irenic' ideas. These were taken up to some extent by figures such as Bucer, who held that the dispute about the Eucharist should not divide Protestants. But true Irenians argued against any confrontational politics between Catholics and Protestants. Maximilian II's (1564–76) Viennese court shows that such ideas could become temporarily important in specific settings. Their main advocate was Maximilian's court physician, Johannes Crato.[26] Crato had come to Wittenberg via Breslau and spent six years living at Luther's house. He regularly corresponded with Calvinists, seeking to reinforce the many areas of agreement with Lutherans. He also sought to unite the Bohemian Brethren and Utraquists. Maximilian II not only employed the Protestant Crato, but was generally interested in an Erasmian resolution of confessional divisions through diplomacy. He allowed Protestant Austrians to study in Vienna and permitted Protestant schools, as well as advocating communion in both kinds and clerical marriage. These concessions were largely politically motivated, since a substantial section of the Austrian nobility and urban elites had developed Protestant sympathies. Maximilian thus, for instance, wished to rein in the exodus of elite sons to study at German universities. But he also genuinely sought compromises in Austrian and Bohemian religious matters, while maintaining the goal of preserving a united Western church. He fought for discussions, rather than divisions. And he continued to do so during the second half of the century, that is, after discussions at the Regensburg Imperial Diet in 1541 under Gasparo Contarini – Pope Paul III's cardinal, who was similarly open to Protestant thought – had finally broken down because of discord over how to celebrate the Eucharist. Attempts in the German Catholic Imperial duchy of Jülich-Cleve during the second half of the century to tolerate Calvinists and Lutherans and allow services to integrate different confessional elements are likewise remarkable. Finally, Erasmus's ideal of a republic of letters, which promoted the exchange of ideas among intellectuals throughout Europe, found continuity in scholars like the Dutch neo-stoical writer Justus Lipsius, who corresponded with Spanish Jesuits and Danish noblemen, or the Hungarian Protestant writer Janos Rimay.[27] We need to remember, though, that Lipsius recommended rulers to insist on confessional unity, and if necessary burn dissenters, for this shows that people's tolerant attitudes often applied merely in specific

[26] Howard Louthan, *The Quest for Compromise. Peacemakers in Counter-Reformation Vienna* (Cambridge, 1997), pp. 85–106.
[27] Peter Burke, *Kultureller Austausch* (Frankfurt-on-Main, 2000), p. 98.

contexts.[28] R. J. Evans has followed Friedrich Heer in calling all active attempts to find a true *via media* between opposing views a 'third force' within sixteenth-century Europe.[29] But its defenders remained few, as confessional conflict deepened after Trent through the consolidation of Calvinism and Reformed Catholicism in the second half of the century. 'Tolerance' continued to be granted mainly because there was no alternative, or for economic reasons, and in highly circumscribed ways.

---

[28] This pattern is interestingly set out in Judith Pollmann's article The Bond of Christian Piety: The Individual Practice of Tolerance and Intolerance in the Dutch Republic, in Ronnie Po-Chia Hsia and Henk van Nierop (eds.), *Calvinism and Religious Toleration in the Dutch Golden Age* (Cambridge, 2002), pp. 53–71.

[29] Robert John Weston Evans, *Rudolf II. and his World. A Study in Intellectual History 1576–1612*, 2nd edn (London, 1997), pp. 92f.

3   Calvinism

The following is an example of the language and imagination of religious hatred so characteristic of these centuries:

A miracle happened on 15 March . . . There was a woman who had been hanging on the gibbet for a year. She had died in the faith of the Holy Mother Church. Miraculously her corpse turned to face the body of a Lutheran youth (executed for murder) who had been hanged on the gibbet after her. Her corpse turned and bit him. This was a wondrous event and talked about everywhere in the city. The Lutherans came along with their spears to separate them . . . but the woman kept turning back to bite the youth. This was seen by more than four thousand people, from every level of society.[1]

This frightening 'miracle' happened in Calvin's Geneva and was recorded by the nun Jeanne de Jussie, who soon had to leave the city with several other sisters amidst the mockery of bystanders. Jeanne still categorised all Protestants as 'Lutherans', and yet, something of exceeding importance was about to happen in Geneva: the emergence of a faith which was to challenge not only Catholicism but also Lutheranism to its core, inspiring in turn its own visions of hatred.

Much about the profile of this Reformed, 'Calvinist' faith, which proved to be so successful during the second part of the sixteenth century, becomes easier to grasp if we characterise it through the sociologist Max Weber's categories. Calvinism was less connected to a specifically new Protestant doctrine than to a renewed religious practice. It was linked to stricter notions of membership and exclusion. Not only birth and baptism determined whether or not one belonged to this church but, more importantly than before, religious knowledge and moral purity. Insufficient knowledge and especially insufficiently moral behaviour were closely monitored and could lead to a temporary exclusion from communion or to total excommunication. Liturgical elements followed Zwingli in breaking more radically with Catholic traditions than Lutheranism. Calvin wished to rid churches of images or sculptures and of all music except

[1] William G. Naphy (ed.), *Documents on the Continental Reformation* (London, 1996), p. 64.

Religious confessions in Europe at the end of the sixteenth century.

psalm singing. His understanding of the Eucharist differed subtly from that of either Luther or Zwingli. These nuances seem mostly arcane to us nowadays. But since communion was at the very heart of medieval and early modern religion and of the most fervent debates, it is important to try to understand its meaning. For Calvin, the Eucharist was a sign of Christ's presence, through which He communicated vividly and which embodied His promise to nourish mankind through eternal life. But the nature of His presence could not be determined more precisely. Bread and wine were not materially completely separate from God. Thus for Calvin, they were *not* mere signs, but it remained God's divine prerogative to define his presence in all that was material. Calvin is now also best known for his comments on man's possibly 'predestined' status from birth as either elect Christian or condemned sinner. In fact, he was much more careful and reassuring than has often been assumed; he certainly did nothing to drive despairing doubtful people to commit suicide. Calvin emphasised that one should not trouble oneself by trying to unravel God's decisions. 'All', he wrote in his 1551 treatise 'On the Eternal Election of God', 'who are truly bound to Jesus Christ in their faith can be completely sure that they belong to God's circle of eternal election and count among His children.'[2] One simply had to remain devout and humble, follow the word of the Bible and remain on the Christian path that had already been taken by the faithful. The communal strengthening of faith through sermons, prayers and communion was far more important than any individual self-questioning. In regard to Calvin's most important works, the successive versions of the *Institutes of Christian Religion*, historians of religion now mostly agree that they do not contain any original theological principle; they selected from several existing doctrines, summarised them clearly and added new emphases, without harmonising conflicting elements.

Calvin's success

We thus need to ask how we can imagine Jean Calvin the man, and what explains his success as Europe's most important reformer after Luther. Here, researchers divide. Some regard the Frenchman as quite dull – 'not so much a personality but a mind', as William Monter suggests – a man who lived for his work and had a remarkable ability to comprehend, systematise and represent ideas as well as an extraordinary memory for biblical passages and commentaries.[3] Alistair McGrath likewise characterises Calvin as a man who lacked humour and warmth and regarded himself as a prophet on a divine mission, which he pursued as conscientiously as possible.[4] The historians Bouwsma and Crouzet, by contrast, regard Calvin as a far more complex man. They portray him as a tragic person of considerable inner depth, who suffered inner conflicts fuelled by the anxieties of the age. According to Bouwsma, Calvin saw himself partly as subjected to an earthly chaos, which he tried to regulate through strict divisions between the good and bad, pure and impure, and partly as exposed to a world resembling a claustrophobic labyrinth in which he tried to create some space. A paradoxical man, Crouzet agrees, who found himself placed on a stage in the middle of a play directed by God.

---

[2] 'Car ceux qui par foy communiquent vrayement en Iesus Christ, se peuvent bien assurer, qu'ils appartiennent à l'election eternelle de Dieu, et qu'ils sont de ses enfants', cited in Eberhard Busch (ed.), *Calvin-Studienausgabe*, vol. IV (Neukirchen-Vluyn, 2002), p. 140.

[3] William Monter, *Calvin's Geneva* (London, 1967), p. 99.

[4] Alistair McGrath, *A Life of John Calvin* (Oxford, 1990).

He exhibited an anti-individualism based on a strict disciplining of sinful people through the church, while his universal ethics revolved around love.[5]

Calvin was born in 1509 into a well-off family. His father worked as scribe for a bishop and other influential people in Picardy, a region north of Paris. Jean belonged to a new generation: he became a student at a time when Erasmus and Lefèvre d'Etaples (see pp. 69–82) as well as humanism already enjoyed great influence. Everybody talked about the *lutheriens*, and some of Luther's works circulated. Luther as a person, as we have already seen, was not regarded with much enthusiasm in France. Here, as elsewhere, reports portrayed him as a man of too much passion; aspects of his criticism seemed overdrawn. Calvin studied law as well as some theology. He moved in Paris humanist circles and in 1532 he published his first book, a commentary on the ancient philosopher Seneca's work *On Clemency*.

The image of Luther as a man lacking in virtue (Calvin himself wrote to Bucer in 1538 that he believed in Luther's deep piety, but found his need to succeed, his arrogance, ignorance and unbridled anger deeply offensive[6]) and Calvin's early interest in the Greek Stoical movement provide important clues in assessing his character and mission. Calvin's own success crucially relied on his attempt to balance Christian ideas with the Renaissance ideal of virtuous 'civility' to serve the public moral good. He developed a Christian ethics of measured, civil behaviour in daily life. Luther, by contrast, emphasised far more that everybody remained a sinner despite any attempts to live a pure life. He himself was no icon of purity. Cranach's depiction of a quiet, devout monk and scholar had little effect: people were well aware that Luther was passionate, whether he was scolding opponents, praying for hours, enjoying drinking wine with his Wittenberg men or even enthusiastically having a bowling green built for students living with him. Although Calvin in principle shared the view that man was eternally sinful and vulnerable to the devil, he devoted himself to developing a sense of a Christian life in which passions were tamed, reason and emotion stood in a proper balance to each other and man's behaviour honoured God. This vision formed the basis of Calvin's charisma.

The attractiveness of this 'religion of civility', especially for the nobility and urban citizenry of sixteenth-century Europe, therefore reflects their search for a Christian-humanist view on life. The same sentiment had

---

[5] William J. Bouwsma, *John Calvin. A Sixteenth-Century Portrait* (Oxford, 1998); Denis Crouzet, *Jean Calvin. Vies parallèles* (Paris, 2000).
[6] Bouwsma, *John Calvin*, p. 18.

already turned Erasmus's 1530 treatise 'On Good Manners in Boys' into a European bestseller. Erasmus believed that the young, regardless of their class, should be taught basic rules of politeness in dealing with others. His examples nowadays make surprising reading. Uninhibited farts, spitting, loud snoring in shared beds and grabbing for chicken thighs with bare hands over the table were specifically mentioned as bad behaviour. For Norbert Elias, a German-Jewish sociologist who grew up during the Third Reich, Erasmus's treatise marks a shift from medieval ways of behaving to the beginnings of a 'civilising process' that has shaped Western man ever since.[7] Spontaneous physical urges now had to be far more controlled. Shame about them was internalised. People became more closed up and were constantly aware of the proper boundaries between themselves and others. Elias's theory has been convincingly questioned in regard to his assumption of an uninhibited medieval age and of the control of 'modern' man, not least under fascism. Nonetheless, Elias rightly points to the enormous sixteenth-century interest in 'civil' kinds of behaviour outside court and convent walls. For, thanks to the Renaissance and humanism, this was a society that often valued people more strongly on the basis of their education and virtue than their inherited social status. Trust in a person's reliable moral conduct became essential. People subscribing to this value system had long ago lost most of their trust that fat monks and forced nuns inevitably led a true Christian life. Calvin stood for a movement that wanted to generate trust that a 'truly' Christian life was possible for ordinary citizens in their homes and communities. And he had clear ideas about its institutional control.

Self-centredness, vanity and shamelessness were outmoded, and 'politeness' highly valued. All aspects of human behaviour now formed part of a desired habitus. Thus, a Genevan cart driver was once excluded from communion because he had urinated on the street without turning his back towards it, and did not even seem to regret this. The notion of 'withdrawnness' became an important virtue for men and women. It did not imply closure, but rather finding proper personally, socially and religiously responsible means of relating to others. What kind of control over the body, passions and emotions was to be exercised was widely discussed during this period and had the potential to transform much of the social and political order of the time. Attitudes towards sexuality came under scrutiny (were humans able to live a celibate life?), as did the right measure of emotional expression such as anger or laughter, the proper display of learnedness (was eloquence desirable, or was a plain style true to God?), beauty (did it have any meaning?), feasts and even

---

[7] *The Civilising Process* (New York, 1978).

dress. One question inspired by the Italian writer Castiglione's influential book on Renaissance courtiers' behaviour remained pertinent: how could some spontaneity be retained despite general self-control? Last but not least, people vigorously debated the social and political rank appropriate to women, since men regarded them as naturally more immoderate than men.

Like many of his contemporaries in the burgeoning educational institutions of early modern Europe, Calvin first systematically confronted moral questions through his humanist studies and classical literature. His commentary on Seneca was directed at rulers and attempted to identify the right measure of severity in government.[8] In doing so, it touched on far wider themes, for instance by sketching out the spectrum of classical views on happiness, from an endorsement of hedonism to Stoic views of how emotions could be balanced in the face of an ever-changing world. Calvin's commentary also probed the question of whether human depravity was a matter of character or influenced by deficient social structures and laws. To what extent was human consciousness influenced by one's fear of other people's judgement? How much tolerance should a state signal through its legislation? The 23-year-old clearly sympathised with Stoic views, but he was soon to revise them in a traditional religious way: no amount of commerce with the classics, but only a measured Christian life could create the most peaceful state of the soul. Nonetheless, God must still be feared. Likewise, joyfulness had been created by God and was to be expressed in regard to the right objects. Such varied emotions, hope and anxiety rendered humans alive; they reinforced a will for change and betterment and sharpened one's sense of danger. A perfect measure of reason, calmness and temperance, as envisaged by Stoic philosophers, would never replace them. Anxiety about death could be mastered but not avoided, while the ability to empathise deeply with others and to feel sad were important virtues. We thus see Calvin advocating everything but rational coldness.

He was similarly open to sensory experiences, and cannot be called an outright ascetic. How, for example, did he discuss the sense of taste? Calvin thought that the nourishment given by God should not simply be consumed but enjoyed. Temporary fasting could heighten this sense and at the same time display the mind's and emotions' control over the passionate body, the precondition of life in the spirit of the Lord. Like parts of the mystical tradition, therefore, Calvin advised measured restraint to enhance the sense of taste. The 1545 Geneva catechism described the

---

[8] Ford Lewis Battle and André Malan Hugo (eds.), *Calvin's Commentary on Seneca's De Clementia* (Leiden, 1969).

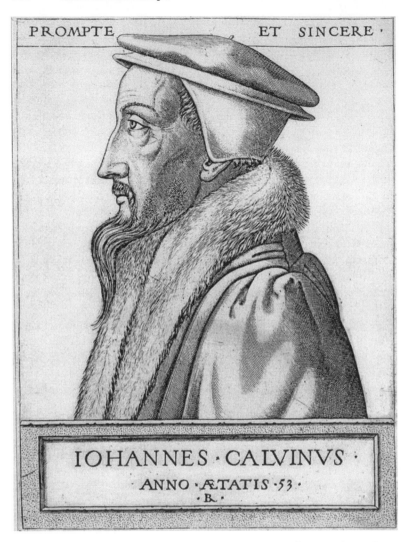

PROMPTE   ET SINCERE ·

IOHANNES · CALVINVS ·
ANNO · ÆTATIS · 53 ·
· B ·

Figure 14. Anon., *Johan Calvin*, 1553, exuding gravity and restrained elegance; contrast the beard with Dürer's depiction of Melanchthon's!

Eucharist as the most sensuous meal: 'In the Eucharist two things come together, bread and wine, which are seen with the eyes, touched by the hands and perceived through one's taste, and Christ, through whom our souls are fed internally.'[9] Among the other senses we find again the sense

---

[9] 'Duas in coena res esse asseris: nempe, panem et vinum, quae oculis cernuntur, attrectantur manibus, percipiuntur gustu: deinde Christum, quo interius animae nostrae,

of hearing particularly privileged: Calvin cherished spiritual music and wanted to create harmony between words and melody. This would open people's hearts and enable the meaning of the words to touch the whole human being. Musical instruments distracted. Only singing, and in particular psalm singing ensured the highest spirituality. Similarly, words of prayer were never to be cold, but must come from the heart and from true feeling. The Geneva catechism set out in detail which disposition God required for prayer: 'First we should feel our helplessness and misery, so that it creates sadness and fear; afterwards a deep and serious desire for God's grace shall burn in ourselves, which then fires us up to pray to Him.'[10] The power of these emotions was not natural: they already resulted from divine grace. As in medieval traditions, they were not seen as spontaneous, but as part of a penitential practice and dialogue with God. In these ways, Calvin's whole thought tried to spiritualise the ethos of temperate behaviour and proper emotional expressiveness in a Protestant way, firmly embedding intense emotional and sensuous experience within religious practice. He developed this ethos in his sermons, biblical commentaries and liturgical practice in regard to all aspects of life. He had designed for himself an emblem – or, in modern speech, logo – showing a hand pointing to a heart and the motto *Prompte et sincere*. Calvin wanted to be a reformer and role model just like this, a man demonstrating a high degree of integrity, reliability and honesty, fused with a piety that fundamentally affected human hearts (figure 14).

Speaking, writing, demonstrating

How did these aims influence the career of a man who soon regarded himself as a divinely chosen prophet? In 1534, after the Placards affair, Calvin escaped from France and never again set foot in his fatherland. In Basle, the 25-year-old wrote a first version of his *Institutes of Christian Religion*, which was influenced by Luther's small catechism. The first edition appeared as a pocket-sized book. By the time its final edition appeared in 1555, the *Institutes* were spelt out in around half a million words and had become a tome. Calvin stayed in Switzerland and in 1536 the former Meaux preacher Farel offered him a position as Bible exegete in Geneva.

It is significant that from the very beginning of his career as a prophet, Calvin tried to distance himself from Catholics, Luther or 'radicals' by

tanquam proprio suo alimento, pascuntur', quoted in: Busch, *Calvin-Studienausgabe*, vol. II, p. 130.

[10] 'Primum, ut inopiam miseriasque nostras sentiamus: utque is sensus moerorem in animis nostris et anxietatem generet: deinde ut vehementi serioque obtinendae a Deo gratiae desiderio aestuemus: quod precandi quoque ardorem in nobis accendat', ibid., p. 88.

emphasising the importance of rational form in his speech and writing. One of his early writings, an open reply to a cardinal called Sadolet, elaborated that he did not intend to use any harsher expressions than Sadolet's injustice against him merited. He wished to purge his language of any impatience or passion that might displease others. His treatise 'Against the Sect of Libertins' stated that God had created language to enable one to express one's thoughts and to communicate. To make hot air with confused, incomprehensible sounds or make 'listeners dream' therefore constituted a reversal of 'God's order'.[11] By emphasising formal conventions, Calvin presented himself as a master of civil rhetoric, and thus an honest and trustworthy man.

Nonetheless, he was certainly capable of sharp and witty polemic. His famous treatise against relics in 1543 joked, for instance, about pieces of fish which St Peter allegedly had given to Christ at Lake Gennesaret and which were now displayed as relics. They would have had to be salted amazingly well, he quipped, in order to last for centuries! It also seemed strange to Calvin that the Apostle should immediately turn a dinner into a relic. He further proposed that a Europe-wide inventory of relics should be drawn up: parts of Christ's foreskin or garments simply turned up in too many places to be real! The treatise went through twenty editions by 1622 and became Calvin's greatest ever publishing success. Polemic of this kind was permissible in the Christian-humanist economy of emotions, because it bespoke a controlled, reasoned disagreement rather than wild anger. Calvin's comments thus continued to contain polemical elements. His catechism, for example, talked about the Catholic ritual of the second communion as an extraordinary

whore, with huge ceremonial make-up, but as they decorate her, they slander her terribly when they boast that she is a sacrament higher than baptism. Who has not been besmirched by their stinking oil only counts as half a Christian. But the whole process contains nothing but deceitful gesturing about or wild ape-like acting.[12]

Polemical rhetoric thus itself easily became 'slanderous'; it also invited an overly illustrative style.

---

[11] Calvin also claimed that 'les Quintinistes ont une langue sauvaige, en laquelle ilz gasouillent tellement qu'on n'y entend quasi non plus quáu chant des oiseaux', ibid., vol. IV, p. 282.

[12] 'Adulterinam enim illam confirmationem, quam in eius locum subrogarunt, instar meretricis magno caeremoniarum splendore, multisque pomparum fuci sine modo ornant: quin etiam dum ornare volunt, exsecrandis blaspemiis adornant, dum sacramentum esse iactant baptismo dignius: vocantque semichristianos, quiunque foetido quam histronicas gesticulationes continet', ibid., vol. II, p. 15.

This was why Calvin on the whole subscribed to simplicity and manly clarity in his presentations, which strengthened his charisma. He also wrote just as he spoke. Increasingly, texts he had dictated or speeches taken down by others were printed, swelling the volume of his works – around 800 sermons, and from 1557 onwards lectures delivered to Genevan pastors three times a week. Calvin's readers thus witnessed his stylistic integrity in all contexts and could participate in the authenticity of the appearance of the chosen exegete. Calvin's successor, Theodore Beza, immediately affirmed such an image after Calvin had died: he had hated pure eloquence and had used as few words as possible, without being a careless author.[13] No theologian, Beza claimed, had written in a purer, more important and justified way. His judgement on each issue had been clear and correct and had often seemed like a prophecy. He had loved truth, simplicity and directness. Despite becoming deeply involved in matters of truth, God had given him the ability to tame his anger, so that he had never uttered a word unbecoming a good person. Calvin's rhetorical style in itself was therefore a proof of truthfulness. Form crucially mediated the contents of religious writing and the position of a preacher as prophet and divine man.

But just as Luther needed Wittenberg, it is clear that for all the charisma Calvin could generate in print Calvinism would never have got off the ground without Geneva. The social history of Calvinism as religious truth was first of all linked to Calvin's ability to present his Protestantism as vital to solving local political problems and securing social order. It furthermore depended on his enduring ability to use the legitimating power and resources of local institutions and of his supporters to implement his ideas and secure the coherence of his teaching. Geneva became a laboratory of true faith. Whereas Wittenberg lost Luther in 1546 and immediately plunged into deep conflict about the legacy of his thought, Calvin used the years between 1546 and 1555 to revive a dream central to the early modern period: that a European city might be a New Jerusalem – and this time not somewhere in the depths of Saxony or Westphalia, but in the middle of the Alps at a lake site. Calvin himself, however, did not want to create a unique Jerusalem. He wanted the whole world. In contrast to Luther, he thought not primarily in terms of his fatherland and ultimately the desired end of the world, but of the world. His sermon on 29 June 1562 is generally taken to express his political will. It ended: 'Let [God] work this miracle of grace not just here and for us, but for all people and nations of this earth' – *tous les*

[13] G. Baum, E. Kunitz and E. Reuss (eds.), *Joannis Calvini Opera* (Braunschweig, 1887), vol. XXI, pp. 815–17.

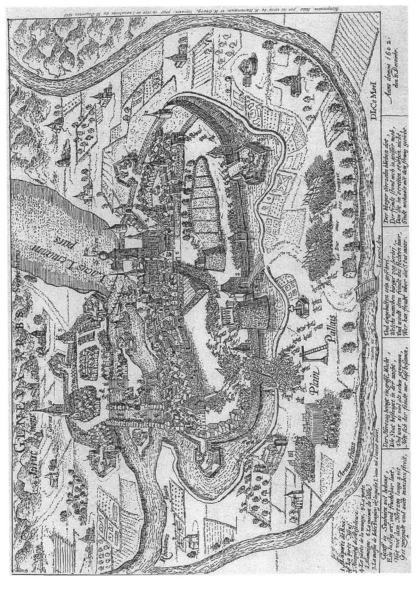

Figure 15. Hogenberg, *View of Geneva*, 1603. This print refers to the battle of the city to maintain itself as a republic.

peoples et nations de la terr, a sentence that would have been unthinkable for
Luther.[14]

Calvin and Geneva

Conditions in Geneva, however, were initially anything but favourable to
Calvin.[15] In 1537, around 10,000 people lived in the city; it was about
four times as large as Wittenberg (figure 15). There were old elites, factions, traditions and institutions, but no university or large humanistic
circles. The first citizens to show Protestant sympathies had done so as
late as 1532. Then, however, everything happened fast. Guillaume Farel,
the man from Meaux, was one of a group of French immigrants who
created a Protestant community in Geneva, and took on the fight with
its bishop. The first religious conversation was held in 1534. A second
followed in 1535, after a cleric tried to poison one of Farel's chief supporters with spinach and then paid a good lawyer to get himself cleared
of all charges. This scandal obviously helped the Protestants. Just as in
Leipzig, Breslau, Zurich and by now many other places, the religious
conversation redefined how theological truth could be arrived at in a
Protestant way (see pp. 37–42). In 1535, the town council decided to
implement reforms, but largely for political reasons. The city tried to free
itself from the bishops' and the church's privileges and to attain independence from the Duke of Savoy. It needed military protection – and this
was offered by its powerful Protestant neighbour Berne. Genevan Protestantism was therefore made to fit a political language of urban liberty and
proper rule among *Eidgenout* citizens and catalysed a conservative, patriotic rebellion of Genevans against their overlords. Of course, Berne in
turn wanted to take control of Geneva. In 1536, Calvin thus entered a
city which had already been largely Reformed, but which continued to
fight for its autonomy. Parts of the elite had gone into exile and taken
their money with them, the town council's rule was unstable and there
were continuing tensions between a patriotic Swiss *Eidgenout* faction and
French immigrants.

Calvin was still unknown to a broader public; his *Institutes* were published only in the year of his arrival, and he left Geneva again by 1538.
Calvin and Farel had opposed the town council's wish to decide church
matters without necessarily consulting church representatives. The city
had already claimed all former Catholic property as its own, and the

[14] Heiko A. Oberman, *The Reformation. Roots and Ramifications* (Grand Rapids, 1994),
p. 216.
[15] Inspiring accounts are provided by Monter, *Calvin's Geneva* and William G. Naphy,
Calvin and the Consolidation of the Genevan Reformation (Manchester, 1994).

reformers did not want to support an all-powerful magistrate. Three years passed before Calvin was persuaded to return from Strasburg. In the meantime, the Strasburg reformer Martin Bucer (see pp. 85–92) had strengthened Calvin's view that the church must be in control of ensuring the religious conformity of the general population, especially in regard to sectarians.

Between 1541 and 1546 Calvin concentrated on implementing his concept of a Reformed church. In retrospect, he declared that he had sought a consensus on how to proceed that could satisfy all parties concerned. Public peace and mutual agreement had been all-important to him; the rhetoric of civil politics entailed the notion that no decision would be taken under pressure or be one-sided; truth was to emerge through mediation. In fact, things were different – the 'consensus' was manufactured by institutional means. Calvin's control first of all had to attend to the sizeable new clergy in Geneva and its territory. The pastorate was organised as a Compagnie, which met regularly, listened to Calvin's Bible exegesis, criticised any deficiencies in each other's lifestyle and teaching in a 'brotherly' way and took a range of decisions over church matters. It was therefore vital to secure the publicly visible coherence of this body. To do so, Calvin systematically recruited well-educated French colleagues of high social standing, who were strongly motivated and able preachers. This selection in turn guaranteed that the preachers possessed the proper social attitude, crucial if Calvinism were to succeed: *Prompte et sincere* – this implied political prudence, when necessary, but also a clear sense of principle, a world-view privileging the importance of temperate behaviour and the clear acceptance of hierarchies. Such attitudes among the pastorate generated trust in Calvin's authority, doctrine and church politics, for they reassured believers that there existed a consensus on how to attain salvation. Doctrine, anyone in doubt would have been told, could always be defended through further religious conversations – and Calvin had proved himself a doughty debater and extraordinarily skilled theologian. Nobody wanted to repeat the conversations – least of all the non-academically trained merchant elite who sat on Geneva's council. Neither did this elite absorb theological arguments in detail; their support for Calvinism relied less on purely theological ideas than on their favourable impression of those embodying the movement and their trust in them as reliable proponents of a new status quo. This status quo was backed up also by Calvin's radical dismissal of 'sectarians', most famously Hieronymous Bolsec and Michael Servetus, as well as by the doctrinal consensus reached among post-Zwinglian Swiss reformers (*Consensus Tigurinus*) in 1549.

Apart from the Compagnie des Pasteurs the second institutional pillar of Calvinism was the 'consistory'. Twelve elders and pastors heard cases concerning conflicts and sinful behaviour in the community; they mediated and punished. The consistory's aim was to ensure that those taking communion had a pure heart. A pure heart was attained by the ability to repent one's sins and forgive others. Most cases dealt with proper behaviour in everyday life: doctrinal dissent or 'superstition' was less central than 'civil' behaviour. Thus, in 1550, the consistory dealt with around 584 cases: 238 concerned quarrels within families or neighbourhoods, 160 sexual misdemeanours, gambling or dancing. Anyone criticising Calvin or the presence of foreigners in Geneva likewise had to appear before the consistory court. Those unwilling to repent and reform were passed on to the city court and threatened with a whole range of punishments, mostly fines, sometimes banishment, or even the death sentence. Church and council cooperated solidly. The 'elders' were recruited among civic officers; they were respected people with a high continuity of office. One citizen, Jacques Gruet, tried to defend his political relativism and hedonism against this new Christian moralism:

Do not rule yourselves by the word or will of one man. For you see that men have many and diverse opinions amongst them! . . . But I am a man who, wanting to eat, will do so according to what pleases me . . . If I want to dance, leap, lead a joyful life, what business is this of justice? None. For each time this crudest form of justice engenders many machinations, one man is able to be the cause of several evils and the perdition of a thousand men.[16]

In 1547, Gruet was sentenced as a blasphemous traitor and executed; others, such as a married woman who had been admonished for dancing and responded by calling the minister a 'pig's groin' had to be careful as well.

As a consequence of such rigorous policies, old tensions between segments of the population hostile to Calvin and the town council remained. Calvinist preachers, for instance, rejected christening children with names that were also saints' names. Boys to be named Claude were quickly baptised Abraham, or other Old Testament names, and without their parents' consent. Moreover, there were growing fears about the huge number of Frenchmen immigrating to Geneva – around 3,000 to 5,000. Not least, a faction of town councillors, the so-called Perrenists, sections of the population and some observers in other Swiss towns regarded Calvin's policies as too rigorous. Did this allegedly temperate man not reveal that he, too, was driven by a passion to be right and follow his

---

[16] Quoted in Pamela Johnston and Bob Scribner (eds.), *The Reformation in Germany and Switzerland* (Cambridge, 1993), p. 151.

mission? Should the consistory really be given the right to excommunicate Christians without previously consulting the magistrate?

On the other hand, the Calvinists now preached all over town, day after day. Calvin alone gave around 4,000 sermons between 1538 and his death. Wedding and funeral sermons presumably created strong affective ties; the views of the pastorate thus gained more and more influence over people's sense of the world. These views concurred in any case with the mentality of respectable artisans, which emphasised thinking for the common good and behaving 'properly'. Children and adults were taught their catechisms on Sundays to firm up on Reformed doctrine. The Compagnie also sent teachers to schools, but was never able to install deacons or gain control over local welfare.

Around 1555 – that is, fourteen years after Calvin had returned to Geneva and after many conflicts – the institutional consolidation of Reformed belief was mostly accomplished. The remaining families of town councillors fully supported Calvin, while about one third of the old ruling elite had gone into exile. The consistory now began a much stricter policy of exclusion. Whereas in 1553, for example, only sixteen citizens had been excommunicated, the annual figure for 1560 was around a hundred. Even though pastors thus saw no reason to be content and told their parishes that God would punish Geneva for its sins, the Calvinist church had clearly demonstrated by now which political and religious order it supported. There were no sects, no communities of goods, no calls for greater democracy. Geneva's elites had committed themselves more and more to a conservative republican politics, which was obedient to authority and prized pastoral care, peaceful families, sexual 'purity' and social unity. At this point, the permanent trickle of Reformed French immigrants turned into a flood. They entered the only European Protestant town that now seemed significant and institutionally stable.

Calvinism's increasingly international character was a consequence of clever ways of disseminating its ideas, and this is what enabled it to become much more than merely a religion of French exiles in a Swiss enclave. From 1540 on, Calvin successively widened his network of correspondents. Like Heinrich Bullinger or Martin Bucer he dedicated publications to high-ranking people in other countries and systematically sent his writings to likely sympathisers in Poland, Scotland or Scandinavia. As the example of Renée of Ferrara has already shown (see p. 96), he invested similar energies in creating and maintaining Italian contacts and modified the role of the spiritual confidant-confessor in his correspondence with several high-ranking French women. Even so, as with Luther, we need to emphasise how laborious all this work was. By 1600, there existed thirty Latin and French editions of the *Institutions*, but only one Italian and one German edition, two Dutch editions (the first dating from 1560) and three English ones.[17] And just as in Wittenberg or Zurich, local book production was used strategically to make an author successful: twenty of the editions of the *Institutions* were printed in Geneva. From middle of the century on, most of the printing and publishing business was looked after by an old friend of Calvin, Laurent de Normandie, who financed several poor printers and provided an excellent network of colporteurs in France. His inventory numbered 35,000 books; 10,000 titles were by Calvin and over 12,000 were Bibles or parts of the Bible. In the early 1560s – the final years of Calvin's life – thirty-four printing presses existed in Geneva, which were able to print tens of thousands of psalm books in a few months. From 1555 onwards, pastors were sent secretly from Geneva to France and other European countries in order to further the mission of the 'church under the Cross'. All their suffering would be healed by God's love and the eternal life, the pastors were told. They built up parishes, consistories and a structure of regional and supraregional meetings; this firm institutional framework again made it easier to maintain a consensus and organise resistance. In 1556, missionaries were even sent to Brazil.[18] In 1559, the Genevan Academy was founded – the first Genevan and Calvinist institution of higher education. The city paid the professors, but the Compagnie decided appointments. The chief aim was to educate Reformed students from across Europe; they all had to obey the Compagnie's rules. Calvin himself had become a famous man and the city would now forever be linked to his name. Geneva had grown from a Savoyard town into a Reformed republic of rank.

It was a peculiar and unique place – a city whose population had been doubled within a short time by tens of thousands of immigrants. Foreign students and visitors added further diversity. Tensions regarding the presence of foreigners and welfare problems were largely resolved within the second half of the century. What was visible, above all, was the wealth created by well-off immigrants through their trades, know-how, capital and good business connections; printing and silk manufacturing especially had taken off – two luxury trades with which Calvinism apparently had no problem, and which linked them firmly to the nearby French centre of trade, Lyons. The remaining immigrant families produced a second generation born in Geneva. Intermarrying became more frequent.

---

[17] Francis Higman has investigated many aspects of Calvin's publishing career; an English article on the subject of translation is printed in A. Duke, G. Lewis and Andrew Pettegree (eds.), *Calvinism in Europe 1540–1620* (Cambridge, 1994), pp. 82–99; Jean-François Gilmont, *Jean Calvin et le livre imprimé* (Geneva, 1997) is likewise indispensable.

[18] Frank Lestringant, *L'expérience Huguenote au nouveau monde (XVIe siècle)* (Geneva, 1996).

Everyone had got used to the boundaries preferred by those belonging to the 'nations' of the Italian, English or French churches and to different intensities of contact and exchange with people from elsewhere, the Spaniards and Scots, Poles and Transylvanians to be found on the narrow streets of the town. No further significant moral faux pas troubled the Genevan elites. In 1558, the town council even began to encourage councillors to criticise each other's behaviour, like the pastors of the Compagnie: 'With love', the minutes note, 'each of us was tested, from the highest to the lowest, to reveal the mistakes and sins of every person. May God give all of us the strength to learn from them.'[19] The perfection of moral Christian behaviour was firmly embedded within this collective framework, whose order, ethics and punishments for dissenters had by now won over almost everyone.

The prophet's death

Any religion influenced by a strong notion of spiritual leadership has to deal with a foreseeable crisis: the prophet's death. Catholicism affirmed that the only authorised Pope would be elected by cardinals in Rome, and Popes were never prophetic. The new Protestant religions needed to work out how to create a sense of leadership. Nobody – even among international Calvinists – contemplated a similar system of electing an official leader through Europe-wide gatherings. The spiritual head of the church was Christ. Even so, the status of the first leading reformers became iconic. A clear cultic identification of the faith with a place and a 'prophet' had to be developed. This was all the more important, since the transmission of the first prophets' charisma to a second or third generation proved difficult. Lutheranism was shaken by conflicts immediately after Luther's death, in which Melanchthon, his best-known follower, came under attack. The cultic veneration of Luther and of Wittenberg as a 'place of memory' nonetheless developed extraordinarily successfully and was sustained over centuries (see p. 157). In Zwingli's case, the transition after his unexpected death was smooth because his young, loyal follower Heinrich Bullinger (1504–75), who lived a long life and widened the European significance of the Zurich Reformation, was ready and waiting to take over. After Bullinger, however, no reformer of similar calibre emerged.

What happened in Geneva? Calvin and the Compagnie decided that Theodore Beza should be Calvin's successor. He had only moved to the city in 1559 and at a mature age. But Beza lived longer than any European

---

[19] Monter, *Calvin's Geneva*, p. 161.

reformer – eighty-four years, from 1519 to 1605. After Calvin's death in 1564 he was thus able to influence Genevan matters and international Calvinism for another forty-one years. After his death, Geneva too faced the problem of the third generation, that is, of how to bestow charisma on a leader who could not claim any personal connection with the first prophet and had not been selected by him. The sense of a special religious identity remained tied to Calvinist institutions, liturgical practice and the increasing veneration of Calvin and Reformed martyrs; even miniature medallions from the sixteenth century depicting Calvin in precious and base metals survive.

Calvin had clearly articulated his expectations for the future when he last spoke to the Compagnie: the pastors were to support Beza, they were not to quarrel and not to introduce any change. This bequest may at first surprise, coming from a man often seen as an agent of change. But it corresponded to Calvin's view of history: he had only returned to proper tradition and the institutions of the early church which had been forgotten about or 'darkened' during the Middle Ages. 'It is not as if I want to maintain my innovations as they are . . . out of ambition' he stated, needing once again to affirm his selfless integrity, 'but it is just that all changes are dangerous and can cause damage'.[20] Beza and the Compagnie mostly followed this line. Changes, such as the introduction of law courses at the Academy to attract wealthy noblemen, remained contested. Beza proved to be a loyal rector of the Academy and not just a reliable, but a clever successor. He developed the cultic narrative of Calvinism through writing Calvin's biography and editing the *Icons* of Reformed religion, a popular hagiography of Protestantism, which was even accompanied by woodcuts. Beza, who came from a provincial noble family, was moreover valued because of his excellent diplomatic skills, his political clear-sightedness and self-control. He energetically maintained a Europe-wide network of contacts, controlling information about the international Calvinist cause. Radical ideas were never discussed in Geneva; everything moved smoothly. Emblematically, clock production began its long-lasting ascent in the city.

In many senses the wheels of this society moved slower than at the end of Calvin's life. The Academy, which had mainly recruited French students, changed as the French Reformation was curbed in 1572 and institutions of Reformed education were founded elsewhere. Geneva became a place where travelling students from Reformed Europe spent a limited

---

[20] 'Je vous prie aussi ne changer rien, ne innover. On demande souvent nouveauté. Non pas que ie desire pour moy par ambition que le mien demeure, et qu'on le retienne sans vouloir mieux: mais par ce que tous changemens sont dangereux, et quelquefois nuisent', see Busch, *Calvin-Studienausgabe*, vol. II, p. 300.

amount of time. The Pope had never approved the Academy's status, and so it had never been able to award internationally recognised degrees; its profile remained stuck between that of a theological seminary and a university. From 1587 onwards, funds to recruit innovative and distinguished professors were chronically lacking; but then 'innovation' was not particularly sought after in Geneva anyway. Professors were mainly recruited internally to cultivate a 'simple, serious' style, a traditional curriculum and to continue to minimise the potential for controversy. French communities likewise chose their candidates to train in Geneva not so much because of their academic brilliance, but because the Academy ensured a reliably 'pure' doctrinal training, free from heresies, and was guaranteed to monitor students' lives.[21] Once again, grappling intensely with theology proved less important than embracing established ideas and the appearance of civil behaviour.

Genevan Calvinism, in sum, does not add up to a linear story of progress and success. It established itself after many conflicts. After Calvin's death it increasingly became a shadow of its great past over the course of a mere nine years (1555–64). It nonetheless proved stable. When the House of Savoy once more threatened to invade the city between 1589 and 1590, the Calvinists' international alliances worked. Prayers and money came in from as far as Scotland and the Pyrenees. Geneva, the first and only Calvinist republic, could not be defeated.

Reform and revolt in France

All of this poses the question of how we should imagine the Reformed tradition in a country in which it was supported from below. Genevan citizens had to accept it without much choice. People of a different faith were merely given the choice to go into exile. Calvinism in Geneva shaped the lives of a strangely 'gathered community'[22] of Reformed immigrants and residents who had stayed on. In 1555, pastors who had been trained in Geneva began their secret missions abroad. By then, around seventeen Reformed exile churches already existed in Europe. What happened in France after 1555? How did missionaries influence the previous 'shapelessness' (see p. 82) of proto-Protestant convictions? What did their audiences look for in sermons and conventicles? Could the Genevan model be repeated? Calvin himself held that different places and historical situations necessarily influenced local practices of belief and church

---

[21] Karin Maag, *Seminary or University? The Genevan Academy and Reformed Higher Education, 1560–1620* (Aldershot, 1995).

[22] William G. Naphy, Calvin and Geneva, in Andrew Pettegree (ed.), *The Reformation World* (London, 2000), p. 321.

organisation. But how far removed were these other practices from 'pure' Calvinism?

In France, interest in Reformed ideas had steadily increased since the middle of the century, especially in the larger towns and among the nobility, despite the continuing persecution of heresy.[23] Around 500 Protestants were burned between 1523 and 1560, and many more suspects imprisoned. Meetings took place in private and secretly. As participants became more courageous, they aimed to form a national church; in 1559, a national synod affirmed principles of faith and discipline corresponding to the Genevan model. By now, Catholic priests and their pamphlets spoke fervently about impurity and sin, notions that Calvin's supporters spread. Catholic citizens and noblemen wanted control; fifty Calvinists were massacred by the Duke of Guise, a successful military commander, at Vassy. In 1562, the wars of religion started. Their extraordinary violence is now best remembered through the massacre of St Bartholomew in 1572. For many Calvinist Huguenots the destruction of the old order had likewise become a matter of divine destiny – 'Kill the papists! A new world!' – *Tue les Papistes! Monde nouveau!* they shouted at a massacre in Nîmes in 1567.

The year 1561 was the 'wonder year' of the French Reformation: the monarchy was weakened by a boy king; the financial situation was disastrous; noble alliances were fragile; the prosecution of heresy hardly worked; and Reformed believers had agreed on their church order at the national synod. Communities from all over France wrote to Geneva and asked to be sent a pastor. The movement grew exponentially. Around 1,240 Huguenot communities were formed between 1555 and 1570, and most of them before 1562; about 10 per cent of the French population were involved in them. In Rouen, a third of all inhabitants were Protestants. In a few cities, like La Rochelle or Nîmes, more than half of all inhabitants were 'Huguenots' – a slightly obscure label, which either derived from the word 'Eidgenouts' or from a ghost said to come at night time, with which the Reformed were identified because of their secret meetings.

Protestants represented a cross-section of society, except for the very lowest income groups; professions requiring advanced literary skills and high geographic mobility on average were overrepresented. The social make-up of Protestant groups and its meaning have been particularly

---

[23] The best monograph on the subject is Denis Crouzet, *La Genèse de la Réforme Française 1520–1562* (Paris, 1996); excellent English introductions are Philip Benedict, Settlements: France, in Thomas A. Brady Jr., Heiko Oberman and James Tracy (eds.), *Handbook of European History 1400–1600* (Leiden, 1995), vol. II, pp. 417–54 and Mark Greengrass, *The French Reformation* (Oxford, 1987).

well constructed for Lyons. Sixteenth-century Lyons was the second largest city in France. The number of inhabitants had grown by one third since 1530. By the middle of the century, 60 per cent of the male population and one third of the total population had been born outside Lyons; 16 per cent of male immigrants were not even French. When the Reformed movement experienced its high point in 1562, 68 per cent of male supporters were born outside Lyons, and many of them belonged to new, skilled professions.[24]

Can these facts help explain why people took up Reformed convictions? Yes, if we relate them to the political and religious contexts of everyday life. In the town council, for instance, the Huguenot group distanced itself from traditional elites, such as lawyers, and new citizens generally voiced their disapproval of traditional networks of power and privileges, above all those of the clerics. Their vision centred on turning the city into a 'holy and free community' of families connected to each other by Christian love and in which everybody had to obey the same moral norms; this order would fully integrate new citizens as equals. Lyons Catholicism was deeply rooted in local traditions, but these meant little to newcomers. The bodies of two local bishops were particularly venerated as relics; the cathedral offered St John the Baptist's jaw, while one of the key processions led to a hill containing the blood and bones of the first martyrs and founders of Christianity in Lyons. Local hills, rivers and shrines thus formed a sacral topography; processions connected these places and honoured traditional office-holding elites. Churches were decorated with stained glass, paintings, statues and tombs, paid for by elite families to eternalise their faith. Feasts honoured saints as well as old guilds and professions attached to them.

All of this meant little to the new and mostly young clock-makers, printing journeymen and publishers. They sang psalms in public, profaned, smashed and de-mystified statues and images and used churches for secular purposes, redefining 'how the sacred should be present in the world'. Notre Dame chapel, for instance, was turned into a clockmakers' workshop. Only places in which the pure Word of God was preached could be sacred. Reformed piety, moreover, was here seen as a regular routine, as something like a clockwork mechanism, while ceremonial extremes such as feasting and fasting, or public exorcisms of devil possession were a Catholic show. The Reformed clockwork was transparent, too – each person's moral behaviour decided whether she or he wanted to play their part. Natalie Davis sums up that in looking at Lyons

---

[24] See the pioneering work of Natalie Zemon Davis, *Society and Culture in Early Modern France* (Oxford, 1965).

Protestantism we are not dealing with an abstract theological doctrine removed from people's lives: religious expression was influenced by the specific experience of the people who used it. The geographic mobility of new Calvinist citizens and their presence in skilled professions and advanced places of fabrication influenced Reformed belief and ritual. These social facts created a 'specific view of space, time and social bonds in the city', in short, a different view of the world and the meanings of religion. Catholics continued to understand spaces, rhythms and the urban community differently.

Looking at French Protestantism more widely, the geography of the movement is much more striking than its sociology. Support for Protestantism stretched from the towns near Geneva in the south-eastern region of Dauphine in the shape of a sickle to Poitou on the Atlantic coast. Four southern towns – Castres, Bazas, Nîmes and Montauban – even officially introduced the Reformation in 1561. In northern France, most supporters came from Normandy, the Loire region and parts of the north-east. Central France remained almost wholly Catholic. There was only a small Protestant minority among c. 300,000 Parisians. Some Catholics were always ready to attack anyone denounced as Huguenot in the streets. The tiny Civic Guard capitulated and tolerated such informal violence.

1561

In order to understand the explosive atmosphere during the years in which the Reformed movement gained so many supporters in many parts of France, it makes sense to look closely at a contemporary source. One of the best is a letter written by a Reformed pastor in Normandy to Calvin.[25] 'Dearest and honoured brother', so the pastor began his report on the extraordinary things which had happened in August 1561, at a large fair in Guibray. For days he had been pressured to preach there. Some merchants had even sent horses to his house. He had hesitated, fearing unrest. He was compelled, in any case, to write like this to Calvin, who wanted the law against Reformed preaching in public to be obeyed.

Having arrived at Guibray, the pastor asked for a proper space in which the service could be conducted 'in an orderly manner'. Between two and three thousand listeners were expected. An open space near Guibray was found to which access could be controlled, and all sympathisers were told to keep the place secret. The service accordingly took place 'in proper stillness', and a psalm was sung at the beginning and end. One can be

[25] Printed in Duke, Lewis and Pettegre, *Calvinism in Europe 1540–1610. A Collection of Documents* (Manchester, 1992), pp. 81–6.

quite certain that most listeners simply absorbed an atmosphere of listening to the Word, rather than understanding details. The 'proper' form of disciplined, quiet listening thus in itself served to convey the message that one differed from Catholics or 'Sectarians'. Such quiet devotion was, however, clearly embedded in a completely different feeling: a sense of danger and excitement about how things would develop from now on.

The next day, rumours abounded that another service would be held. At the same time, people grew more anxious, fearing that they would be rounded up. In nearby Falaise, shops that had sold Genevan pamphlets and books had been closed. Still, boys at the fair ran around with broadsheets denouncing the Catholic mass. They shouted that if God did not provide help soon, the world would come to an end through Catholic falsity. By five o'clock on the Sunday morning crowds of people had gathered to attend the service; they were also waiting to see whether any troops had been sent. But nothing happened, and once more a quiet and 'uplifting' service was held. A Franciscan monk who preached in the evening was interrupted by shouting, and was later attacked. The Reformed pastor, too, preached again in the evening; this time he addressed between 5,000 and 6,000 people. A tense atmosphere prevailed. Suddenly, loud noises filled the air. The men jumped up, and reached for their swords; much confusion ensued. When everybody had calmed down again and no enemy was visible, the parson told the crowd that Satan had come among them, wishing to prevent the coming of God's Kingdom. Later, at ten o'clock that night, a number of the traders still sat in front of their stalls singing psalms. Some Parisian rosary makers began to insult them as rebels and sang indecent songs. 'Long live the Bible' was the resounding Huguenot rallying cry in which even the Parisians finally joined. Afterwards the stall-owners went to the crossroads of the main alleys nearby, where they lit candles, knelt and prayed. This they did every night until the fair ended.

The next day, the bishop arrived from Falaise, and, to everyone's surprise, he preached a message of peace and unity. Catholics and Reformed supporters, he proposed, differed not so much in their faith or because of the notion of good works, but simply in their understanding of proper ritual. He himself agreed that mass should be celebrated in a modified way. The Normandy parson now became even more courageous. His evening service was publicly announced, and in it he vigorously attacked the mass. People were afterwards left wondering 'We can no longer go to mass: how shall we live now?'

On the final day of the fair, noble families from the surrounding area attended the parson's service. He told his audience that he preached not a new faith, but the true traditional faith of the forefathers and prophets.

Each family should be well educated in this true faith, read the Bible, change its life and pray for kings and princes that God should help them to attain a proper understanding of Scripture. 'Away with the stinking mass', the booksellers meanwhile shouted openly. They sold broadsheets entitled 'The Divine Laws Compared to Those of the Papal Antichrist' or 'A Treatise on Relics'. 'Go and work, it is high time, go and carry the baskets at the wine harvest, you have eaten for too long without doing anything', they shouted at priests wanting to debate with them. Some were thrown into the mud. 'This is where things are at', the report closed, 'we continue to hold services in private houses and wait for the moment to show ourselves in public.'

What does a source like this tell us? It shows first of all that Calvin was of course unable to control the Huguenot movement from Geneva – even if the parson suggested that he was waiting to be told what to do. Yet he had gone to Guibray and preached publicly. He strongly suggested that the crowds who no longer wished to attend Catholic mass, too many to fit into private homes, could not be left without an alternative. The report moreover shows that listeners created independent spiritual traditions, which did not necessarily fit Calvin's notion of proper belief – such as the lighting of candles at crossroads to pray. This was a ritual, mediated by spiritual objects, in which participants asked for God's protection. Crossroads were traditional places of popular piety, which the Churches condemned as 'superstition'. But this was precisely how ordinary people put new elements of faith together with traditional forms of belief to express their needs (see pp. 150–2).

Intriguingly, these events provide no evidence that a belief in predestination was specifically deployed to assure believers that they would reach eternity. The assumption that it was undergirds Denis Crouzet's explanation of the success of the Reformed movement in these years; it supposedly made people overcome their enormous spiritual anxiety.[26] What is far more apparent, at least in this case, and far more profane, is that the atmosphere of danger, secrecy and confrontation created an exciting mix (for men in particular?). The report also reveals the extent to which, given the right audience, preachers displayed their faith as a cornerstone of social order, affirmed that it encapsulated true tradition, that they respected social hierarchies (apart from those imposed by the Old church) and the monarchy. Finally, the source points to the important group of 'moyenneurs', like the bishop, who tried to mediate between the parties and were rooted in a critical Catholic tradition. For many listeners, their

[26] Denis Crouzet, Les guerriers de Dieu. La violence au temps des troubles de religion, vers 1525–vers 1610, 2 vols. (Paris, 1990).

preaching must have posed the question of whether it was really necessary to plump for a new religion and faith. The response of Reformed
preachers, however, made it absolutely clear that this was indeed essential. Such preachers felt increasingly safe to express themselves: in 1562
they gained the right to hold assemblies in public, on noble estates and
outside towns.

Wars of religion

The right to assembly was a truly amazing concession, reflecting the fragile political situation.[27] After the tragic death of Henry II in a tournament
and Francis II's death after only one year of rule, Catherine of Medici
took over a regency government in 1561 as her son Charles IX was too
young to be king. Catherine tried to defuse the tense situation by grant-
ing Protestants some rights of expression. This policy was continued by
Charles when he began his reign at the age of eighteen. Many Catholics,
fearing a dangerous power vacuum, felt they had to fight the extraordinary growth of the Reformed movement; they described the Huguenots
as wild animals that had infiltrated the Lord's flock and must be extinguished. This was why, in 1562 at Vassy, the Duke of Guise and his
men killed Protestants who dared to hold a service within the town. A
Protestant national synod soon designated the high-ranking nobleman
Louis Condé as the 'Protector of Calvinist Churches and Defender of
the French Crown'. The synod aimed at creating a 'better' monarchy
that obeyed divine law. Noblemen on both sides, some of whom like
Guise became popular heroes, were in part motivated by the wish to gain
power over other nobles and in court. The history of the wars of religion
cannot, nonetheless, solely be described as a political chess game between
influential families, the Crown and foreign interested parties. The first
war of religion, after the Vassy massacre, and the seven subsequent wars
were above all conflicts in which substantial parts of the population fought
over conflicting visions of the right religious, social and political order.

The first war of religion ended with the peace of Amboise, which
restricted Protestants' rights to assemble to noble estates and the suburbs
of each department. The peace agreement – and all those to follow – had
been necessitated by the fact that no party was able to establish its military
superiority. As the Crown was never able to guarantee that agreements
were implemented, tensions between Catholics and Protestants continuously resurfaced. From 1568 onwards, this process was accelerated

---

[27] For the following see esp. the excellent textbook by Mack Holt, *The French Wars of
Religion 1562–1629* (Cambridge, 1995).

by the militancy of new Catholic fraternities. In towns, Catholics and Protestants constantly provoked each other. In Dijon in 1570, for example, one Protestant took his dog, baptised him at a well, tied the figure of St Anthony round his neck and paraded him through the streets. The overwhelmingly Catholic population was furious to see saint veneration mocked. Protestants elsewhere sang in processions that Catholics honoured the host as God, only to eat and digest him; they branded the host 'Jean le Blanc', God of flour. They also disrupted Catholic processions, while Catholics would ridicule Reformed psalm singing or try to stop it. The situation thus remained explosive.

In 1570 – after two further wars – Protestants retained strong military and political power. They controlled four fortified cities: the western port town of La Rochelle, from which alliances with England and the Netherlands could be stabilised; nearby Cognac; La Charité on the Loire and Montauban in the south-west. Some compared their fight to that of the Hebrews against the Pharaoh and, like radical Catholics, developed ideas on how legitimately to resist a tyrannical monarch. These ideas gained currency despite important concessions granted to Protestants by the edict of St Germain after the third war of religion in 1570. For the first time services could be held inside towns (or two in each region or *gouvernement*). By now, many Protestant communities had introduced consistories. Keeping up discipline was especially important, because Catholics accused Protestants of being immoral and sexually licentious heretics. Quarrelling, gambling and dancing were the most frequently registered sins.[28] In contrast to Geneva, these were mostly dealt with autonomously by the church: a structure independent from secular authorities was held to be more secure.

What happened in 1572 – ten years after the first war of religion – when Paris witnessed the massacre on St Bartholomew's Day? The massacre spread quickly. A total of 5,000 Protestants lost their lives, 2,000 of them in Paris and 3,000 in other cities. Catholics were gravely worried about the Protestant minority; many Catholics felt they had a divine mission finally to purify the country and regarded the Edict of St Germain as intolerable. Moreover, the Court was perceived as insufficiently supportive of the Guise, while moderate Catholic nobles were felt to have overstepped the mark in strengthening Catherine's policy of mediation; her daughter Marguerite was now married to the Protestant Henry of Navarre. Just after the wedding, an attack on the Protestant leader Coligny misfired. The King's Council, Catherine and Charles completely misjudged the political explosiveness of events; so worried were they about Protestant

---

[28] A table is provided in Janine Garrison, *Les Protestants au XVIe siècle* (Paris, 1998), p. 72.

revenge that they ordered several Huguenot noblemen to be put to death to prevent conflict. It achieved exactly the opposite; rumours circulated that the king had finally ordered Catholics to exterminate Protestants. The Duke of Guise himself killed Coligny, whose body was mutilated, dragged through the streets, set on fire and hurled into the Seine; this was how heretics were traditionally punished and communities symbolically purified of them. The remaining 2,000 killings were approached in a similar way. They were not wild and unplanned, but drew on a repertoire of brutal practices well known through public punishments, and also on symbols used in Catholic ritual and images of heretics suffering in hell. All of this legitimised gruesome violence. The many supporters of the Parisian Catholic militia now finally triumphed as 'God's warriors', empowered by the king to complete their crusade against heretics and uphold the one Christian world.

Massacres followed in twelve other cities containing a substantial Protestant minority. Afterwards, countless remaining Protestants formally pledged to abandon their heresy. In some places, such as Toulouse, the number of Protestants was negligible after 1572. In Rouen, too, their numbers were decimated: 165,000 members of the Reformed Church in 1564–5 had been reduced to a mere 3,000 by the late 1570s; they now formed a small, but still important minority. Cities controlled by Protestants, like La Rochelle and parts of the Protestant Midi, had entered a state of official warfare with the king. Protestant services continued to be held and international military alliances bolstered. Of the old Protestant military leaders, however, only Condé's son was left. In 1574, a Huguenot constitution was published, which also openly rejected the monarchy. In the same year, Charles IX died aged twenty-three. Three further wars of religion followed by 1584, aiming finally to implement the maxim 'one king, one law, one faith' and to convert any remaining Protestants.

The year 1584 marked the second decisive point of change in the French wars of religion: the Protestant Henry of Navarre of the House of Bourbon unexpectedly became heir to the throne, and began his reign ten years later. Though he converted to Catholicism, overtly practised Catholic ritual, healed scrofula and accepted the traditional programme of *un roi, une loi, une foi*, fears persisted that his heart had not changed. Already during the rule of Henry III – who had no children and no surviving brothers, and whose only sister had been married to Henry of Navarre at the fatal blood wedding – an extremely militant Catholicism developed, directed against the king, which led to the creation of further fraternities and a wave of public penitential piety. Barefoot Christians from the rural areas around Paris came to the city in white penitential cloths for the 'processions blanches'. All this activity certainly affected the king.

In 1583, the chronicler Pierre L'Estoile reports, the king ordered all lions, bears and bulls that performed battles at feasts at the Louvre to be killed. He had dreamed that they would eat him; L'Estoile interpreted the nightmare as a prophetic dream about Henry III's fights with the Catholic League. The general atmosphere was again extraordinarily tense. Astrologers predicted the end of the world. League supporters felt themselves sufficiently legitimised by God to become His warriors once more and fight for a new, pure society and city. Pamphlets attacked the luxury at court and all those who went to theatre plays on Sundays. The higher orders were blamed for a decline in morals and the subversion of hierarchies, because they provided such a bad example. The church itself was criticised. There were no more carnival processions in Paris, a chronicler noted, only 'fine and pious processions', and contemporary paintings show how militant citizens, priests and armed soldiers paraded through the streets while women and children stood and watched. A war over who should become the next king finally began even before Henry III had died. John Casimir of the Palatinate once more supported the Huguenots with troops and money; Spain backed the Duke of Guise and the League. Guise was killed in 1588, Henry III one year later.

Henry IV was Margaret of Navarre's grandson and son of her dedicatedly Calvinist daughter, Jeanne d'Albret. When Henry became king he followed a politics of mediation, which perpetuated each party's unease about the other side. His approach nonetheless proved feasible; he deployed a rhetoric of stoicism, reason and reflection, which appealed to those tired of endless wars and confrontations. Only compromise could create a united faith, and all concessions to the Huguenots were in time limited. In 1598, the Edict of Nantes reintroduced the Catholic mass in all towns still controlled by Protestants, which now comprised around one million supporters in all of France. Protestants were ordered to obey all Catholic feast days. At the same time, they were granted freedom of conscience and guaranteed to suffer no disadvantages because of their faith. Reformed services and discipline could be upheld in certain places. Publishing was subjected to censorship and its output was only allowed to circulate among Protestant groups. Two articles were added and were to be in place for only eight years: Protestants were allowed to maintain troops and would receive money to pay for their parsons. The edict launched a stable peace that endured until 1620. Henry IV was killed in 1610 by a fanatic Catholic, but no further war erupted until Louis XIII attacked the last bastions of Protestantism – such as the small Pyrenean state of Béarn, which Jeanne d'Albret herself had energetically Reformed, by creating an Academy and having catechisms translated into Bearnese and Basque. La Rochelle, the most important Protestant fortified city, fell in 1628. The small Protestant minority dwindled further, until it had reached a stable proportion of hard-line Huguenots, who no longer constituted a real threat to the king and whose rights were slowly eroded over many years; Huguenots were completely evicted by Louis XVI, the new 'most Christian of all kings'.

One of the chief concerns underlying all wars, murders and massacres was the question of the meaning of a symbol that in France had taken on a particularly loaded political significance: the Eucharist.[29] Catholics depicted Calvin's understanding of the Eucharist as if he regarded the host and blood as mere signs, lacking divine immanence. Calvin however, as set out at the beginning of the chapter, merely insisted that nothing created by mankind could be ascribed divine immanence with any certainty. For Catholics and supporters of the monarchy this was not just subversive religiously, but politically. For since the Middle Ages the French monarchy had been legitimised as a sacred institution to an unusual extent. France was a vast and heterogeneous country with strong interest groups that were difficult to rule. The Crown needed powerful symbols to create a myth of its supremacy and inspire loyalty. Thus the Holy Ghost imported holy oil directly from heaven at every coronation. Rituals of this kind legitimised royal power as divine; they made the king almost God's equal. This representation was underlined by the healing powers attributed to French kings, who cured those suffering from scrofula in mass rituals. Anyone thought to be questioning a direct connection between sacred, superior humans, such as regents, priests or saints, and material elements, like holy oil or the host, which communicated God's will, thus fundamentally attacked the French political order. The Catholic mass therefore formed part of a specific system of symbolic power, which adhered to clear hierarchies. For Huguenots, by contrast, communion was mainly a social symbol, which ritualised the purity, proper faith and thus privileged position of those attending. In 1561, for instance, the Venetian ambassador Suriano feared that a France under the Huguenots would become a Swiss-style federal republic, in which there was no secular ruler and politics was determined by elites and the populace. The manner in which the Eucharist was celebrated and the way in which the church was organised (such as how much was decided locally or nationally or whether regional synods were organised in a democratic way on a national level) were thus taken to be symbolic of a political world-view at large, and this brings out once more how religion and politics were

[29] Christopher Elwood, *The Body Broken. The Calvinist Doctrine of the Eucharist and the Symbolisation of Power in Sixteenth-Century France* (New York, 1996).

interwoven at the time. Nor did much change or a 'de-confessionalisation' of politics occur until the end of Louis XIV's reign.

Another refugee town: Emden

The Reform movement in France would have struggled to get off the ground without the Genevan missions and organisation. Its shapelessness would have persisted, or it might have been reshaped by the Catholic Renewal. Is this similarly true of the relationship between the Dutch Reform movement and Emden? Who now has ever heard of a place called Emden? This east Frisian town was situated in the north-east of Germany and seemed to be at the periphery of any influence even in the early six-teenth century. Nonetheless it temporarily played a historically impor-tant role.[30] As in Geneva, the example of Emden shows how the religious confrontations of the sixteenth century generated a substantial move-ment of refugees who could change a city's character. For the first time in European history, such a movement was made up of younger, morally principled women and men who were artisans and traders, and could provide a city with a new economic and technological profile. Around 1570, thanks to such immigrants, Emden's merchant fleet outgrew the English one. Early modern princes, nobles and magistrates welcomed such well-mannered and industrious exiles. They now began to shape the history of several towns.

Emden itself had between 3,000 and 4,000 inhabitants at around 1550; this had grown to about 20,000 by 1595. New buildings and plans abounded. In 1574, work even began on a new town hall, which emu-lated the Antwerp Renaissance town hall and embodied a desire proudly to proclaim the city's new status. Most of the new citizens came from the Netherlands, and a substantial number of them had already lived in exile communities in London, Germany or Geneva. The first superintendent of the Reformed churches was Johann à Lasco, a Polish nobleman with an unusually international career. Born in 1499, he studied in Bologna and Padua, became an Erasmus devotee in 1524 and took over his library after Erasmus's death. Lasco was an ordained priest, and only formally broke with the Catholic church in the second half of his life. He married in Leuwen, was appointed as Emden's Reformed superintendent in 1542 by the east Frisian duchess, Anna, but left the city after the Interim in 1548

---

[30] See Andrew Pettegree, *Emden and the Dutch Revolt: Exile and the Development of Reformed Protestantism* (Oxford, 1992); Heinz Schilling, *Civic Calvinism in North-western Germany and the Netherlands: Sixteenth to Nineteenth Centuries* (Ann Arbor, 1991); Heinz Schilling (ed.), *Die Kirchenratsprotokolle der reformierten Gemeinde Emden 1557–1620* (Cologne/Vienna, 1989).

(see p. 87). He then organised the London Reformed exile church. Under Queen Mary's Catholic rule he led the exiles first to Denmark and then to Emden in 1554, where he remained for two years. During the last four years of his life he worked in Poland, where the Reformed church had meanwhile attracted a following.

Like Calvin, Lasco insisted on firm church institutional structures: Emden pastors answered questions relating to doctrine on Sundays, elders decided about who could participate in communion, deacons oversaw welfare matters and thus decided who received poor relief, while other deacons were tasked with looking after immigrants in need of support. These four activities were supervised by the so-called presbytery, which in turn was responsible to the synod of 'classis' within the Reformed East Frisian Church. Cohesion was particularly important, for, in contrast to Geneva, many smaller religious groups existed in Emden with which one had to coexist: Lutherans, Mennonites, 'radicals', Jews and Catholics.

Shortly after France had experienced its 'wonder years' with the rapid growth of the Protestant movement in 1561/2, the Reformed movement in the Netherlands in 1566 took over several cities, cleansed the churches of all images and statues, and legitimised its resistance against the Habsburgs and hostile magistrates. The movement again drew on the support of a section of the nobility. Reformed preachers had large audiences in many areas. To turn up required some courage. Since 1523, the Inquisition had condemned more than 1,300 'heretics' to death, by far the largest number in Europe. But a clear commitment to Protestant ideas was now strengthened by the many 'hedge preachers' and through French and English influences. The Reformed church immediately built up its institutions. By the end of 1566, consistories existed in eight towns in the province of Holland, even though no Churches under the Cross had been rooted there beforehand. Emden became the Protestant centre of print. As usual, however, religious printing had to be approached carefully. The printer Gilles van der Erve, for instance, had come from London and was nearly ruined by an Emden pastor's New Testament translation. The work lacked stylistic fluency, but had been calculated for a print run of 2,500 copies. Since even in good times printers thus needed to rely on safe products, Reformed printing was intellectually innovative only to a limited extent. Moreover, the high tide of the Reform movement only lasted for a short time. The 'wonder year' of 1566 was followed by a renewed Catholic offensive, and by unease among many about iconoclastic attacks.[31] This strengthened the so-called *middengroepen*, who regarded Catholic as well as Reformed ways of proceeding as too extreme.

---

[31] See esp. Alistair Duke, *Reformation and Revolt in the Low Countries* (London, 1991).

In 1567, between 30,000 and 40,000 Reformed supporters from areas that today make up the Netherlands, Belgium, Luxembourg and parts of northern France went into exile. Hundreds of houses stood empty in cities like Antwerp or Valenciennes. London, Norwich, Frankfurt, Heidelberg, Cologne, Frankenthal, Aachen and Duisburg were the destinations of many of these exiles. Emden integrated another 4,000 refugees, some of whom could be seen on the streets wearing mass vestments they had plundered the year before. When the Heidelberg and Frankenthal exile communities called for a general synod in Emden in 1571, only sixteen Churches under the Cross were left in all of the Netherlands. The Spanish Duke of Alba seemed to have completed his mission brilliantly.

Any Spanish offensive, however, in turn caused a reaction against the Habsburgs' limiting the rights and liberties of the Dutch. Alba moreover had not just fought heretics and hanged some high-ranking nobles. He had also raised taxes. Thus, in 1572, the provinces Holland and Zeeland decided to raise troops against Spain under William of Orange's leadership. During the following years, Emden became a recruiting ground for pastors of Reformed churches, which now practised openly in these provinces. Again, as in the case of Geneva and France, Emden's institutions served as a model, and Emden helped to mediate and give advice in any controversy about proper doctrine and Reformed life. It renewed its role as publishing centre of Reformed writing. The printer van der Erve had learned his lesson and now overwhelmingly invested in reprints of translations of the Bible that had already been successful, reprints of small catechism books, and church orders to be used in the new communities, as well as books of psalms, well-produced martyrologies and an elegant Dutch edition of Calvin's *Institutes*.

Emden's 'great time' lasted roughly as long as Geneva's: the Baltic trade took off amazingly well, the exiles providing a ready workforce. As new citizens, they were committed to a church structure that set out to judge everyone by the same moral standards and to discipline the well-off and long term residents if they overstepped the mark. From 1557 onwards, the consistory carefully considered all questions of daily morale – tackling issues such as how to trade in a Christian way and whether or not it might be permissible to play *Kolf*, a kind of ice hockey. After à Lasco had left, the city never again attracted an outstanding European reformer; neither did it build up an institution of higher education. Geneva's Academy, as well as institutions in Heidelberg and Leiden, were after all high-ranking Reformed universities. The big controversies about predestination opened up by the Leiden professor Jacobus Arminius were viewed suspiciously in Emden. Basic doctrinal issues appeared to have been sufficiently clarified by several catechisms, treatises and translations of the Bible. Like French Huguenots, Emden people probably regarded a deep academic training as less important than a stable practice of belief supported by well-run institutions and emotionally intelligent office-holders. Emden saw itself as a model of just such qualities. Its institutions functioned, and by now had confidently dropped participatory elements. No pastor discussed Reformed doctrine after the Sunday services, and none of the officers was communally elected. Nor was this status quo questioned.

In the 1590s, the Reformed church held sway in all the northern provinces of the Netherlands (see below). Many exiles and their children returned from Emden to their homes, or settled in areas of economic promise, like Amsterdam. Frontiers of faith were finally clearly drawn: in 1578, Alessandro Farnese had become Spanish governor general and had gone out of his way to stamp out heresy in the southern Nether-lands. By 1585, the Antwerp Reformed community had to admit defeat – once more thousands of citizens faced the choice of converting or going into exile. Flanders and Brabant became bastions of a vibrant Catholi-cism. In the northern Netherlands, by contrast, even Frisia decided to abolish the Catholic mass by 1580, even though its organised Reformed community had only been active for four years. As in the provinces of Holland, Zeeland, Overijssel, Gelderland and Utrecht, convents were abolished, church property was taken over and Reformed churches and schools financed through these means. The stadtholder governors John and William Louis of Nassau fought their last military offensives in 1594 and 1598 to implement the anti-Spanish and anti-Catholic alliance of the United Provinces in Groningen and Drenthe, both of which lay in the north-east. In Emden the citizenry had to defend Calvinism between 1591 and 1599, during the rule of the orthodox Lutheran Edzard II, and in so doing drew on Dutch support. From 1600 onwards Emden played an important role largely within its own region of East Frisia. It had become a Reformed provincial town bordering a Reformed republic.

The Dutch Reformation

The United Provinces of the northern Netherlands had meanwhile created a confessional structure unique within Europe. There was no state church. The Reformed church was privileged by magistrates and stadtholder governors overseeing the provinces. After 1550, Lutheranism never again attracted significant support. No authority favoured sectari-ans, but different faiths were nonetheless tolerated; after initial prohibi-tions, tolerance was even extended to Catholics and this despite the fact that Calvinists continued to preach vehemently against them and against sectarians, both of whom they regarded as agents of Satan.[32] Still, most citizens regarded the historical battle against Spain as a fight against the tyranny of whatever church and confession; religious freedom had become crucial to the idea of civic liberty. Religious identities remained relatively heterogeneous. Around 1620, for instance, we find the following distribution of confessions in Haarlem: 20 per cent of the population defined themselves as Reformed, 12.5 per cent as Catholic, 14 per cent as Baptist, 1 per cent as Lutheran and *c.* 1 per cent as part of the Walloon church. Reliable figures for nine regions in Holland and Zeeland for 1600 likewise document that only 12 to 18 per cent of the population were full members of the Reformed Church. So what did half of the Dutch, who did not formally belong to any confession, believe in? There were complaints about libertines and atheists – but never to such an extent that a specific part of the population seems to have rejected a religious funeral, for instance. Weddings could already be celebrated as merely secular rituals in most of the northern Netherlands. The broadest confessional group was composed of heterodox sympathisers of Reformed religion, since Reformed Calvinists had settled for an extraordinary compromise: full membership in their church and the right to receive communion was not just a condition of having been baptised, but of knowing the doctrines. This insistence on a clear sense of confessional values was intended to enshrine boundaries between Calvinists and Anabaptists, Mennonites and other 'sectarians', groups that still enjoyed considerable popularity until the middle of the seventeenth century. Full membership moreover required that Reformed parishioners subject themselves to the 'discipline of Christ' in consistory courts. While full membership was thus restricted, the church tolerated the fact that most of those who attended its services would never become proper members. Half of all Christians thus evaded consistorial controls – and were not admitted to receive communion. This fact impressively documents that many early modern citizens were prepared to do without the ritual of forgiveness of sin or the ritualised promise of salvation without becoming paranoid about their afterlives, as historians who portray these centuries as characterised by spiritual *Angst* seem to overlook.

The republic had therefore not witnessed a rapid spread of Reformed religion and discipline. Elders were elected by consistories and not by the council, and largely had to conform to magistrates' vision of their communal influence; most magistrates wanted to remain in control of education and welfare matters and sometimes even decided the appointment of

---

[32] Nonetheless, tolerance was a complex matter in the Dutch Republic as elsewhere, see Ronnie Po-Chia Hsia and Henk van Nierop (eds.), *Calvinism and Religious Toleration in the Dutch Golden Age* (Cambridge, 2002).

pastors.[33] Conflicts between the Reformed church and magistrates were in turn difficult to avoid. Whether, why and when they began to erupt differed from place to place. Dordrecht patricians, for instance, agreed that all school teachers of Latin should first be interrogated by the consistory, in order to guarantee that their sons were taught pure Reformed doctrine. Elsewhere, for example in Rotterdam, magistrates insisted on handling everything they defined as civic affairs, including their increasing control of the poor and of migrants. Dancing and theatre going – which entertained middling and upper classes, but were much despised by Reformed hard-liners – were hardly ever condemned by magistrates. In the countryside, rural elites mostly remained hostile to Reformed religion. Here, Catholicism was at its strongest, while exposure to the new disciplinary urges of the Reformed church, town magistrates and provincial governors remained low. It often proved difficult to find elders. And yet, local circumstances were always interestingly nuanced. Half of the province of Holland's population was rural by 1622. A handful of villages in that province strongly supported Reformed religion; in many others, only four people would turn up for communion (figure 16).

The Reformed church had thus managed limited gains in the Netherlands: at the time of the Edict of Nantes and the final offensives against Huguenots it was protected and privileged in the northern regions of the country. But its ideal of Christianising society had been watered down in the land of canals. Its peculiar profile becomes even more obvious when we consider that about two thirds of full members were female. As Judith Pollmann explains, membership enabled women in particular to demonstrate their *eerlijkheid* and honour and thereby raise their public status.[34] This was important to them because they were precluded from membership in other 'honourable' associations, such as guilds, and from most official functions. Membership documented respectability in an age that above all blamed women for their passions and excessive nature. To be Reformed therefore had important social rather than merely religious meanings: it showed that one was happy scrupulously to subject one's lifestyle to the demands of civility. Non-members meanwhile agreed, across confessional boundaries, that anyone leading a pious life deserved trust and respect as well. A pious life manifested itself principally through a moderate lifestyle, which those who cared could observe by looking at one's interior decoration, appearance, and shopping and leisure activities.

---

[33] Andrew Pettegree, Coming to Terms with Victory: The Up-building of a Calvinist Church in Holland, 1572–1590, in Duke, Lewis and Pettegree, *Calvinism in Europe*, pp. 160–80, sets this out extremely well.

[34] Judith Pollman, *Religious Choice in the Dutch Republic. The Reformation of Arnold Bucholius (1565–1641)* (Manchester, 1999), p. 197.

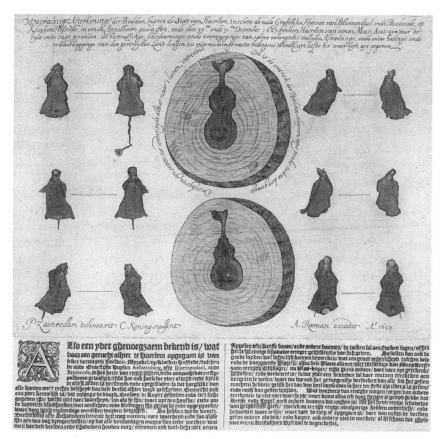

Figure 16. Cornelis Koning, after Pieter Saenredam, 1628, *Print to Belie Rumours about the Images Found in an Apple*. This etching represents cross-sections cut through an old apple tree on a farm near Haarlem. It was to repudiate another print which had claimed that the dark core of the apples represented the miraculous appearances of Roman Catholic priests, who might take over Holland. Saenredam, a pious man himself, published this print 'out of love of truth', against such superstition. Precision and a magnifying glass revealed that there were only dark cores which meant nothing. Disputes in religious interpretation thus could strengthen natural observation. The print is discussed in Svetlana Alpers, *The Art of Describing. Dutch Art in the Seventeenth Century* (Chicago, 1983), p. 81.

Hungary and Transylvania

Dutch tolerance perhaps found its sole counterpart in Transylvania.[35] In 1564, the estate assembly officially recognised the Reformed religion in addition to Catholicism and Lutheranism, and most of the Hungarian nobility regarded itself as Reformed (see p. 98). Four years later Anti-Trinitarians were also recognised. The clergy was told to preach according to the wishes of the majority of believers in each town, while each majority group taking over the communal church had to make sure that places of worship were provided for minority congregations. Noble magnates usually determined what was defined as majority faith. Even so, many local traditions of multi-confessional cooperation evolved. This tolerance was based partly on the experience of multi-ethnic cooperation, and partly on political anxieties about the fragmentation of the country through confessional conflict. Since about 1570 it had become clear that most noblemen and magistrates in the market towns preferred a Calvinist Reformed religion and that the other parts of Hungary not under Ottoman rule were likewise predominantly Protestant. Around 80 per cent of all communities are estimated to have been Protestant in 1600. Protestantism was a vehicle for the aristocracy to assert their autonomy against the Habsburgs and to connect with a 'purer' religion, which pleased God and was also intended to protect them against the Ottomans. When the Habsburgs tried to expand their power, the Hungarian Reformed nobleman Istvan Bocskai was elected as prince of Transylvania in 1605 and the Reformed faith now became the dominant and privileged state religion. The church glorified Bocskai and his successors as guardians of the people of Israel and profited from their donations. Hungarian students who were financed by bursaries still made up a significant portion of foreign students at Reformed universities – until 1629 in particular at Heidelberg and Frankfurt an der Oder, and afterwards at Leiden, Utrecht and the east Frisian town of Franeker. These students functioned as important cultural mediators who, for example, brought books to Hungary, which they donated to local libraries.

However, neither Reformed communities nor noblemen in Royal Hungary or in Transylvania ever showed great interest in taking over Reformed institutional models. There were hardly any consistories or elders. Discipline was mainly overseen independently by the pastorate, local judges and noble magnates, even though local judges were sometimes confirmed by the church. Parsons differed individually in the extent

---

[35] For the following see esp. Graeme Murdoch, *Calvinism on the Frontier 1600–1660. International Calvinism and the Reformed Church in Hungary and Transylvania* (Oxford, 2000).

to which they collaborated with magnates to push through penitential notions of punishment in courts. Public penitence was privileged, in which 'true repentance' had to be documented. Moreover, the Synod of Debrecen in 1567 had decided that two to three annual church visitations should be conducted by Reformed superintendents and archdeacons; they were to deal with any serious problems in the churches and the behaviour of members and insist that weekly catechism classes be held. The rules of church membership, however, were not primarily tied to the notion of a pure Eucharistic community and were thus hardly ever regulated through excommunication; only a few church court minutes survive, pointing to the relatively low significance of church surveillance over an explicitly Reformed lifestyle. Campaigns against feasts, blasphemy, dancing or the profanation of the Sabbath did occur. But all this fitted within the general framework of moral reforms in Europe by the end of the sixteenth century, and did not mark out any specifically Reformed identity.

With which social norms was Reformed as opposed to Lutheran belief in Hungary thus enmeshed? How did the majority of illiterate peasants, who now found themselves in whitewashed churches, respond? How did noble families and magnates change their lifestyle? How did Reformed belief affect these specific milieus, and what difference did it make to mentalities? Whereas the Dutch Reformed church insisted on the purity of those admitted to communion and paid the price of a small membership, the spreading of Reformed beliefs in Hungary and Transylvania was obviously based on much looser principles. Membership was not dependent on attendance at catechism classes and moral behaviour. True Reformed convictions were bound to these practices, and we thus need to pose the question of what exactly historians mean by stating that 80 per cent of communities were 'Reformed' by 1600.

Court Calvinism – Brandenburg

Christmas Day in Berlin, 1613: the Lutheran Brandenburg ruler Johann Sigismund declares himself a Calvinist. Did Brandenburg in turn become Calvinist? Were its churches emptied and schools staffed with new personnel? How did the so-called 'Second Reformation' proceed in a formerly Lutheran territory within an Empire ruled by Catholics? Could Genevan principles be implemented here?

Far from it. The example of Brandenburg on the contrary shows that the introduction of Calvinism could have complex ramifications and heighten religious and political pluriformity. The prince's motives were partly rooted in a desire to advance his dynastic claims in another small

German state, Jülich-Cleve.[36] Johann Sigismund nonetheless stressed that these were minor motives – and it is credible that they at least did not outweigh his religious motives. The prince belonged to a generation that had been educated strictly as Lutherans but had followed the development of Calvinist ideas, particularly at Heidelberg, which had become the intellectual centre of German Calvinism since 1559. It was located in the Palatinate, the most important territory that a prince had Reformed according to Calvinist ideas. Frederick III had published Reformed church and government ordinances in 1562 and 1563, and the so-called Heidelberg Catechism had been formulated as a religious manifesto. After sustained controversies, the organisation of church discipline was aligned to the Genevan rather than the Zurich model in 1571. The right to excommunicate sinners, however, remained in secular hands. The prince's church council was staffed by secular officers and continued to play an important role in controlling church matters. Institutionally German Reformed religion in this respect remained largely a princes' Reformation. Unlike in the Netherlands or France, Reformed religion was not supported by movements from below. The northern city of Bremen was an exception; and here the council insisted on the Zurich model of magistrates' control over morals. A number of smaller principalities, such as Nassau-Dillenburg in the Wetterau (which most clearly adhered to the Genevan model of more autonomous church control over communal discipline and church institutions), Lippe (except for the city of Lemgo, which defended its Lutheranism), Zweibrücken, Baden-Durlach and, significantly, Hesse-Kassel followed the Palatinate and had all introduced the Second Reformation by 1605. Reforms at Hesse-Kassel, however, mainly concerned the liturgy, catechism and educational reforms, rather than parish discipline. It has been estimated that about one million of the 16 million inhabitants of the German lands were Reformed Calvinists by 1618, when the Thirty Years War broke out. But, as in the case of Hungary, to give meaning to estimates of this kind we need to ask how this Second Reformation really affected people.

Johann Sigismund of Brandenburg was the last important ruler who converted to Calvinism; he had already formed his convictions by 1606. The Catholic Renewal had strengthened the sense among Protestant elites that everything happening in the world was part of the great battle between good and evil before the end of time. Catholicism was satanic and allied to the Antichrist – and Lutheranism still did not seem to dissociate itself enough from these beliefs. How, Heidelberg theologians insisted on asking, could one maintain that bread and wine at

---

[36] See Bodo Nischan, *Prince, People, and Confession. The Second Reformation in Brandenburg* (Philadelphia, 1994), and Bodo Nischan, Confessionalisation and Absolutism. The Case of Brandenburg, in Duke, Lewis and Pettegree, *Calvinism in Europe*, pp. 181–204.

communion were materially related to Christ? Reformed communities broke the bread they received into pieces; they rid their churches
of images, and were convinced of their more thorough Reformation.
Reformed eschatological convictions also seem to have differed from
Lutheran eschatology in one important respect: whereas the latter
assumed that the world was being ineluctably torn asunder by the power of
the Antichrist and that its end would be sudden and dramatic, Calvinists
believed in their victory against the powers of Satan. They were, according
to Bodo Nischan, more optimistic, militant and politically more involved
than Lutherans. Calvinist preachers and professors described princes as
'God's regents' who represented God on earth and were the only ones who
could confront Catholicism. People could be forced to accept a prince's
confessional change in the name of this proper belief, which was propagated with the old slogan 'pure, without any human additions and against
any papal superstition'.

But every ruler relied on the money and cooperation of his or her aristocracy. And Junker on Brandenburg estates were decidedly Lutheran.
Johann Sigismund was therefore only able to support Calvinism at his
court and at institutions where he directly controlled appointments, such
as at the university of Frankfurt/Oder and some elite schools. But he now
had to reckon with the resistance of his estates for confessional reasons,
and could not risk appearing as a religious tyrant who caused rebellion.
Pastors and parishes in towns and villages were similarly hard to convert.
The introduction of the Reformed religion was therefore a limited elite
phenomenon, which created more religious and political problems for the
prince than it helped to solve. How could an openly multi-confessional
territory be ruled? Could the prince be convincingly presented as its spiritual guardian, legitimised by God? Within two years more than one hundred polemical writings against Johann Sigismund had been published in
Lutheran territories. Berlin churches and churchgoers, too, had decided
by 1615 that Reformed practice held no appeal for them. As in Lemgo,
Lutheranism had become so popular with congregations that they simply resisted the *cuius regio, eius religio* imperative. This is why the Second
Reformation in Brandenburg remained a 'court Calvinism'.

In contrast to the Netherlands and Transylvania, confessional plurality
nonetheless aggravated confessional conflicts to a considerable degree.
Only by the 1630s, when Brandenburg had been occupied several times
by the Catholics during the Thirty Years War, were Lutherans and
Calvinists ready to join forces. 'Fraternal unity' was demanded, and it
was argued that Protestant divisions had delayed the Papacy's collapse.
Among many writings, a pamphlet entitled 'Apocalyptical, but Political
Consideration' appeared in 1631. It held that only unity could com-
bat the power of the Antichrist. Seventeen further years of war passed

before all three confessions in the Empire agreed to recognise each other fully.

Calvinism in Europe

'History is made accidentally and through the power of specific places and people' (see p. 61) – is this proposition equally true for Calvinism? The social history sketched out in this chapter does indeed point in that direction. Calvin, a young, ambitious man in exile arrived accidentally in the emerging republic of Geneva. He began to build up institutions (the Compagnie des Pasteurs, the Academy) and used the authority of civic institutions (the town council and schools) and their resources (money for the Academy, the city's potential to absorb immigrants) effectively. In contrast to Wittenberg, this programme unfolded in a merchant city without a university, but with its own factions and traditions. It took years to consolidate Calvinism through prolonged conflicts. Calvin's will to reveal his truth in thousands of sermons was crucial, and so were thousands more sermons by his 'team' of carefully selected and super-vised pastors. Moreover, by the time of Calvin's death, half the popula-tion were religious exiles. Calvin's truth also formed part of a political order in which the church offered to cooperate with the new republic to establish a civic moral regime, even if the church maintained its institu-tional autonomy more strongly than in Zurich. The religious conversation (see p. 41) remained the primary convention of doctrinal truth finding. Calvin demonstrated rhetorical civility through his speech and writing, and by not using visual propaganda as a tool. He and his pastors moreover demonstrated civility through a habitus, that is, all behaviour, including bodily comportment. This expressed a Christian ethos of human integrity in everyday life. Even beards were cut in a certain way to signal a modest, elegant kind of gravity. Beer had to be drunk in proper quantities and without failing to honour the Lord who had created it.

This civil religion was adapted by different Reformed milieus in differ-ent ways. We still know far too little about this. For many Dutch women, who made up two thirds of all members of the Reformed Church, it socially affirmed their *eerlijkheid*. For noble Huguenot women, Reformed civility was far from puritanical. These women defined their own notions of what constituted measured behaviour. They wore elegant, but not overly frivolous or luxurious dress at court, endorsed civil dancing and even enjoyed a modest flirt.[37] In Utrecht, similarly, the lady of Brederode only blushed slightly in 1626, when elders reprimanded her about dances

---

[37] Nancy Roelker, The Appeal of Calvinism to French Noblewomen in the Sixteenth Century, *Journal of Interdisciplinary History*, 2 (1972), pp. 391–418.

at her house. She then replied firmly that 'her house was no convent'. Her case was not even minuted by the consistory court.[38]

How important was the religion of civility for Polish and Hungarian noblemen and women, many of whom identified with the new Reformed faith? What did it mean for the habitus of Heidelberg professors?

European Calvinism evolved *through* these interpretations in everyday practice. It was adapted to different milieus and shaped by gender as well as by social and cultural factors. The dissemination of Reformed norms did not lead to uniform, self-controlled, anti-sensual and rational behaviour among Calvinist Christians. The next chapter investigates which Protestant identities emerged during the sixteenth and seventeenth centuries; it reinforces the argument that Protestantism helped to 'discipline' the population only in specific milieus and places. Discipline could not simply be imposed by the church, but had to be supported by different social groups, such as the unusually large groups of exiles in Geneva and Emden or the Dutch women who sought affirmation of their decency. Historians need to attend to social places and people and work out what it meant for them to be 'Reformed', that is, how their creed made social sense.

It is similarly questionable to assume a Europe-wide alliance of the early modern 'state' and the Reformed churches in indoctrinating and disciplining the Christian populace.[39] In east-central Europe it was not the state but the nobility who were responsible for spreading religious ideals. And even when a Transylvanian prince made Calvinism a state religion and was hailed by the church as King David, this did not result in a programme of reforming peoples' behaviour. The Dutch Republic similarly does not fit the model of a clear cooperation between state and church. The example of Brandenburg shows in the extreme how isolated a ruler with Reformed views could remain and hence be unable to implement corresponding policies. In Scotland Reformed religion only secured definite state support by 1590; in England the Old church retained its jurisdiction and the relationship between state and 'church' was marked by substantial conflicts. The concept of a 'confessionalised' Europe, marked by such joint efforts of state and church to create a subservient population is, even for the Reformed tradition, of little relevance.

[38] Judith Pollman, Off the Record: Problems with the Quantification of Calvinist Church Discipline, *Sixteenth Century Journal*, 2 (2002), pp. 432f.
[39] Heinz Schilling, Confessional Europe, in Thomas A. Brady Jr., Heiko Oberman and James Tracy (eds.), *Handbook of European History 1400–1600*, vol. II (Leiden, 1995), pp. 641–82; Philip Benedict's recent, masterly overview, *Christ's Churches Purely Reformed. A Social History of Calvinism* (New Haven, 2002) succeeds in providing solid and subtle arguments in view of these themes.

4   Truths of everyday life

The preceding chapters have shown how leading reformers legitimised their Christian truths and tried to sustain these truth claims through institutional, political, social and emotional strategies as well as through publishing and propaganda. How effective were such truth claims? Did Protestantism ever become a 'popular' religion? Most Europeans had never asked for Protestantism to be introduced and nobody had asked them about their opinion. Even so, with time, an everyday Protestantism evolved in which old and new elements merged in fascinating ways. The following stories provide us with a sense of this process.

The piper of Niklashausen

In 1476 the Virgin Mary appeared to a humble shepherd and musician. He was called Hans Behem and guarded the sheep at night, just as did the shepherds at Bethlehem when Mary gave birth to her son.[1] This time, Mary proposed clear political demands: tolls should be abolished, and water, woods and meadows belong to everyone. Behem went to the nearby village of Niklashausen and started to preach. He said that the clergy were living in great opulence. All people would be able to live properly, if only princes, the clergy, lords and knights were to share their wealth, but even princes would have to work as day-labourers one day. The Pope and the Emperor were worth little. Germany was living in great sin – one single glance at people's appearances proved as much. Pointed shoes, men's long hair and women's low-cut dresses had to be done away with.

People came to listen to Behem in their thousands. Artisan wives from the nearby city of Würzburg collected wax for candles and donated them. Servants and harvest workers threw their sickles away, and as the new wine

---

[1] The most reliable account is Klaus Arnold, *Niklashausen 1476. Quellen und Untersuchungen zur sozialreligiösen Bewegung des Hans Behem und zur Agrarstruktur eines spätmittelalterlichen Dorfes* (Baden-Baden, 1980).

arrived everybody began to be in pilgrimage mood: street taverns were set up, sermons were listened to, pointed shoes were indeed shortened and long hair was trimmed, dresses were taken off, so that some went 'naked' (presumably in their underclothes). Pregnant women touched Behem's cap, and radical songs against the priesthood were sung. Behem started telling people that if they wished to honour Mary, men should bring their arms. As a result, the Bishop of Würzburg threw Behem into prison and reminded his followers of their oath of obedience. Two peasants were hunted down as 'ringleaders' of this failed rebellion; Behem was burnt and his ashes were spread in the river Main; the bishop also prohibited pilgrimages to Niklashausen.

Manuscript and printed chronicles kept mentioning Behem's story throughout the sixteenth century. Some clearly thought him wrong, others did not take him seriously, some even showed sympathy. But they all helped document that the church had been criticised in this way, with extraordinary popular support which had been radically extinguished.

Hans Keil, a Lutheran prophet

Some 150 years later a vintner in the nearby Lutheran territory of Württemberg had another vision.[2] In 1648, shortly before the end of the Thirty Years War, an angel appeared in the vineyard. He ordered Hans Keil to tell the Duke of Württemberg that God was greatly aggrieved and would bring more ill over the country. The angel took Keil's knife to cut six vines: they bled! He then listed everbody's sinful and bad behaviour: the new tax, the clergy's greed, swearing and cursing, female vanity, to name but a few. The country had only six months in which to repent. Otherwise hell would open, and the devil and his thousand assistants would tear up everybody. God himself had sent the angel because he wanted everybody to be saved. If everybody repented, a brief time of happy sunshine would begin, leading to eternity.

Keil was one of around 200 known male and female prophets in Lutheran regions. The clergy and rulers had to deal with their warnings and predictions. Some rulers, like Emperor Charles V or the Swedish king Gustavus Adolphus, were themselves interested in prophecies. Collections of prophecies were printed in huge numbers – Luther edited one such collection in 1527. The Württemberg court, however, did not treat Keil as a prophet, but as a problem. He was far too critical, so the duke prohibited Keil from leaving his village. But once more thousands

---

[2] David W. Sabean, *Power in the Blood. Popular Culture and Village Discourse in Early Modern Germany* (Cambridge, 1984), pp. 61–9.

Figure 17. Anon., Broadsheet depicting the prophecy of Hans Keil, 1648.

of people began travelling to the village, called Gerlingen. And afterwards they would spread Keil's prophecies on streets, at markets and on boats, from the river Neckar to the Rhine and Main, in Switzerland and France. Small printers took up the news. Within four weeks, several cheap prints had been published (figure 17).

How did the duke deal with Keil and his followers? The theologians who sat on his church council produced a long report to decide whether the vision could be true. Their position was that there had been authentic prophets about whom the Bible wrote, and that new ones were not needed. Discipline, repentance and prayer were certainly important. The war rendered this obvious, and the church itself kept saying so; again, there was no need for a prophet. Keil, by contrast, believed that every further nail of sin hit Christ's body and could hurt everybody – urgent renewal was needed to appease God. The local pastor whose sermons he had listened to believed that God severely punished every trespass against the Ten Commandments and that punishments affected sinners themselves just as much as those allowing them to do evil. The theologians agreed. But they also believed that humans could not help but be sinners. A wise government had to make sure that procedures were in place to reprimand or punish wrongdoers. During the Thirty Years War, the duchy of Württemberg had thus introduced local church courts staffed by pastors and village judges. These 'church convents' were inspired by Geneva's consistory court, and their mission was to punish those who danced, swore, quarrelled or profaned the Sabbath with fines, admonishments or even imprisonment. The duke meanwhile could not be punished by anyone; certainly not for demanding new taxes.

In the end, the theologians proved that Keil was a false prophet. He had alleged, for instance, that the angel had talked about ten wise virgins wanting to see Christ. But the Bible only ever mentioned five of them, since the whole point of the tale had been that the other five virgins had stupidly fallen asleep in the dark! Since angels never fail, Keil had clearly invented everything. But why had the vines bled? Many villagers believed in the miracle. Although Württemberg had been Lutheran for more than a century, they declared the vineyard a sacred place and told all visitors to take off their hats and caps when they entered its ground. People from a neighbouring village came to pray in the vineyard. Afterwards, the vines had once more started bleeding. Some pastors and educated people from the region wanted experimentally to test the truth: they took the stalks and tried writing down words such as 'Jesus Christus' and 'Gott mit uns'. God would have prevented the blood turning into sacred words if the angel had not been real. In these ways, religious words were believed to manifest the presence of the Lord. Lutherans often carried prayers and sacred words with them as amulets, to protect themselves from Satan and misfortune. Religious books could be used in a similar way: Keil, for instance, put a Bible on his chest once he was imprisoned and promptly had another vision. Village women nonetheless successfully pressurised the duke to release him, so that his wife would not be left working all by herself.

Miracles

Among the thousands of people who had come to listen to Keil's prophecy and to see the bleeding vines was one woman with a truly special history.[3] She had been born nearby, as one of thirteen children. Her father was unknown, and even her mother had left the family when Katharina was ten years old. Guardians looked after the girl, but soon nothing of the family's property was left. Katharina had to go begging and this in the middle of a war. She fell ill, and as her wounds failed to heal, her feet became crippled and Katharina had to move about on hand crutches. She managed to earn a living in the town of Leonberg through spinning and looking after sick children. Eight years went by like this. Then, one Sunday, Katharina attended a service at which the duke and his entourage were also present. The sermon narrated the story of the merciful Samaritan. And as the community was listening, a miracle happened: Katharina was suddenly able to get up. Her feet had become straight again! She no longer needed to crawl, or wear skirts made for children! She kneeled down, tearfully thanking God. Her hand crutches were left in Leonberg's church, where they can still be seen today.

How can we make sense of miracles? One of the most interesting explanatory attempts holds that people who powerfully express their suffering and deep wish for improvement through religious idioms sometimes gain trust that their situation might change and that they might leave behind past experiences, which have blocked and embittered them. Religious practice offers the possibility to experience existential feelings, such as fear, weakness, bitterness, love, hope, the desire for forgiveness and the dependence on 'higher' forces. Most importantly, it provides a sense of a self which can be transformed, and can therefore facilitate 'healing'.[4] Thus, Katharina Hummel, who survived emotionally and physiologically crippling experiences, seems finally to have found through religion the strength to reveal herself as a woman who could walk upright and independently, after having demonstrated that she could provide for herself and do without her uncaring family. Church council theologians checked that Katharina lived a pious and humble life and permitted the publication of her story to show what wonders Protestantism worked. Katharina nonetheless continued to assert her independence: she started having relationships with men, she had a child, accepted an invitation to see the

---

[3] Nicole Bauer and Renate Dürr, Die Wunderheilung der Katharina Hummel 1644, in Renate Dürr (ed.), *Nonne, Magd oder Ratsfrau. Frauenleben in Leonberg aus vier Jahrhunderten* (Leonberg, 1998), pp. 85–93.

[4] Ruth Harris, *Lourdes. Body and Spirit in the Secular Age* (London, 1999) provides an excellent discussion of this issue.

duke and commented critically on the church and on local authorities. She cheekily told the ducal bailiff's wife that if she, Katharina, was to be expelled from Leonberg for such criticism she would sing Halleluja happily! And in 1648, she went to Keil.

Stories about ordinary people like those of Hans Keil and Katharina Hummel document a fascinating spectrum of early modern Protestant beliefs and how they modified Catholicism rather than radically breaking with it. Keil's prophecy was not mediated by the Virgin Mary, but by an angel. Katharina was not healed by a saint or during a pilgrimage but during a church service, while hearing a particular sermon, that is, through the Word and amidst a praying, singing community. Württemberg theologians believed in Katharina's miracle and proposed propagating it – even if orthodox doctrine allowed for miracles as little as it did for prophets. Their views were thus far from consistent, partly because of confessional politics, and partly because they knew full well that the Bible could be interpreted in different ways. In any case, visions and miracles had not vanished from Lutheran belief.

The stories' rich context moreover introduce important motives which shaped Protestant identities in Europe and which this chapter explores: they range from people's need for a spiritual language, support and comfort, for being heard and saved through prayers and song to the force of providentialism and attitudes towards the Word; they point us to a Protestant material culture and questions about the laity's relationship with the clergy, as well as the impact of increasingly institutionalised modes of clerical and state discipline for 'sinful' behaviour. This discussion aims not only at underlining that historical change principally took place through modifications rather than radical transitions, but also that Protestantism was no rational religion. Rather, it was a religion fired by emotion – by anxieties about God's punishment, by someone like Keil's determination to explain why there was so much suffering in the world and his deeply felt wish for everybody's salvation, and by intensely private emotions about life and life changes.

Providence

So how did religious world-views become modified? How did cultures whose religion had for centuries been deeply rooted in saint worship, Marian veneration, pilgrimages and processions, or the reading of masses for the souls of the dead, deal with the far-reaching changes introduced by Protestantism? Let us turn to England. After the death of the Catholic Queen Mary, Elizabeth I succeeded to the throne between 1559 and 1603 and thereby became head of the Anglican church. Around 1570,

Reformed convictions became more deeply rooted among ordinary people. It was the culmination of a long Reformation, which, despite all medieval heretical movements, had never been supported by the majority of the population. By the end of the sixteenth century, most English men and women in the north as in the south regarded themselves as Protestants. They went to church, bought catechisms and Bibles in ever increasing numbers, decorated their houses with prints from hymns and broadsheets, celebrated Protestant feast days and developed a vibrantly patriotic Protestantism, principally directed against Spain.

Just as for the Hans Keil in his Württemberg village, divine providence was essential for English Protestantism and eased its transition from Catholicism.[5] One of countless examples may suffice: in 1595, an ancient oak tree in Essex moaned for three days like a dying man. It was cut down immediately, and a report was entered into the local chronicle. There was no question as to the tree's importance, not least just because it was so old, rooted, as it were, in the local topography. God had sent this sign to remind everybody of their sinfulness, pride and the possible proximity of the world's end, and his grace was revealed by the fact that he gave people time to repent. In Elizabethan England, and until the Civil Wars, people from all social levels believed that God communicated with them through such signs: unusual cosmic or other natural events, plague, or the experience of healing were often interpreted as divine messages.

God made and moved everything in his universe. Since all other mediators between heaven and earth, such as Mary or the saints, were no longer relevant, God had become omnipotent. And he was certainly not perceived as running his universe smoothly like a clock. There were leaps and standstills, reminding everyone of the Last Days. No episode of human behaviour escaped God. Corpses of murderers, who had not confessed, for instance, would turn black, and corpses of innocent victims would bleed. Individual sins, such as murder, were already punished during a person's life-time, and not in purgatory. Widespread sins, such as heavy drinking, were believed to cause collective punishment. It remained disputed whether grave individual sins, such as infanticide, might also result in collective punishments. Those excelling in piety, on the other hand, could achieve both individual and collective rewards. Such 'hotter' Protestants, as Patrick Collinson has termed them, are better known under the label 'Puritans', as they demanded purer forms of Reformed worship and doctrine than Elizabeth allowed for, but their

---

[5] For the following see the brilliant monograph by Alexandra Walsham, *Providence in Early Modern England* (Oxford, 1999). See also Kaspar von Greyerz, *Vorsehungsglaube und Kosmologie. Studien zu englischen Selbstzeugnissen des 17. Jahrhunderts* (Göttingen, 1990).

general religious outlook in fact did not differ substantially from mainstream Protestantism. Even so, they held particularly strong convictions that they personally received a whole string of signs, such as illness, which made them suffer on earth rather than in hell, or reminded them of being humble. The better one was at interpreting these signs, the closer he or she might be to God's kingdom. Hence, some of the hotter Protestants registered all their observations obsessively in diaries.

Cheap broadsheets relating miraculous stories as well as compendia of providential signs were frequently translated and thus documented to believers that God acted similarly in a pan-European way: English people read or heard about cosmic signs in Bohemia, Silesia or France. In 1580, prophetic utterances from a young German woman were translated into English, as they had already proved to be a publishing success in Baltic port towns such as Danzig, Lübeck and Hamburg. Around 1620, an elegant copper-engraving provided up-market clients with extraordinary news about a Dutch maid who had fasted for fourteen years and been kept alive solely through God's care. The number of such prints and woodcut ballads had increased significantly from 1560 onwards. Sermons, too, made much of providential examples. Most people now at some point in their lives experienced spectacular signs themselves: for instance swords of flames or a peculiar river flooding. They would look at many memorable pious broadsheets at tavern walls, such as one about a pregnant noblewoman who had denied a woman vagrant alms and had given birth to rabbits! The sins and virtues exemplified by these stories remained completely traditional, as they affirmed the values of the Ten Commandments and the evil of the Seven Deadly Sins. Reformed Anglicanism, in short, clearly allowed and built on important mental continuities. Fasting miracles and prophecies were still believed in, and perhaps more cosmic signs and demonic appearances were witnessed than ever before. The religious consequences of all types of behaviour were described with textual and visual vigour. This providential world-view, moreover, was not solely disseminated through print. In London, Oxford and Norwich, puppet shows might, for instance, stage the story of 'Jerusalem's glory and destruction' in several parts by the early seventeenth century. Audiences were by now steeped in a forty-year-old tradition of Protestant sermons which viewed England's history as directly mirroring that of Israel – a history of a chosen people which was nonetheless close to ruin because of its sinfulness. History could repeat itself, fatefully and frighteningly so.

Which psychic dispositions resulted from such an outlook? The spectrum ranged from some 'hotter' Protestants' confidence in their election to bouts of anxiety in bad times and collective calls for repentance during crisis years. Most people, however, thought of themselves as neither better nor much worse than others, at least most of the time, and once more kept to traditional notions of sin and repentance. They presumably regarded talking trees and other miracles with a mixture of curiosity and awe, tried to live their lives as best as possible and hoped for God's final grace if they repented their sins. A 'rational' or more individualised faith had certainly not emerged.

Providential beliefs shaped the world-view of countless Protestant clerics not just in England but across Europe. The sixteenth-century Zurich parson Johann Jakob Wick, for instance, bought hundreds of coloured broadsheets about providential signs and everyday disasters. He kept an extensive handwritten chronicle of further stories he had heard about, and often illustrated them with watercolour miniatures, as if the visual rendered them even more present.[6] Such stories demonstrated to Wick the wretched existence of mankind between the Fall and Last Judgement, a humanity caught in warfare, illness, death, quarrels, greed and the abuse of power before salvation. This condition had to be accepted, and the only remaining question was whether one did so quietly or decided that human sin nonetheless had to be dealt with rigorously.

From among all these divine signs, abnormal births strangely were the most revealing for many Protestants. German pastors would inspect the corpses of oddly shaped newborn babies with horror; in Württemberg, clergymen had to report abnormal births to the church council and even supply sketch drawings of them. These 'monsters' also revealed human depravity. The much bemoaned addiction to wearing fashionably wide 'Turkish' trousers, for instance, would manifest itself clearly in a monster's fleshly folds – and once again point to the approaching end of the world.[7] Thick folio volumes and thin pamphlets were written about such creatures, and woodcuts depicting them were to be meditated on, just in the way fifteenth-century broadsheet images had been designed to guide penitential meditation. Other medieval modes of perception likewise continued in modified ways. Thus, in 1594 a Saxon clergyman reported on a woman from Magdeburg who had died after long labour pains. After she had been buried, sounds could be heard from her coffin. When the midwife opened it, she saw that the corpse had turned snow white. She opened the women's belly, and found in it a monstrous baby laden with jewellery! During the Middle Ages, some saints had been recognised only after their coffins and bodies had been opened, and hieroglyphs had

---

[6] Matthias Senn, *Die Wickiana. Johann Jakob Wicks Nachrichtensammlung aus dem 16. Jahrhundert* (Küssnacht-Zurich, 1975).

[7] Philip M. Soergel, The Afterlives of Monstrous Infants in Reformation Germany, in Bruce Gordon and Peter Marshall (eds.), *The Place of the Dead. Death and Remembrance in Late Medieval and Early Modern Europe* (Cambridge, 2000), pp. 288–309.

revealed themselves inside the corpse. The Magdeburg woman was also believed to be God's messenger. But in accordance with an orthodox Lutheranism shared by the pastor, her body could no longer be a bearer of sanctity. It remained strictly tied to its nature as sinful flesh, and so the women and her monstrous child were taken to symbolise the unleashed force of human evil in the world.

A 'disenchanted' world?

Each of these examples demonstrates how strongly people's perceptions during this period differ from ours. They saw angels, demons and ghosts in the shape of black dogs, monsters and many other creatures. They lived with these realities, and hardly ever fundamentally questioned them, even though they would debate the precise nature of their powers. There was no unified Protestant doctrine regarding the question of how God and the devil wielded their power. The most basic consensus was that much about God's creation and faith itself transcended reason. Opinions likewise divided over the question in which ways the body could be a bearer of divine messages or of the devil. Many believed in fasting miracles and miraculous healing. People who thought themselves possessed by a demon were still helped in all Protestant cultures, although with prayers and psalms, rather than Catholic exorcisms. This further underlines that faith was not just believed to be a matter of a reasoning spirit; the body and senses were part of the experience of divine or demonic intervention.

Protestants, moreover, were characteristically hazy or disagreed about whether religious behaviour had any efficacy. Did good behaviour matter for salvation, and did good works, reading Scripture and attending sermons make any difference to one's relationship with God? Would penitential services avert plague and God's anger? Did collective prayers have any different effect than private prayers, and were prayers able to protect one from the devil and bad spirits? All of these questions were left open or answered differently and remained contested. Clear answers were nonetheless urgently sought, as many Lutherans and Calvinists kept stating that there was an eternal fight between God, Satan and the Antichrist and that the end of the world was near. This battle once more constantly manifested itself in everyday life through supernatural signs: a Hungarian Calvinist peasant, for instance, who destroyed a Catholic crucifix on the roadside, claimed that he saw it turning into a monster before his very eyes.[8] A transformation of this kind left unsettlingly unclear whether this

---

[8] István György Tóth, The Missionary and the Devil. Ways of Conversion in Catholic Missions in Hungary, in E. Andor and I. G. Tóth (eds.), *Frontiers of Faith, Religious Exchange and the Constitution of Religious Identities 1400–1750* (Budapest, 2001), p. 86.

happened because of Satan's power in order to punish the peasant, or whether God used the monster to affirm how horrific Catholicism was. Either way, people who found themselves faced by monsters needed to know.

Questions such as these were in any case particularly important in people's everyday life because they expected religion to protect them against misfortune, such as infant death, crop failure and the like.[9] Catholicism offered protection through 'sacramentals' – objects which had been blessed by a priest, such as candles, and possessed a divine power. They were put into corners of rooms, cradles or stables. Devotional signs from pilgrimage places possessed similar powers, and so did water from holy wells or holy oil. Amulets were often worn as a protection against illness and witchcraft. What happened to these traditions in Protestantism? There were no longer any blessed objects which the laity could use independently in their everyday lives. Such practices were now defined as 'superstitious'. Even so, Protestant rituals, sermons and prayers often retained the notion that they might influence God or convey his influence. Pastors' gestural behaviour, such as when they put their hand on a person's forehead after he or she had been absolved from sins after confession likewise suggested that there was a direct and physical link between God, the clergy and laity. In general, Protestantism continued to maintain such notions until the middle of the seventeenth century and often for much longer.

So, clearly, and even though we must be careful not to overemphasise similarities between Catholics and Protestants, this was not a 'disenchanted' religion, to invoke the sociologist Max Weber's famous formula, which drew clear and tight boundaries between 'religion' and 'magic'. Protestants merely redefined the meaning of these terms, just as they redefined what was 'proper' ritual, rather than doing away with it.[10] Lutherans processed through fields to avert hail, and pastors charged high fees for such services. There continued to be sacred objects, such as the blessed bells, which protected church and parish. The bells of the Genevan church St Pierre carried the following inscription since 1407: 'I praise the true God, I summon the people, I assemble the clergy, I cry for the dead, I avert all plague, I embellish feast days. My voice is the horror of all devils', and it continued to ring for Calvinists, even though few may have known about the inscription and it would have been expensive

[9] The most important discussion of these issues can be found in R. W. Scribner, The Reformation, Popular Magic, and the Disenchantment of the World, *Journal of Interdisciplinary History*, 23 (1993), pp. 475–94.

[10] See Susan Karant-Nunn, *The Reformation of Ritual. An Interpretation of Early Modern Germany* (London, 1997).

to commission a new bell. But we know from archival records that many communities wanted church bells to be rung during bad weather to frighten off evil spirits. Some eighteenth-century communities, by contrast, refused to have lightning conductors on their bell towers, so that God's punishments would remain manifest. Sacred places, such as the Gerlingen vineyard, were supported by communities who thereby created local sacred topographies, no doubt partly out of wish to bolster local prestige and attract religious tourism. The Danish church even officially recognised holy wells; 650 (!) of them were discovered after the Reformation.[11] In 1650, the clergyman Erik Hansen wrote a treatise in which he admonished the laity to link the wells' healing power solely to God, and to visit them at any time, rather than on particular days or during special seasons. Sick people should ask God (rather than the saints) in the name of Jesus Christ to heal them through the waters. Archaeologists have discovered crutches which seem to have been thrown away and left behind at a well located on the small island of Fünen, first mentioned in 1580 – an extraordinary and moving find. In England, Ireland and Scotland, people also kept visiting ancient holy wells. In Germany, places linked to Luther were usually held to be imbued with sacred power, and the Wartburg became a kind of Protestant pilgrimage place, as Lutherans looked for the mark left on the wall when the reformer had fought off the devil with his ink. By 1574, a guide book suggested that visitors should touch the walls behind which Luther had sought protection and take away tiny pieces of wood or material that showed some of the ink. Zedler's *Universal Encyclopaedia* noted that by 1735 more than a thousand visitors had inscribed their names on the walls.[12]

The world of the Word

Such graffiti, the fact that educated Württemberg elites wrote down 'Jesus Christ' with bleeding vines to test Hans Keil's vision, or the popularity of sermons document that Word and Scripture had become exceptionally important in Protestant culture. This is why Protestantism is often characterised as a more rational religion than Catholicism and as non-sensual. As has already been suggested in earlier chapters, this view overlooks contemporary attitudes towards the Word and the sensual practices surrounding it. For early modern Protestants, the Word was not just a communicative sign. It could mediate the divine.

---

[11] Jens Christian Johansen, Holy Springs and Protestantism in Early Modern Denmark. A Medical Rationale from Religious Practise, *Medical History* (1997), pp. 59–69.
[12] Etienne François, Die Wartburg, in E. François and H. Schulze (eds.), *Deutsche Erinnerungsorte*, vol. II (Munich, 2001), pp. 154–70.

Art historians are by now well known for their claim that each period sees differently, as attitudes towards the visible and perception change. Those interested in how art was looked at must reconstruct the 'period eye'. It is rarely noted, however, that until the late seventeenth century commentators on the senses frequently privileged hearing over seeing. The sixteenth-century essayist Michel de Montaigne, for instance, possessed a great library and was an avid writer, but nonetheless preferred to lose his sense of sight rather than his hearing. Historians therefore need to rephrase the question posed by art historians and explore what 'hearing' meant for people in the Middle Ages and during the early modern period in order to reconstruct 'period ears'. In doing so, one needs to pay attention to contemporary attitudes towards the voice and rhetorical techniques (equivalent to the gaze and pictorial techniques) and to the rich layers of oral culture, including singing.

Once more, however, we should not expect to find unified and unchanging views, for instance about how the Word was supposed to affect its hearer. Whether hearing transmitted the Word first to the heart or to reason, or to both, were difficult questions occupying learned contemporaries. Even so, it is perhaps not too far fetched to suggest that the popularity of Protestant sermons in the early years of the movement may partly be explained by the fact that they often suggested that the mere hearing of the 'pure' Word implied that the faith was fully understood, so that believers would be saved through merely listening to the Word – as the principles *sola scriptura, sola fide, sola gratia* were interlinked. In later years, the notion that particular powers attached to the biblical Word persisted, and likewise that it was most fully apprehended if body and soul played their part.

Hence sermons, prayers and singing had become central in Protestant services, and words could occasion spiritual transformations. This becomes easier to understand if we remind ourselves that early modern people regarded everything that existed, including language, as God-given, and language could therefore be imbued with divine power. Some sectarians spoke in tongues, and the story of Katharina Hummel shows that seventeenth-century Lutheran orthodox elites believed instantly in the possibility that merely listening to a sermon might heal a person. English Protestants, too, widely held that God's Word miraculously effected change and salvation.[13] Anglicans turned sermons into the climax of any service. They could be highly emotional and imbued with a quasi-sacramental power. One parson, for instance, announced that his congregation's tears which had been collected in 'God's bottle' would

---

[13] See Walsham, *Providence*, pp. 281–325.

lead God to forgive the community and protect it from plague and epidemics. Liturgical sayings were regarded as similarly powerful, so that Lutheran laypeople used them in their everyday lives to avert illness or misfortune. Any parson who found this superstitious was told that God's Word had miraculous powers: since it changed hearts and souls, it could also help in accidents. The Word, in short, made God's power manifest on earth and in the flesh and was perceived as being able to transform despair into hope, bad into good. Hence, for many Protestants, the Word was linked to a mystery of a transformation previously only witnessed in the Catholic celebration of mass. This might even explain reports of church-goers who abruptly left as the sermon ended. Late medieval people often went to church just to see the elevated host. For Protestants, the Word itself could mediate protection and salvation, the highest sacred powers.

It comes as no surprise then that the Bible became a specifically Protestant object of veneration – Hans Keil, as we have seen, put it on his chest when imprisoned. The Bible protected him from evil and mediated the divine. Such practices, bizarre as they may seem nowadays, become more easily explicable if we question our normal assumption that books are used primarily for reading. For many early modern people books possessed a representative or almost totemic character. Complete Bible editions or parts of it were proudly displayed in one's best chamber and demonstrated that the owners were good Christians. This implied that God protected their home, family and visitors. The inventory of a Dutch couple in 1659 thus listed that their *stave*, their living room, displayed five landscape paintings and one portrait of Luther, a Dutch Bible and a high-German Bible, a book in German by Jan Hus and a Lutheran sermon amidst a set of fifteen or so books on geometry, medicine, antiquity, war, politics and everyday morals as well as *veele kleijne verscheijdene andere soo Duitsche als franse boexkens* – lots of other small books in Dutch and French.[14] Bibles were put into cradles, held closed in one's hands, or randomly opened to find passages offering comfort or future guidance. This latter mode of Protestant divination was practised for centuries: Goethe's mother still resorted to it in order to find out when and how her son's life might improve.

In order to assess properly what religious books could mean, it is, of course, necessary to attend to a broad spectrum of practices in different milieus and places. Educated people, for instance, could certainly pride themselves on working through their Bibles, hymn-books, prayer-books

---

[14] Hester Dibbits, *Vertrouwd bezit, Materiële cultuur in Doesburg en Maassluis 1650–1800* (Nijmegen, 2001), p. 335.

and catechisms through annotations, marginalia, by underlining text passages, entering spiritual verse or pasting in images. All of this documented their intense involvement with these texts and the sheer time spent with them – it was a Protestant equivalent of good works. Gradually, typically Protestant modes of handling books evolved, relating to their character and to class. More or less expensive ways of binding were significant, pages were carefully turned, hands were washed before taking up a Bible, the time of the day and the day of the week mattered and so did the space. Even the writing tools with which notes might be entered and their colours were never chosen accidentally but according to cultural codes, as were the typography, the places where books were shut away or shelved, the clothes which were worn for reading and the mental and emotional disposition before one began reading. Most of this was not new. Books of hours and other illuminated manuscripts, the Vulgate and other 'high' religious writings had been similarly treated during the Middle Ages, and humanism had likewise matched its unparalleled veneration of classical authors with corresponding reading habits: Machiavelli or Thomas More would never have read Socrates without putting on a fresh shirt. But among Protestants these attitudes diversified and spread outside convents and universities to the nobility and middle classes. Pious reading habits were also evinced through the ability to memorise large numbers of hymns, biblical verses or psalms. Print reinforced a vast oral culture which turned on the ability to recite from memory.

Protestant appropriations of sacred texts were therefore neither necessarily a quiet pursuit nor did they solely involve the mind. Helena of Asseburgk, for example, was a provincial noblewoman who grew up during the Thirty Years War. Aged twenty, she had already made the dress she wished to wear on her death bed, and stitched biblical verses on it, as if she wanted to inscribe her salvation on her body in anticipation of the very moment when she would witness the Lord.[15] Although she kept the dress for thirty years, the Bible helped the young woman to prepare herself emotionally for the likelihood of an unexpected death because of the war. Another example may demonstrate how a seventeenth-century Württemberg court physician prepared for death at the end of a long life. His funeral sermon specified that, once widowed, he had 'read, prayed or sung' the Old Testament seventeen times, the New Testament thirty-one times, Johannes Arndt's *True Christendom* twenty-nine times, his *Paradise Garden* over a hundred times, Kubach's large prayer book twenty-nine times, and the thick Letvonian hymn-book eight times. This manner

---

[15] Patrice Veit, Das Gesangbuch in der Praxis Pietatis der Lutheraner, in H.-C. Rublack (ed.), *Die lutherische Konfessionalisierung in Deutschland* (Gütersloh, 1992), p. 450.

of accounting not only registered piety. Christian singing and speaking expressed everyday worries and hopes for an eternal life. The voice and repetitive speaking became part of a flow of feelings aiming at reconciliation with the world. It was believed to open the heart physically and intellectually and to protect it from hardening. Reading aloud was part of a way of life which stood in contrast to the silence of those who already had a hardened heart and did not wish to forgive. During the sixteenth century, the witch had been turned into an emblem of such an embittered person, who had made her pact with the devil and was full of ill will. Doctors explained that old witches had become so dry that they were even unable to cry out of empathy or remorse. They were completely fixated on their envy of others and could not return to a state of Christian love. No Christian word would pass their lips. Pious speaking and reading habits thus had no abstract, 'logo-centrical' meaning for people in their everyday lives, but rather emotional and social meanings. They were linked to contemporary views of the embodied self, of age, death, community and love.[16]

Reading aloud or singing therefore constituted important cultural practices among the educated, and even theology students were not necessarily eager to read quietly for hours. Wittenberg University library, for instance, was part of Frederick the Wise's castle until the middle of the sixteenth century. And nobody sat there to read. Early modern people feared that melancholy would soon possess those reading books for a long time. Students stood at high desks, and books were chained, because they were precious. All of this presumably limited the intensity with which folio volumes were used and the number of students able to consult them. In addition, early modern readers often struggled with darkness and cold temperatures, and it is more than likely that students in overcrowded Wittenberg rooms had a difficult time reading at home. Students from a bourgeois background, who typically entered new universities and went to marginal towns such as Wittenberg (which charged reduced fees and where basic costs of life was cheaper) might have also found it difficult to afford books, although we know that pious Wittenberg students walked around with their Bibles for a while. They had become an identity symbol, and we can assume that students generally chose to own few books and invested them with deep emotional meanings.

Hence they began to ask Luther and Melanchthon for autographs in their books and Bibles. This was part of the professorial cult encouraged by Wittenberg scholars, which not just related to the professor as

[16] Ulinka Rublack, Fluxes: The Early Modern Body and the Emotions, *History Workshop Journal*, 53 (Spring, 2002), pp. 1–16.

a man who knew a lot and the truth, but was destined by God. As a result, the so-called *liber amicorum* emerged as a genre in Wittenberg. Students brought books or special albums and asked their colleagues and professors to enter verses or sayings in them to guide the owners' lives and assure them of their friendship. Melanchthon, as his contemporary biographer notes, apparently spent an 'incredible' amount of time and effort on these entries.[17] Many of the books are still preserved. A student called Nicolaus Zeitlos, for instance, brought the Wittenberg Bible, and Luther and Melanchthon both entered biblical quotations and some prose in it. Zeitlos added to this a portrait of Luther by Cranach as well as a double portrait of Luther and Melanchthon, framed by angels and the four evangelists.[18] The Bible was turned into a personified cult object. For generations to come, autographs and texts of leading reformers retained their value. A man called Georg Werner, for example, who had matriculated in Wittenberg in 1584 and became a parson, acquired the seal of a letter by Zwingli addressed to Philip of Hesse for his *liber amicorum*, and also a page with twenty-five lines written by Luther's hand, as authenticated by Melanchthon's son, seventeen lines written by Melanchthon, and his son's autograph.[19] Portraits of Luther and Melanchthon were imprinted on leather-bound *libri* (figure 18). The traditional trade in relics, in bones and cloth, had thus turned into a trade with Scripture and related items. We need to call them *grapho*-relics, for they were directly connected with the body and soul of Protestant heroes, whose hands had written or held the specific piece. In an academic milieu, too, books were therefore frequently relational objects. They not so much manifested abstract ideas as gained their meaning socially. Theologians, noble and bourgeois people even travelled to Wittenberg in Luther's later years and asked him to enter some comforting or explanatory comments in their Wittenberg Bibles or writings by him. Psalm verses were particularly popular. Over three hundred of these inscriptions are known. Not least, they signalled their owners' pious prestige, and were soon themselves collected and published.

Biblical quotations, moreover, served to protect people against spirits and the devil, and were written on walls, beams and gables. Luther himself immediately wrote psalm verses on the walls of Coburg castle to ward off

---

[17] Hans-Peter Hasse, Wittenberger Theologie im 'Stammbuch': Eintragungen der Wittenberger Professoren im Album des Wolfgang Ruprecht aus Eger, in M. Beyer and G. Wartenberg (eds.), *Humanismus und Wittenberger Reformation* (Leipzig, 1996), p. 88.

[18] *Die Handschriften der Stadtbibliothek Nürnberg, Sonderband: Die Stammbücher und Stammbuchfragmente*, Part I (Berlin, 1995), p. 3.

[19] Karlheinz Goldmann, *Nürnberger und Altdorfer Stammbücher aus vier Jahrhunderten* (Nuremberg, 1981), p. 298.

Figure 18. *Album Amicorum* cover, 1579. Luther's portrait is imprinted on the binding.

Satan. He collected biblical verses and edited them. Such verses offered reassurance and enabled believers to express a variety of sentiments, ranging from despair, insecurity and the wish for redemption or understanding, revelation and rejoicing. In these ways, they helped to articulate and accommodate existential experiences.

Within Protestant popular culture, likewise, a whole genre of tales dwelt on Luther and the efficacy of the Word.[20] Stories recounted how Luther had fought off the devil with hymns or biblical quotations, how his prayers had restored Melanchthon's health (see pp. 33–6), how psalms spoken by him had extinguished fires or how his prayers had alleviated a community's need. Yet a further story reported how one prince, upon hearing children sing Luther's famous hymn *Ein feste Burg ist unser Gott*, had said that he wanted to storm this fortress (*feste Burg*), or otherwise die. He had died the next day. Other tales showed that Luther used his prophetic words as an effective punishment. He had condemned all rebellious citizens of Karlstadt's parish in Orlamünde, and their village well dried up. All of these stories enshrined Luther's quasi-sacred status within Protestantism. So did reports about miracles which were linked to him. Luther's birthplace in Eisleben, for instance, was said to have miraculously resisted several fires. Luther-Bibles and portraits of the reformer time and again proved incombustible. After the Thirty Years War, one portrait of him had even sweated when the parson had meditated on the hardships of war. Some portraits resisted Calvinist attempts to paint them over. Such miraculous stories of Lutheran (*sic!*) sacred places and objects were experienced, told and noted down by clergymen until the eighteenth century; educated people could believe in them as much as ordinary folk.

Luther himself certainly thought that biblical words directly related to God – for him they possessed an almost sacramental quality, and so did the very name 'God' in writing. Luther regarded the Word as an important mediator of the divine, and this explains, for instance, why he wrote 'this is my body' with chalk on a table and immediately covered the writing with a velvet cloth when discussing the question of Christ's presence in the Eucharist with Zwinglians at the decisive Marburg colloquy. For Luther, Scripture said 'this is' and this meant that the bread was Christ's body – even if how and why transcended human reasoning. The Word could signify the divine signifier; it was a visible trace of an invisible, supernatural world.

The phrase 'God's Word remains in eternity' – *Verbum Domini manet in aeternum* – therefore became a hugely important, iconic dictum in

[20] R. W. Scribner, *Popular Culture and Popular Movements in Reformation Germany* (London, 1987), pp. 301–54.

Wittenberg early on. Luther used it for his entries in student's albums, implicitly promising them eternal life. One such inscription runs:

The just have a desire for God's word and like talking about it day and night, which is why they can do everything, they do everything and forever remain green and fertile, like a palm tree at the water. The godless have pleasure with their God, bellies and mammon, which is why they cannot do anything, they do nothing, and do not last, but vanish, like a shadow, with all their goods, honour, doings, power, belly and Mammon, *quia Verbum Domini Manet in aeternum,* and all those who remain with it with desire and love Amen Mart Luther D 1542.[21]

The Wittenberg circle soon built up such a strong identification with this programmatic slogan that the capital letters VDMI(A)E functioned as a Lutheran logo, and was later even reproduced on household tools (figure 19). In 1530, Philip of Hesse nonetheless attempted to appropriate the slogan at the Diet of Augsburg, when his 120 guardsmen all had VDMIAE stitched on their left sleeve. Their entry made a big show. It was directed against the Catholics, but also meant to demonstrate that Philip, despite mediating with Zwinglians, nonetheless fought for the true biblical word and embodied a political order blessed by God. Lutherans in Augsburg nonetheless immediately joked that the letters meant *Und Du must ins Elend* – 'and you have to go into misery' – while Catholics said they meant *Verbum Domini Manet in Ärmeln,* 'God's word remains forever in sleeves.'[22] Early modern educated people used wit as a fast and biting weapon.

The capital letters used for the slogan VDMIAE finally point to specific typographical techniques distinguishing the Protestant culture of the word. Capital letters could signal spiritual elevation, as in GOD, or the LORD. Luther's entries in Bibles and books were designed with some words in capital letters and carefully arranged on the page – Lutheran layout, so to speak. Bibles continued to ornament the first letter of every chapter; Calvinists frequently copied Bible passages with calligraphic perfection. Religious writing was therefore connected to a visual and symbolic aesthetic of its own, and this once more shows that Protestants did not simply read and process their faith with their minds, but also with their senses. It moreover demonstrates that Protestant religious thought was mediated by specific cultural techniques; its messages and effects were thus interlinked with its representation and the materials used to represent them.[23]

---

[21] Hasse, Wittenberger Theologie, p. 94.

[22] Maximilian Liebermann, *Urbanus Rhegius und die Anfänge der Reformation* (Münster, 1980); Frederick Stopp, 'Verbum Domini Manet in Aeternum: The Dissemination of a Reformation Slogan, 1522–1904', in S. S. Prawer, R. H. Thomas and L. Forster (eds.), *Essays in German Language, Culture and Society* (London, 1969), pp. 123–35.

[23] A stimulating discussion of such issues is provided by Juliet Fleming, *Graffiti and the Writing Arts of Early Modern England* (London, 2001), pp. 9–21.

Figure 19. Mortar, 1590, north German.

Hence it is fascinating to explore how attitudes towards the Word influenced Protestant domestic culture. In England, for instance, tiled stoves never proved a lasting success during the early modern period.[24] Open fireplaces were the norm, and since smoke damaged canvases, wall hangings, cloths or wall paintings remained a common form of decoration. As they were less durable and costly, they were frequently not registered in inventories. But we must not imagine English houses as whitewashed;

[24]   For the following see the pioneering study of Tessa Watt, *Cheap Print and Popular Piety, 1550–1640* (Cambridge, 1991).

rather, the lost wealth of church decorations was to some extent trans-
ferred to the domestic realm and to 'public' houses, in particular taverns.
This domestic iconographic culture is mostly dealt with by archaeologists
and historians too often fail to notice their findings. The evidence gathered for England, however, reveals that wall cloths with short sayings,
such as 'Fear God' were extremely common, and so were painted biblical
scenes, or a series of broadsheets pinned onto cloths. Wall paintings can
now mainly be traced in manor and other substantial houses, but it is
more than likely that they were copied by locals onto their own walls. A
Buckinghamshire farmhouse, for instance, still shows a simple painting
of Adam and Eve dating from *c.* 1627, and surprises with the following
black-letter placard, 'As by the disobedience of one mane many weare
made sinners so by the obedience of one shall many be made righteous',
a comforting collective notion of salvation and election. Psalm verses,
too, were easily and frequently painted on domestic walls. These practices once more document that we are not dealing with a culture in which
the Word was seen to mediate abstract, 'logo-centric' meanings, but in
which religious or, more specifically, biblical words had a decorative, protective and emotional function. Quite simply, they helped people to make
sense of and get through life. Psalm 112: 1–4, 'Riches and treasures shall
be in this house, and his righteousness endureth forever', was a success for
obvious reasons. Likewise, the admonishing words 'Feare God' achieved
an iconic status which presumably possessed a 'mystical authority' even
for the illiterate. The Hebrew Tetragrammaton which emblematically
depicted God did the same for educated elites. In wealthy households,
printed wallpapers could line wooden chests, combining decorative elements with biblical phrases on secular matters turned into couplets, such
as 'A virtuous wife gives husband life.' Finally, nearly everybody was able
to afford pious broadsheets and could paste them on her or his walls.
These were not just about providential signs and miraculous stories, but
might also, for instance, explain the Ten Commandments. Good house-
holders and masters were supposed to fix them on the wall, read them
aloud to their wives, children and servants, and help them to memorise
the written Word.

These broadsheets therefore formed part of a much broader and historically specific culture of religious words, signs and oral performance,
rather than being a separate 'print-medium' requiring completely new
responses. The doors of English plague victims, for instance, were marked
with a red cross and a large printed sheet with the words 'Lord have mercy
upon us' was fixed next to it. This wish was taken up in a broadsheet dating from 1636, which carried 'LORD HAVE MERCY UPON US' as a
huge headline, like a cry for help (figure 20). Its rough woodcut depicted

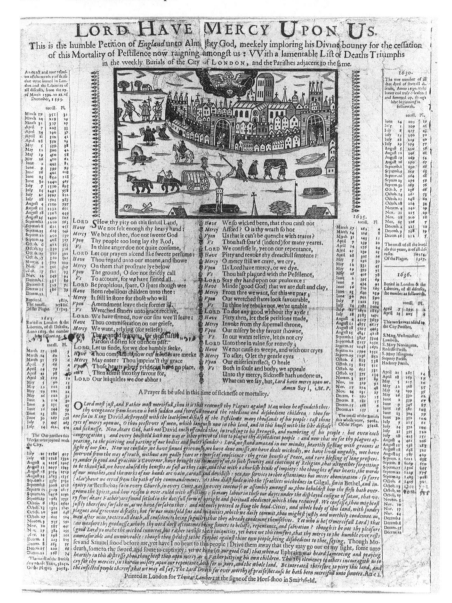

Figure 20. *Plague Broadside, c. 1636.*

the city of London, with an angel of the dying hovering over it, while the dead, coffins and death itself dominated the rest of the scene. Two columns at either side listed funeral statistics. Columns in the centre featured a dialogue between man and God. Printed next to it were over and over again the words 'LORD HAVE MERCY UPON US'. In times of crisis, which otherwise could have led to sheer despair, faith facilitated a dialogue which made sense out of punishment, offered hope for the future and thus enabled people to articulate their wish for protection again and again, thereby exerting at least some kind of agency. The wish 'Lord have mercy upon us' must have created its own topography of the sacred, deeply emotive word throughout London. It could be heard in churches and was set in letters in print workshops. It reached the doors of victims and hung on the walls of houses whose inhabitants were still alive.

Sermons

God's Word and his name were to be praised in sermons, which had become an essential element of every service. We can distinguish at least three types of Protestant preaching: first, a dramatic style, which described the miracles and punishments of God's creation and reminded everybody of the Last Judgement, and that it was close. Secondly, admonishing sermons, relating current crisis to the sinful behaviour shown by all ranks of society. Individual sinners might be alluded to, the parishioners might be insulted collectively, even the whole nation was possibly blamed and God's punishment portrayed as a necessary and just response. Finally, the plain style, which distanced itself from all dramatic devices, as well as from elaborate rhetorical strategies and humour, all of which were regarded as 'Catholic' acting. English handbooks for preachers, for instance, advised them to display 'pious seriousness', modesty and firmness, not to use any entertaining anecdotes and never to provoke laughter. Eloquence was unnecessary. The sermon had three elements: an exposition of doctrine, its justification and meaning for life. Plain preaching was to create an atmosphere of dignified revelation for honourable citizens and lend authority to the new Protestant faith.

Handbooks, however, only ever capture part of what was practised. At least at fairs, markets and in the churchyard of St Paul's cathedral we see a type of preacher in action who would have been successful as a mendicant preacher during the Middle Ages and might now work as an evangelical television preacher.[25] Those gathering in front of

---

[25] This passage is based on Walsham, *Providence*, pp. 281–325.

St Paul's, for instance, once more heard the nation being condemned. The preacher William Perkins apparently pronounced the very word 'condemned' in such a terrifying manner that it would echo in the audience's ears and make people's hearts race. Other preachers rolled their eyes up to heaven, their voices trembled and at the end some preachers had to be patted dry because they were wet with sweat. If national disasters happened soon after such sermons the preachers' prophetic gift seemed to be beyond doubt. Some showed concern that 'common people' might imitate these zealous preachers and ridicule them, so that the caste of preachers might lose its dignity altogether. On the other hand, one knew full well that audiences needed to be attracted and held. On weekdays, tens of thousands of Londoners already went to Shakespeare's and others' plays. In view of such competition, the church and churchyard were to be defended as 'the nation's stage' and its 'main theatre', since here, at last, play was serious and the nation's survival dependent on it. But this means that boundaries between dramatic 'acting' and a proper, serious, 'pure' exposition of the word remained difficult to establish for Protestants.

Routine sermons in smaller parishes in any case caused some structural problems. Thus, Nuremberg pastors created a prayer against sleeping in sermons, while Calvinists sometimes used sticks to wake up sleeping members of the congregation and widely used hour-glasses during the service, on which the eyes of the parishioners were fixed. Churches could be bitterly cold during winter, and lay people would sometimes cover themselves with two hats, which somewhat impaired their hearing. Attentiveness was variable even at the best of times. For attending a 'plain' service often meant not to talk or to laugh, to sit in semi-darkness, to kneel or stand, and to control all physical expressions, like yawning, as well as possible. Peasants and aristocrats, artisans and maidservants had to concentrate on simply hearing, singing and speaking liturgical words – a considerable achievement to interact in a limited way.

If a parson always preached in a punitive way, the laity simply switched off, demanded a different preacher or just stayed away. The upper Swabian town of Memmingen thus introduced some house searches during the seventeenth century, because its churches were empty. At least one person of every household was ordered to attend church. Situations of this kind reveal a structural tension between preachers and parishioners. Clergy understood it as their spiritual duty to preach God's law and repentance. But this frequently weighed heavily on their relationship with the laity. On the whole, we thus do well to assume that parsons were only able to keep their parishioners on church benches if they comforted as well as admonished their audience. German printed sermons generally show that such a balance was aimed at.[26] Sermons engaged with everyday life and endorsed norms adhered to by respectable, honourable house-holders. Sin was linked to social misbehaviour and traditional values. People were told to live in a modest (neither frugal nor luxurious) way and to avoid meanness and greed. Parents were to be honoured, every-body was to eschew laziness; women had to be their husbands' obedient helpmates in looking after business and household affairs; needless to say they were also expected to give birth and patiently endure the pains Eve had bestowed on their sex. Death ended a life of misery; peace and happiness existed only in heaven. As we can see, ideas about guilt or the meaning of life had thus not become more individualised, and there is no hint either that Protestantism promoted more 'capitalist' values than medieval Catholics had done.

While communities listened to sermons, they could participate more actively in services through singing. Even so, Protestantism only 'democratised' spiritual music to a limited extent.[27] Lutheran hymns were nearly all written and composed by theologians, or used existing tunes from monastic or urban culture; Calvinism created melodies for psalms and relied on trained musicians. In urban Lutheran churches, the boys' choir of the Latin school, the pastor, Kantor (choir director) and Kantorei (adult mixed choir) would sing.[28] Lutheran Kantoreien were choirs for gifted lay singers whose social background was 'respectable'. They therefore somewhat resembled Catholic fraternities, and allowed women in particular to play a public role in parish life. The Kantorei sang at weddings, feast days, baptisms and funerals and thus accompa-nied the key rituals in people's lives. There would be much sociability and an annual feast as well. But a high percentage of urban laity usually remained silent.

Village churches, especially in Reformed areas, usually found it hard to find people capable of singing church music at all – or perhaps even willing to do so, since Genevan music can even today easily strike one as rather joyless, overly sombre and slow. A Calvinist village pastor near Geneva thus reported that he only started the service once the few parishioners who could sing at least some of the eleven psalms he used had appeared. Often there was not a single man who could sing properly. Most people were only able to sing by stumbling over words and mistaking notes – and,

---

[26] Hans-Christoph Rublack, Lutherische Predigt und gesellschaftliche Wirklichkeiten, in H.-C. Rublack, *Lutherische Konfessionalisierung*, pp. 344–95.

[27] See the argument in Francis Higman, Music, in Andrew Pettegrew (ed.), *The Reformation World* (London, 2000), pp. 491–504.

[28] Helga Robinson-Hammerstein, The Lutheran Reformation and Music, in *The Trans-mission of Ideas in the Lutheran Reformation* (Worcester, 1989), pp. 141–72.

of course, there were no organs to support them. The pastor knew exactly whom to count on: Gervaise's daughter, Jeanne, who lived with the Monets, another woman and two men.[29] In Calvinist Hungarian churches, too, the laity found Marot's psalm melodies uncomfortable and at the beginning simply too difficult. In the end, psalm singing was completely abolished.[30]

If the laity was able to identify with texts and melodies and knew them well, they did, on the other hand, sing passionately and singing would create a strong sense of community. In English churches, for example, typically only between 4 and 10 melodies were ever used. They were only three lines long, followed a simple rhythm and relied on little variation and standardised cadences.[31] Spiritual singing outside the church became increasingly popular in many parts of Europe. It was less intimidating, and simple songs could easily be memorised. Hymn-books offered an enormous range of 'joyous' or comforting songs, which even pious servants and labourers would pick up from their mistresses and masters at work. They were sung in fields, during long journeys on foot or in coaches. The repertoire of these hymns changed and expanded with time: during the crisis years between 1580 and the end of the Thirty Years War in 1648, for instance, many hymns about war, plague, want and human misery articulated the fears of the time and tried to offer comfort.[32] Other seventeenth-century hymns related to specific regional experiences, such as the dangers connected to living near the sea or in mountainous areas, or they commented on problems associated with the life-cycle or work. They were thus attuned to the needs of different groups of the laity and could serve specific purposes, i.e. to ward off the devil, or to ask for good harvest weather or for marital fertility. It was easy to understand them as a direct way to communicate with God and to demand favours. Together with prayers they expressed people's existential feelings and could help them to manage their lives. Illness and dying, for instance, were accompanied by singing, and the middle and upper classes often chose the songs they wanted to be sung at their funeral long before they died. Huguenot campaigners sang happily about their salvation in eternal life. Fear about whether or not they belonged to the elect apparently played no role in their song culture.[33] Their melodies were often borrowed from popular

---

[29] Alastair Duke, Gillian Lewis and Andrew Pettegrew (eds.), *Calvinism in Europe 1540–1610. A Collection of Documents* (Manchester, 1992), p. 50.

[30] Graeme Murdoch, *Calvinism on the Frontier 1600–1660, International Calvinism and the Reformed Church in Hungary and Transvlvania* (Oxford, 2000), p. 166.

[31] Watt, *Cheap Print*, pp. 57–66.   [32] Veit, *Das Gesangbuch*, pp. 435–55.

[33] Barbara Diefendorf, *Beneath the Cross, Catholics and Huguenots in Sixteenth-Century Paris* (New York/Oxford, 1991), p. 141.

songs: *Dame d'Orleans ne pleurez plus* was turned into *Pauvres papistes retournez vous* and sung at street marches alongside psalms. In England, godly ballads, such as one about the 'Dream of a sinner matyred by Satan' (1624) conveyed an upbeat version of justification by faith alone to the sound of a dancing song called 'Rogero'.[34] A pious patriotic song 'Prepare ye the plough' used the tune of another popular song, called 'Pepper is black', and the equally popular melody of a song entitled 'Row well, ye Mariners' featured several times. Such English spiritual ballads depicted errors as human and provided a generous religious ethic; they also introduced few changes to medieval notions of Christian living and dying. From 1570 onwards, ballads were increasingly pushed aside, however, as they were regarded as man-made and psalms as infinitely superior.

Calvin himself regarded psalm singing as a form of public prayer; its tunes had to be created by divinely inspired, chosen musicians. He emphasised that psalms were to be sung not only in church, but everywhere. Singing led to a depth of joy and feeling, which manifested itself in the whole human being. Thus, the pious could attain a special connection with the divine and almost taste their heavenly state as elect. Once more we therefore need to register how Calvinism regarded the civilised body and soul, and not just the mind, as spiritually interlinked with the divine. This also explains why Calvin thought that no organ or other instruments should distract from this experience of pure singing. Tunes and harmonies ideally were plain, 'serious and clear' and had *majesté*. Psalm singing was yet another, and crucial, manifestation of a faith which set out to recognise reasonable emotions and cultivate them in such a way that they fitted into a deeply spiritualised ethos of civility that promised transcendence.

Material culture

In which places were psalms sung and sermons listened to? What did Protestant houses look like? Such simple questions about Protestant material culture are rarely posed. They are nonetheless extremely important, because material 'things' were interlinked with certain kinds of behaviour and religious identities. Church benches, for instance, made it much more likely that people would stay for a whole service. Protestant material culture, moreover, helped to root these new religions in everyday life. It enshrined notions of 'typically' Protestant ways of behaviour, by creating a sense that 'things were now like this' and different from other confessions. Material culture, in short, helped to symbolise a new faith.

---

[34] Watt, *Cheap Print*, pp. 57–66.

Clothes worn by Protestant clergymen, for example, helped to fabricate the authority of a social group no longer considered as sacred. A considerable extent of cultural work was invested in clarifying questions such as how elegantly they could be dressed or what kind of decorations were appropriate in churches, and thus in drawing social and symbolic boundaries. These, of course, remained flexible and contested among Protestants, and so a whole spectrum of material cultures ensued. This means that we need to consider Protestantism as the most important cultural movement since the Renaissance and alongside the Catholic Renewal: it created new visual and musical traditions, a new culture around the Word, novel architectural elements and festive customs. It changed people's interior decoration from London to Malmü and introduced a very particular social group with a distinctive lifestyle in towns and villages: the parson with his family and household.

Let us, first of all, turn to churches. Cranach's altar paintings became hugely influential in Germany and Scandinavia, and ideas of transformation and salvation were made concrete through their visual language. The Weimar altar-piece even depicted Cranach himself between John the Baptist and Luther under the Cross, and a later addition to the painting showed a flow of blood from Christ's wounds blessing Cranach's head. Figures of death and the devil were rendered with dramatic realism in the background – Lutheranism, the painting told the onlooker, would overcome their power, but once more it could not but thereby turn them into such striking enemies.[35]

Calvinist, Reformed traditions are usually associated with whitewash everywhere, covering medieval wall paintings and bright colours. Whitewash once more tends to be seen as typical of a rational, austere religion, pitting itself against the senses. Such a position, however, wrongly assumes that white was a symbolically neutral colour. What we need to ask is what meaning Reformed people at the time gave to this colour. White was certainly regarded as a colour full of high spiritual and sensual qualities, as was the light which ideally would flood into the house of the Lord 'purely', that is through unstained glass windows, and reflect from white walls. The colour white and heavenly light were the very materials found to mediate a superior form of sacredness. A Reformed church inaugurated in the Hungarian town of Bekecs in 1625 displayed four windows and undecorated columns.[36] The inauguration sermon proudly referred to the white walls as symbolising the purifying power

[35] Joseph Leo Koerner's book, *The Reformation of the Image* (Chicago, 2004) discusses Cranach's art in particularly interesting ways.
[36] Murdoch, *Calvinism on the Frontier*, pp. 153f.

of Christ's blood and of the Holy Ghost to wash away the sins of repentant believers. White could thus even be seen as the most powerful spiritual colour which materialised salvation. And here, white was not just a plain white, but connected to the redness of Christ's blood, which could turn into white. This mode of perception seems strange to us now, but it made sense within cultures which for centuries had taken for granted that matter could transform mysteriously. White, moreover, would remind people of repentance and tears – and the latter were materially linked to the water bound in colour. White was therefore by no means an ascetic, bland colour, but could be ascribed sensual and sacred properties in a characteristically Reformed manner. The Bekecs sermon surprisingly even suggested that church decoration could emanate a quasi-sacramental efficacy: to be in this room meant to be put in touch sensually with the proposition that sins could be 'washed away'. White had to be connected to repentance, purity and salvation already in medieval traditions, and several monastic orders had already begun to emphasise the power of pure light and simple church spaces without side chapels. These elements now dominated Calvinism and were interlinked with the Reformed notion of an aesthetic of worship which would materially and mysteriously connect the laity with the experience of salvation. Despite the whitewash over medieval frescoes, incidentally, nearly every Hungarian church 'made some effort to decorate its ceilings, pews or galleries,'[37] with beautiful ornamental flower paintings or striking naïve renderings of angels, Adam and Eve and symbol-laden animals.

Protestant churches were either newly built or existing buildings were taken over. What we need to ask is what happened in them as they were used, and how social and political factors could influence their use. Contemporary paintings of churches by Emmanuel de Witte, Gerrit Beckheyde and Pieter Saenredam provide us with interesting clues in regard to Dutch Reformed churches (figure 21). Immediately, we register with surprise that we are not seeing sparsely decorated buildings here either. Graffiti were spread on columns, windows and walls were adorned with biblical words. Coats of arms and flags decorated walls, and elegant chandeliers hung from ceilings. High, light spaces drew the gaze towards the sky and its changing appearance; they connected parishioners with heaven, the imagined seat of the divine. And people, it seems, often had to look up rather than straight ahead, for we see many men wearing high hats in the pews, which must have somewhat impaired the congregation's view. But meanwhile, far from everybody was seated, so that there would

---

[37] George Starr, Art and Architecture in the Hungarian Reformed Church, in Paul Corby Finney (ed.), *Seeing Beyond the Word, Visual Arts and the Calvinist Tradition* (Grand Rapids, 1999), pp. 321.

Figure 21. Emmanuel de Witte, *The Interior of the Oude Kerk*, 1651.

have been a permanent coming and going. Church pews were only introduced slowly after the Middle Ages, and sometimes people were asked
to bring their own chairs. The paintings also depict people listening to
the sermon with their dogs, which no doubt would sniff each other out,
and, presumably, occasionally bark and run about. Babies and children
of all ages were a further part of a congregation's soundscape. In sum it
seems then that church services were not quiet affairs and it must have
been hard to focus one's attention solely on a parson.

Putting together such evidence from art with historical findings, it is
indeed easy to verify that Dutch Reformed churches were only radically
cleansed after 1787.[38] Before then, here, as in many other places, one
usually did not invest the money to order new windows, and instead
simply cut out depictions of the Virgin Mary or God. Organs likewise often remained in Reformed churches and retained their decorations, just as pews might retain medieval wood carvings of the heads of
animals, monks or nuns. In the countryside in particular, overseers of
churches or noble families, who were themselves not Reformed, often
sabotaged change. Wealthy Protestants everywhere had elaborate family
tombs built in side chapels of larger churches. Citizens imitated aristocrats
and invented colourful coats of arms for themselves which they placed in
Reformed churches, even if they were not full members of the church (see
pp. 136–9). Important town churches, moreover, operated as a space for
civic self-representation, and were used by guilds, the town council and
other corporate bodies. Especially during cold, dark seasons or during
hot summers, churches became a communal meeting point. The so-
called *Wandelkerk* was a part of the church permanently used by Dutch
citizens for *wandelingen*, that is, to wander about, even during the services. Reformed congregations protested frequently about disturbances.
Hungarian visitations complained about yet another use of churches: in
villages, churches doubled as a space in which to dry meat or to store
wheat, in which mice might nest.

Moreover, we know that congregations which now increasingly were
seated constantly mulled over one question: did their seat correspond to
the social rank they either held or aspired to within their community?
Seats closest to the altar were best. Ruling members of local society or
elders were in any case given separate, wider and more comfortable seats.
Men sat separately from women on the privileged right-hand side. All

---

[38] C. A. van Swingen *et al.* (eds.), *Een huis voor het Word, Het protestantse kerkinterieur in
Nederland tot 1900* (The Hague/Zeist, 1984); Judith Pollmann, The Cleansing of the
Temples. Church Space and its Meanings in the Dutch Republic, in José Pedro Paiva
(ed.), *Religious Ceremonials and Images. Power and Social Meaning (1400–1750)* (Coimbra,
2002), pp. 177–90.

further details of the seating order had to be fixed precisely, and even so there was continual fighting about it. Church-going thus served in part to negotiate and mark social geographies within a parish.

For the same reason, Sunday dress was not just worn to honour the Lord, but to demonstrate a person's rank and perhaps increase his or her social capital. Even maidservants would make sure that their dresses and caps were washed and well ironed, since attending church and looking neat might secure them a better future position, or, better still, the attention of handsome journeymen, who might marry them. Which clothes could be worn in church remained contested; Calvinist preachers in Amsterdam and elsewhere certainly condemned any satin, velvet and brocade they spotted, even if it was black. Still, all over northern Europe, churches quite simply were the most important space where both sexes and all ranks regularly met and accordingly church-going had social and profane functions, which once again would always influence how much people concentrated on the Word (figure 22).

Which symbols decorated the exterior of churches? Many Hungarian churches (and also the one in Bekecs) used a cock as a weather vane from the early seventeenth century onwards. This was an anti-Catholic statement, alluding to St Peter's lies that he did not know Jesus. In northern Germany and the Netherlands a swan became a widespread symbol. The Lutheran church in Den Haag made up for its minority status by placing four swans on its church tower. Swans were associated with Luther, who had famously said that he would forever 'sing' like one, and never be silenced by the Papacy. Placed on churches, swans were expected to protect communities against storms, hail and fire. In fact, the swan generally became one of the most popular Protestant symbols.[39] Thus, even an English seventeenth-century emblematic broadsheet to be used for private meditation depicted a swan and had written below it 'Oh the pure consciousness sings until the last hour'. In Lutheran churches, portraits of the reformer with the swan were – and still are – common; they decorated medals, which were collected by elites, and beakers which were used by broad sections of society in their daily lives.

This takes us to the topic of how domestic goods, such as ceramics and stove-ceramics, became part of Protestant material culture, and once more archaeologists produce fascinating findings. Stoves were a technological invention of the fifteenth and sixteenth centuries and spread from Germany to wealthy households in other countries. They were typically introduced by migrant merchants, and hence are represented in

---

[39] Katalog Lutherhalle Wittenberg, *Luther mit dem Schwan, Tod und Verklärung eines großen Mannes* (Berlin, 1996).

Figure 22. Church decoration in Reformed Fife, Scotland.

all English coastal towns and all Baltic towns trading with Hanse cities. Fifteenth-century tiles often depicted saints. Already the Hussites began to produce different images, while sixteenth-century tiles in the south of England or the Baltic regions were imported from Germany and now offered a standard Lutheran iconography: the reformers (mostly Luther and Melanchthon), Apostles and Protestant rulers, among whom Philip of Hesse and John Frederick of Saxony were particularly popular. Tiles which were produced in Lübeck reached as far north as Stockholm and Turku. Thus we can trace how a Protestant culture of home decoration emerged which transcended cultural boundaries.[40] Once more it is easy to see that heroic rulers and reformers occupied the former place of saints.

Wealthy people not only invested in stoves, but more generally in interior decoration. Late sixteenth-century Amsterdam, for instance, was economically booming, and Reformed citizens were far from merely accumulating savings or investing capital in their businesses. They bought houses, art, precious books, furniture made of tropical woods, Turkish rugs, silver and china. Religious books had become valuable objects of veneration and were exhibited as such. Reformed citizens, moreover, owned as many paintings as Catholics. Only what they depicted differed. Thus, 48 Antwerp Calvinists who were interrogated by the Inquisition

[40] David Gaimster, Pots, Prints and Propaganda: Changing Mentalities in the Domestic Sphere 1480–1580, in D. Gaimster and R. Gilchrist (eds.), *The Archaeology of the Reformation 1480–1580* (Leeds, 2003), pp. 122–44.

between 1567 and 1577 owned a total of 249 paintings, about half of which depicted Old or New Testament themes.[41] They visually endorsed how much their owners related to the Bible. Calvin himself approved of such paintings illustrating biblical scenes. In the French town of Metz, however, seventeenth-century Protestants possessed fewer overtly religious paintings than Catholics did. Interestingly, the view of Geneva had become an art object. But most popular were genre paintings, depicting courtesans, the *Four Seasons*, *Five Senses*, or *Twelve Months*. But these could also be seen in religious terms, since an understanding of how to use the *Five Senses* properly was fundamental to a Reformed person's belief.[42] Genre paintings of prostitutes clearly had become a way to illustrate one's adherence to a moral Christian lifestyle. The relative lack of 'directly' religious themes thus does not point to a more secularised attitude of Calvinists to everyday life, but on the contrary to its more direct spiritualisation. And the widespread ownership of images reminds us once again that even Calvinism must not be exclusively characterised as a religion of the Word; it was not necessarily hostile to images or even 'visually anorexic'.

Parish and clergy

What was the life of Protestant pastors like and which cultural techniques were used to lend weight to their status? Celibacy no longer distinguished these men from ordinary citizens, since all Lutheran clergy and usually Reformed ministers as well were married. Catholics had been attacked for their lack of learning and for hiding the truth from the laity for centuries. Protestants therefore needed to cultivate their own appearance as learned men whom the laity needed in order to hear the truth, live in the proper faith and thus reach eternity. Studies, libraries, thick, open folio volumes with foreign alphabets thus constituted the cultural materials with which Protestant clergymen demonstrated their authority. Quiet hours in the study visibly formed part of their routine. In fact, however, the knowledge of rural German pastors until the seventeenth century rarely reached beyond a basic knowledge of classical languages and of fundamental doctrines as explained in catechisms. Establishing their credentials thus required considerable cultural work; pastors needed to know how to bluff and how to fashion themselves as figures of spiritual

---

[41] Guido Marnef, The Changing Face of Calvinism in Antwerp, 1555–1585, in Duke, Lewis and Pettegree, *Calvinism in Europe*, p. 155.

[42] Philip Benedict, *The Faith and Fortunes of France's Huguenots, 1600–85* (Aldershot, 2001), pp. 198–202.

authority.[43] At its most basic level, a parson's credentials depended on his masculinity – the Protestant church never discussed at any length whether women might legitimately preach. For common people, however, manhood required a certain maturity. Theology graduates thus usually spent several years of their lives as single private teachers or in low positions in church. They would become pastors around the age of thirty, but even then their authority was not necessarily secure. This helps to explain why most Protestant clergymen wore beards. Men around Calvin wore them pointed and elegantly trimmed, like the reformer himself; clergymen in Hungary, England or Germany preferred them to be long and full. This made them look older and wiser, like Hebrew patriarchs or prophets depicted in contemporary paintings. Lutheran village pastors complained that peasants did not value clergymen without proper beards: 'It is not rare for a pastor to imagine that he has no authority and carries no respect without having a long, big beard', one commentator observed in 1691.[44] Moreover, Protestant pastors, and especially Calvinists, embodied their spiritual ethos through their body weight. Being relatively slim – neither fat, nor too thin – distanced them from the image of fat monks and Catholic priests who harvested the fruit of others' labour, which polemics had cultivated for a long time. Also, a fat belly was believed to rule over the mind and higher senses, while thinness marked out people who were too scholarly and enclosed, not rooted in the materiality of life, in the social and physical processes which making food and drink, acquiring food and drink, cooking, eating and digesting entailed, which *made* men and man. The clergy's clothing was equally meaningful. German seventeenth-century church ordinances prescribed that 'theological' dress should be worn – but what exactly was meant by this? Bodily contours and any tactile sensuousness were to be hidden, just as elaborate details and unnecessary luxury were to be avoided. Clothing, in short, crucially symbolised the clerical ethos of civility. At the same time, communities did not like pastors' families to be buttoned up in drab colours. This showed that they were mean or removed from normal life. All light or bright colours, on the other hand, could not possibly convey dignity. Parsons therefore mostly appeared in long, black robes, which have since proved to be one of the longest-lasting types of professional apparel in the Western world. Before this kind of standardisation and

---

[43] The most comprehensive work on German pastors is Luise Schorn-Schütte, *Evangelische Geistlichkeit in der Frühen Neuzeit. Deren Anteil an der Entfaltung frühmoderner Staatlichkeit und Gesellschaft* (Gütersloh, 1996).

[44] Hans-Christoph Rublack, 'Der wohlgeplagte Priester': Vom Selbstverständnis lutherischer Geistlichkeit im Zeitalter der Orthodoxie, *Zeitschrift für Historische Forschung*, 1 (1989), pp. 19f.

a shared understanding of which everyday clothes could be worn were reached, Hungarian and Transylvanian synods, for instance, tried to lay down several times which clothes and shoes were permissible, how hair should be grown and whether wigs were acceptable. They only allowed men to wear low heels (!), since pastors were not to resemble courtiers or soldiers. Foreign fashion, gold jewellery and fur linings were prohibited. Any references to Ottoman clothing were to be avoided as well: no family member was allowed to wear short sheepskin, or red or yellow boots.[45] Across Europe, then, proper, 'civil' forms of behaviour were believed to manifest themselves in clothing, and even the physical movements which generously cut, modest dress allowed helped to represent the truth and authority of Protestantism in everyday life.

Being a parson nonetheless remained far from easy. Most of the clergy worked in the countryside and their parishioners had clear expectations of them. Uneducated laymen certainly did not restrain themselves if they thought that a clergyman did too little or demanded too much, and would even pay scribes to appeal to secular authorities for support. Let us look at the example of a small Saxon parish called Ringleben.[46] In 1564, the community, its pastor Phillip Schmidt, the duke and his church council exchanged a flood of letters. Schmidt allegedly held no catechism classes, parishioners complained. He treated children roughly. Confessions easily annoyed him, and he got upset instead of giving people friendly advice or trying to understand them. He asked 'unnecessary' questions about Lutheran doctrine and demanded that laypeople were familiar with basic principles of faith before absolving them. He only collected the tithe when cereal prices were high, and did not even contribute his own share of cereals to pay for the parish cowherd.

Naturally, the pastor saw things very differently. The children, he replied, were too lazy to come to catechism classes. Several parishioners had neither confessed nor attended communion for years. The parish wanted just a mild, sweet 'honey'-preacher. The task of any confession time had to be to distinguish between those who truly repented what they had done and those who needed to be admonished. Schmidt also claimed that he had to beg to get the tithe and that the community had reduced his farmland.

Both lists of complaints point to the importance of property, which crucially determined people's relationship with their clergy before and after the Reformations. Pastors and all other church officials were usually

---

[45] Murdoch, *Calvinism on the Frontier*, p. 232.

[46] R. W. Scribner, Pastoral Care and the Reformation in Germany, in R. W. Scribner and Lyndal Roper (eds.), *Religion and Culture in Germany (1400–1800)* (Leiden 2001), pp. 172–95.

paid for by the community. Old conflicts about the tithe, about special fees charged for baptisms and other services, and about the land which pastors were allowed to farm continued. In contrast to Catholic priests, Protestant clergymen usually had to support whole families and left widows behind when they died. If people paid for the clergy and in support of their families perhaps sometimes more than before, they also had clear demands. They wanted sermons against hailstorms, regularly held sermons which did not relentlessly castigate sinners, and generous absolutions. Parsons were thus faced with several problems. To what extent should they insist on basic doctrinal knowledge in order to absolve someone and approve her or him as a Protestant Christian? Should one continue to teach the catechism even though people were not much interested in it? Low literacy rates in any case required a focus on memorising if one wished to achieve anything.

By the seventeenth century, this structurally difficult relationship between pastors and their laity in Germany got more difficult still. The clergy now predominantly came from urban bourgeois families. A pastor's father was usually a pastor himself, or a lawyer-bureaucrat serving urban councils and territorial rulers. Wives came from similar backgrounds. The clergy therefore were solidly part of a middling culture, but nonetheless entertained a 'special spiritual understanding' of their social role. They revived the medieval notion that society was composed of three social orders – one to govern, one to fight, one to pray – and thus defended its right to criticise all other social groups. Rural pastors, and hence the majority of clergymen, meanwhile were chronically underfunded. Parishes only reluctantly paid their dues and tried to avoid paying any special fees. The clergy were therefore forced to use their farmland more intensely. But for most pastors, preparedness to plough fields, sow them and put dung on them, that is, to be like peasants, had dwindled. This meant that they were more dependent on villagers to work for them. Urban clergymen were usually financed by other sources, such as the council, and this reduced economic conflicts. Villagers, however, had no choice but to accept the clergy's economic privileges. Often relationships hardened, although a parson's threat not to bury a person honourably who was unwilling to help or pay him usually worked wonders. In many places, pastors and their parishes found ways to accommodate their interests and mutual expectations. This meant that pastors could be 'different' from normal people, but had to refrain from getting involved in all political fights and delicate issues in village life. A good parson was supposed to have some spiritual depth, and to lead a modest, pious life and take care of the cure of souls jointly with his wife. Discipline, indoctrination and admonishing sermons only had a limited place in this scheme. The clergy were expected to understand that people were unable to memorise sermons or catechisms. A parson was paid by peasants to mediate between them and God; he was expected to adjust to parish needs and to adapt his notion of piety and superstition largely to theirs.

Discipline and virtues

Clergymen who knew when to compromise and understood the realities of people's everyday lives therefore were most likely to achieve at least some success in Christian education. These compromises, however, were often substantial. Charles Perrot, for instance, had been a pastor in a rural parish near Geneva, and left his successor the following advice: all communicants were required to be present at weddings and baptisms, though Perrot conceded that 'in practice' he often needed to drop this demand, as long as they attended the catechism class afterwards. Breastfeeding mothers could only be expected to try to attend catechism classes. Perrot recommended using an hourglass during services and related that he always finished promptly when the last corn dropped to avoid irritation. Holding sermons on Thursdays was difficult, because everyone worked in the fields. Thus, services needed to be brief and only the head of household could be expected to attend. Perrot likewise tolerated many men leaving after he had blessed the congregation and talked business in the graveyard next to the church. He no longer based sermons on more difficult biblical passages and generally preferred to refer to catechisms rather than to Scripture itself. Catechism classes took place on Sundays, lasted ninety-five minutes and above all had to be attended by children and servants. First of all, the Ten Commandments would be sung. Then Perrot read the Lord's Prayer. He did not even start talking about the sacraments. His main concern was not to confuse people. He therefore briefly set out the main articles of the catechism in a simplified form and got everyone to repeat them twice. During summer time, children sat outside in the evenings and were taught to repeat prayers 'nicely'. All adults were examined before Easter, and in principle only those who knew key doctrines were allowed to participate in communion. Perrot's tactic was to frighten men somewhat in order to make them learn anything at all – they had to be able at least to repeat a summary of the Ten Commandments speedily. Those with a feeble memory (and everybody who claimed to be affected) nonetheless had to be treated leniently. People who had shown some effort were also admitted to communion. In the end, even those who did not seem to care about doctrine but turned up for communion were usually admitted, unless they were known to have committed grave sins. For those willing to do better, Perrot had designed a short catalogue of questions and answers, which went like this:

Q. What is faith?

A: Faith is a firm assurance that God, for love of his son Jesus Christ, extends his grace towards us.
Q. How can we have that assurance?
A: Through the power of the Holy Spirit, in the preaching of the Gospel.
Q. What is the Gospel?
A. Good news.
Q. What does it contain?
A. The letter of the grace of God in Jesus Christ his son, of which baptism and the Lord's Supper are the two seals.
Q. What does the word 'baptism' mean?
A. Washing.
Q. What does the word 'supper' mean?
A. A meal.

This is what one strove for year by year and throughout one's life as much as possible. Clearly, Calvinist doctrine was only conveyed in very loose terms. And one did not even get people to start thinking about what, for instance, the Holy Ghost might be.[47]

But what is important about this revealing source from around 1560 is not to diagnose a 'failure' of Reformed zeal, but to note that Perrot and his parishioners got along well and that he was a young man full of talent and potential, who was to teach at the Genevan Academy in future years. Calvinism clearly was not necessarily an intellectual faith of urban elites. Parishioners knew that Perrot was a conscientious preacher, who did not look down on them. He visited the dying and made sure that the sick were prayed for. He looked after all his other duties reliably and helped to keep children busy on Sundays. He knew how to achieve respect without insisting on a rigid order. We do not know how rigorously he prosecuted sins and referred culprits to the Genevan consistory. But it has to be assumed that in this respect, too, he adjusted to communal norms and only gave notice of notorious cases of drunkenness, adultery or swearing. Repentant sinners would then be readmitted to communion. Compared to medieval Catholicism, people even saved on wax candles and pilgrimage expenses.

Generally, the efficiency of church discipline depended on the readiness of each community to report offences. If church and secular officials

---

[47] This source is printed in Duke, Lewis and Pettegree, *Calvinism in Europe*, pp. 48f.

and elite families cooperated well in smaller communities, church courts could certainly become a formidably repressive tool. They usually targeted the poor and their 'immoral' behaviour, above all their sexual licentiousness, even though this largely resulted from the fact that poor people could not afford to become citizens, form a household of their own and support children. Were these campaigns successful? Illegitimacy remained relatively rare, but 'immoral' courtship and sexual practices hardly changed. The Basle marriage court persistently punished these offences throughout the sixteenth and seventeenth centuries, but even so, its case-load rose.[48] Tough disciplining could not be seen to purify society; rather, it revealed how much understandings of sin diverged.

In the long run, church courts usually were only successful if they prosecuted persistent 'sinners' who offended widely accepted communal moral norms and if they dealt with citizens' everyday quarrels. A powerful 'moral tradition', which had established itself during the Middle Ages, linked Christianity above all to the command to love one's neighbours, to forgive sins and to live in peace.[49] This was a precarious aim, because early modern families and neighbours endlessly quarrelled about property, power and privileges. They expressed conflicts loudly and clearly, by throwing hats, grabbing hair and pulling plaits. Women across Europe insulted each others as whores, and men as thieves. Afterwards they needed to re-establish their reputation, which influenced how much other people trusted them. Trust in turn influenced their economic and social status, for this was a society in which people had no access to health insurance and bank credits. People depended on each other's help. Church courts and elders therefore were kept busy as long as they merely mediated between those who had quarrelled, restored the honour of all parties and asked for no or only modest fines. But despite such persistent court interventions in many places, there is no evidence that Protestants started quarrelling in a more civilised way or feeling guilty about their insults during the sixteenth and seventeenth centuries. Conflicts were part of life. In a large city like Amsterdam church councillors were thus faced with constant complaints about petty insults 'of little worth': *kwesties en krakelen von kleine waarde*.[50] New citizens trying to build up an existence typically lived crowded in temporary accommodation

---

[48] Susanna Burghartz, *Zeiten der Reinheit, Orte der Unzucht. Ehe und Sexualität während der Frühen Neuzeit* (Paderborn, 1999).

[49] John Bossy, *Peace and the Counter-Reformation* (Cambridge, 1998).

[50] Herman Roodenburg, *Onder Censuur. De kerklijke tucht in de gereformeerde gemeente van Amsterdam, 1578–1700* (Hilversum, 1990).

in back alleys and used the courts to insist on their respectability, by asking to be 'purified' after quarrels. In the end, insults were taken back,
women exchanged a kiss of peace and everybody was willing to break the
bread together again at communion. Forgiveness and community, rather
than relentless discipline and individual guilt, were central to Christian
identity.

For the same reason, Calvinist consistory courts, as in Geneva, should
not be described as a 'counselling service' in the modern sense.[51] People
used session hearings as a platform to describe family conflicts and problems in the neighbourhood; they might dramatise their feelings and probably were enabled to release their potential for love and forgiveness within
the mediation process. But no proper, individual therapeutic understanding was offered. The consistory certainly helped people to transcend their
resentment and frustration and to accept their lives; it dealt with some
deeply depressed people, but it never tried to look for individual causes
of problems or individual solutions. It tried, above all, to get people to
behave 'peacefully' within their household and community, that is, to fit
into the status quo.

This is equally true for the ways in which marital problems, on the
whole, were dealt with by Protestants. Protestantism is often regarded
as a more modern religion than Catholicism because it introduced
divorce, but records of marriage courts reveal that divorce was hardly
ever granted.[52] Couples were held together until their death, even if husbands were persistently violent. Society was based on the lives of men,
women and children being organised by the institutions of marriage and
the family, and so marriage was not to be questioned; destitute families
without a father to support them were unwanted.[53] Luther himself had
never intended to introduce the possibility of a divorce to further individual freedom – he merely thought that it corresponded to biblical law.
Luther, Calvin and other Protestant reformers unanimously agreed that
women were to be their husbands' helpmates, and pastors' wives were
to be their model. Notions of partnership remained firmly embedded
within a patriarchal world-view characteristic of the period: men were
still allowed to beat 'quarrelsome' wives, for instance, and girls would be

---

[51] See the argument of Robert M. Kingdon, The Genevan Consistory in the Time of
Calvin, in Duke, Lewis and Pettegree, *Calvinism in Europe*, pp. 21–34.

[52] See Robert M. Kingdon, *Adultery and Divorce in Calvin's Geneva* (Cambridge, Mass.,
1995) and Ulinka Rublack, *The Crimes of Women in Early Modern Germany* (Oxford,
1999), ch. 6; Joel Harrington, *Re-ordering Marriage and Society in Reformation Germany*
(Cambridge, 1995).

[53] A crucial book about gender and the Reformation is Lyndal Roper, *The Holy Household.*
Women, Sex and Morals in Early Modern Augsburg (Oxford, 1989).

treated as harshly for incestuous sexual abuse as men, since women were believed to be the more desirous sex. On the other hand, wives whose reputation was unblemished were often successful in prosecuting husbands who beat them 'for no reason', drank and wasted money, as this fitted into the authorities' goal of creating stable, 'godly' and tax-paying households. Single women were generally regarded with scepticism and those who were pregnant and not, or not yet, married were dealt with harshly. There were no 'holy' women in convents any longer and no whores in civic brothels either. All women were to fulfil their 'office' as mother, wife and co-worker in 'holy households' – even the Virgin Mary now retarded into a sole symbol of a good housewife and mother, and assumed her place far behind God and Christ in the hierarchy of veneration. As Protestantism preached that all sexual desire was to be domesticated in the family, telling pathologies evolved, such as the artist Lukas Cranach the Elder's more and more obsessively voyeuristic depictions of Lucretia, Venus and Judith in see-through dresses, their eyes fixed on the onlooker. Cranach painted these at the same time as his workshop turned out small double portraits of Martin and Käthe Luther for bourgeois interiors across northern Europe in large quantities. Protestants defined narrowly what it meant to be a man or a woman, and generally did not allow for passionate and playful, let alone queer experiences.[54] But as the enticements of lust were described and demonised over and over again, they were lent a presence which had to be dealt with.

This dynamic partly explains why the image of the witch became so powerful during the sixteenth century, and was feared by Protestants as much as by Catholics. The witch was the opposite of a young housewife and mother. She did not nourish but poisoned those around her; she was envious and demanding, a woman who killed infants, not subservient, but a woman who acted as it pleased her. The witch often controlled men, and entered a world of dance, food and pleasure at night. Protestantism defined itself not least through fighting against this figure. Her male equivalent was the heretical and greedy Jew.

An impressive example of this is a stained glass window which the city of Nuremberg commissioned in 1598, representing the victory of Christian liberty (figure 23).[55] Liberty sat on clouds, her opened Bible promising *Verbum Domini manet in aeternum*. The city's coat of arms was

---

[54] For a nuanced discussion see Susan Karant-Nunn, 'Fragent Wedding Roses': Lutheran Wedding Sermons and Gender Definition in Early Modern Germany, in *German History* (1/1999), pp. 25–40.

[55] The artist was Christoph Murner of Zurich. See Charles Zika, Cannibalism and Witchcraft in Early Modern Europe: Reading the Visual Evidence, *History Workshop Journal*, 44 (1997), pp. 99f.

Figure 23. Christoph Murer, *Allegory on the good government of the city of Nuremberg*, 1597/8, stained glass.

depicted below her, its emblem showed a virgin and an eagle. The battle for liberty which Protestants had won was depicted in the last third of the image. A naked, old witch with sagging breasts and a Jew were torturing an innocent Christian boy. A king was turning a blind eye to the scene. This iconography thus revived the old fantasy of the Jew who magically used the blood of Christian children, linked it to the imaginary threat of witches and created a scene which resembled an inverted holy family. Arguably, it was only because of these fantasies of evil that the purity of a commune made up of pious families and their Protestant, fatherly council could be propagated so effectively.

To end our investigation into Protestant culture, we may profitably turn to Scotland.[56] Here a lively Calvinist tradition evolved, but its practices once more defy the assumption that Calvinism must be characterised principally as a rigorous discipline, or as a rational religion. For in Scotland, as elsewhere in Protestant Europe, rituals remained crucial to mediate faith, answering people's need to deal with guilt as well as their search for forgiveness and salvation. On Sundays, churches would be crowded and attendance was precisely controlled. After services, parishioners would split into groups and read the Bible, sing psalms and learn catechisms. Their doctrinal knowledge would be conscientiously tested. At the same time, sermons were deeply emotional occasions. Pastors and their congregations would weep – hearts were to be moved. Sermons were structured around rhetorical questions inviting the response 'Amen', which involved the community in a dramatic dialogue with God. Christ's crucified body was imagined so vividly in words that they took the place of images. The annual spiritual climax was communion, which was preceded by a time of fasting and anxious meditations on a sinful life. These feelings were collectively expressed and shared, as was the joy about the badges people received once they had confessed and been admitted to communion. Communion sermons were all about salvation and how the sacrament mediated an experience of the Lord. A Glasgow sermon, for instance, promised that all senses, gaze, touch, taste and smell, would be satisfied through partaking in the Eucharist. 'Are your hearts in heaven, Christians? . . . Is it him? Is it him? . . . He whom I saw in prayers and the sacraments?', the preacher then asked. Throughout the year, guilds frequently participated in decorating churches; fishermen donated boats and asked for special blessings; wealthy families built tombs with emblems and religious symbols; thus no white and empty churches are to be found in early modern Scotland either, but decorative elements,

---

[56] See the pioneering study by Margo Todd, *The Culture of Protestantism in Early Modern Scotland* (New Haven, 2002).

which communal groups helped define. Elders regularly punished severe domestic violence, helped to mediate in conflicts, made sure that schools were built, distributed alms and got fathers to pay for the upkeep of their illegitimate children. They were clever enough to be lenient about people's behaviour during festive occasions and fairs, and about leisure pursuits such as dancing, unless there was extreme rowdiness. Nor did they object to dancing, sport and theatre plays on weekdays. People still believed in fairies and visited holy wells in May. And they hunted witches, too.

Epilogue: Towards a cultural history of the Reformation

Historical legends are easily constructed and some of their elements seem to last forever. One of the most powerful legends concerning the Reformation posits that Protestantism was a more rational religion than Catholicism, as it was principally based on a 'logo-centric' use of the Word. Protestantism was pragmatic, anti-sensual and so dependent on reading and intellectual skills that it could not become a truly popular religion. It was mostly supported by elites who increasingly adapted to introspection and individualism – that is, to 'modern' ways of behaving. As a result, Protestantism has been regarded as a 'progressive' religion for a long time, even though historians nowadays more commonly assert that elites, often in alliance with secular authorities, turned Protestantism into a disciplining, repressive faith and thus helped to create a modern self on which we ought to reflect critically.[1]

Much of this book has tried to suggest what is problematic about each of these arguments and how questions inspired by the new cultural history can change our account of what the Reformation was about and which legacies it left. Such an account certainly must question whether an emphasis on the Word rules out any sensual involvement with the world. Early modern notions of the self, it is true, generally held that passions dominated the behaviour of people who were perceived as being closer to 'nature', uneducated folk, women, peasants and 'savages' in particular. Cultured manhood, by contrast, was positively associated with proper uses of rationality and self-control. But these uses of rationality were only thought appropriate because rather than obliterating emotions and the senses they integrated them appropriately. Emotions were not thought to be as destructive as passions, and the senses were, on the whole, similarly seen as vital expressions of mankind. Emotions were to be cultivated, rather than disciplined in a repressive fashion, not least through religious culture. Hence, Protestants would have never conceived of religion

[1] Ronnie Po-Cha Hsia, *Social Discipline in the Reformation: Central Europe 1550–1750* (London, 1989) provides an excellent overview.

192

as something that could possibly be rational and a-sensual, but emphasised their attempt to integrate the senses in ways which they thought were in harmony with the uses destined for them by God. Catholics, they preached, had vulgarised or abused the religious gaze, touch and voice as well as smelling and hearing, and had not allowed for 'evangelical' religious reading. Profoundly influenced by mystical traditions, many Protestants therefore tried to define a new spiritual aesthetics which could involve sensual reading as a process of chewing on words and literally incorporating them or psalm singing as a practice of transcendence. Even Calvin, who nowadays is often regarded as an embodiment of the ascetic, anti-sensual and disciplinarian elements within the reform movements, thus turns out to be a man deeply engaged in working out such aesthetics and making it fit contemporary elite ideals of civility and communality. But individualistic, modern and logo-centric his approach to life was not.

Protestantism, we might sum up instead, generated a whole set of cultural expressions and codes about being in the world rather than simply in the mind. It inspired a rich material culture, which has hardly been surveyed across Europe, or properly explored, and stretches from churches, public buildings, taverns, house decoration, ceramics and glass objects destined for everyday use to appearances, medals, tokens, book bindings, lettering and even a lively trade in reformers' autographs, handwritten items, or seals. I have termed such Protestant materials of memory 'grapho-relics'. All of this means that Protestantism did not do away with culture, as is sometimes suggested, through iconoclasm, whitewashing or a 'visual anorexia', but created its own languages, which we still have to learn to read in many cases, and which hold many surprises. Hence this book has used illustrations to convey some of the ways in which Protestantism was not just a culture of the Word, but of the image and object, and has tried to point out what important visual dimension representations of the Word could gain, so that distinctions between words and images lose their shape. Writing, reading, carrying books, annotating books, the customisation of books through binding and inscriptions, moreover, were full of symbolic meanings which likewise defy any easy connection of literacy merely with the realm of the 'rational'. This point is further strengthened once we reflect on the fact that Protestant elites typically believed that writing, the circulation of manuscripts, book publication and the dissemination of books were their instruments to change the world – or even that God had invented the printing press just for them. A particularly striking expression of this view is a broadsheet published in 1617 to commemorate the centenary of the circulation of Luther's ninety-five theses against the indulgence trade. It was called the 'Dream of Frederick the Wise' and relates a dream Frederick was supposed to have had on the evening before Luther allegedly posted the theses on the door of his castle church (figure 24). The woodcut showed how Luther, by then still a monk, wrote with a huge quill on the church door, a quill which magically grew so long that it reached Rome and made the papal throne tumble. The text explained that Frederick had not only had this dream but another one in which some people had unsuccessfully attempted to break the monk's quill. It had produced other quills, taken up by learned folk, whose quills became as long and hard as the monk's. The broadsheet thus unexpectedly leads us into a mental world in which reading and writing could be motivated by forceful fantasies about leadership and pupillage, knowledge, creation, truth finding, male power and potency. The uses of literacy could be deeply intertwined with the realm of the unconscious and thus with sentiments threatening neat boundaries between passion and emotion, which these men were so eager to draw.

Sweeping generalisations about a Protestant character or culture therefore often turn out to be wrong, and to attempt them we still have to build up a much better and European-wide sense of the Protestant world and its transformations across the early modern period and beyond. This book has tried to show, however, that if we ask about practices, contexts, usages, objects and experience – what people actually *did* and how they perceived their worlds four or five hundred years ago – the history of Reformation Europe and hence a key part of the history of Western civilisation open up in new ways.

I have also found it promising to relate approaches used by historians of science to the history of the Reformation. Like scientific ideas, theological thought is often regarded as something universal and abstracted from life, as something that is 'discovered' by a unique intellect at a given time or to some extent revealed by supernatural powers. *When* and *where* such a person lived seems little to affect the *content* of ideas. And it is more or less the autonomous force of an idea which is then thought to have quickly or gradually convinced others. Over the past twenty years or so, historians of science have powerfully challenged such notions in their field. They argue that, whatever a culture regards as factual, 'true' science is historically 'situated' and local to a considerable extent. Galileo, for instance, gathered influence not just because of his intellect. He knew how to behave at the Medici court in such a way as to attract princely benefaction and generated 'scientific' knowledge glorifying the Medici family.[2] Hence historians of science often seek to show how such locally

---

[2] Mario Biagioli, *Galileo Courtier: The Practice of Science in the Culture of Absolutism* (Chicago, 1993).

Figure 24. Anon., *Dream of Frederick the Wise*, 1617.

relevant knowledge can be turned into a more universally acknowledged truth, especially given the fact that new ideas typically are contested. They identify social strategies of securing trust and loyalty, of training observers and standardising instruments as key factors in this process. What might this mean for how we approach the Reformation? It suggests, first of all, that we might like similarly to try thinking about theological knowledge not as fixed, timeless and universal doctrine, but as one of the ways of thinking about notions of the sacred. This does not diminish the sense that there are 'great' ideas, distinguished by the possibilities they point to of understanding human life as well as by their complexity or simplicity, as the case may be. But it draws attention to the historical and local situation in which ideas are generated and defended as factual and divinely sanctioned knowledge; in other words, it draws attention to the process of how certain understandings were successfully established as being true for some interpretative communities. Dominant Protestant ideas, as this book has shown, were lent authority through a range of cultural techniques: a consensus had to be created and maintained among a group of local followers and in the community; local education facilities had to be built up to socialise students and future preachers coherently into new mindsets and ways of behaving; the dissemination of ideas through print had to be much invested in locally, and so on. We can therefore paraphrase a recent writer on scientific culture in stating that the establishment of Lutheranism, for instance, must thus be considered a social achievement and not the inevitable consequence of some inherent theological essence.[3] Of course, it was a political achievement as well. This is no news for Reformation history: most people interested in it know that the German Reformation movements turned into a 'princely' Reformation, or that reform ideas elsewhere were taken up because of their political use. Social historians of the Reformation have spent much of their time working out how Reformation ideas were received and transformed by different groups in different places. But what this book has tried to bring more sharply into view is how the fact that Lutheranism came into existence in *Wittenberg* and Calvinism in *Geneva* mattered for their content and success. Thus, chapter 1 of this book has suggested that the unique situation of that marginal place Wittenberg with its reform university turned Luther into the man we know of as much as his theological expertise and gift to express himself. 'Locating Luther' means understanding that it was crucial for Luther as he was leaving his convent to take up the identity of a university professor and the tools of academic life

---

[3] David N. Livingstone, *Putting Science in its Place. Geographies of Scientific Knowledge* (Chicago, 2003), p. 83.

to gain credibility for his ideas. The 'religious conversation', which was modelled on principles of academic debates and adapted for Lutheran needs after the famous Leipzig debate in 1519, became the key method of introducing Protestantism in many towns in a formally authoritative, semi-consensual and seemingly 'scholarly' way. Wittenberg University was small and could be structured efficiently so as to make sure that no rival knowledge would be disseminated; and everyone in town knew that they lived better because Dr Luther attracted students from Denmark to Hungary in considerable numbers as well as visitors from far way. The Augustinian monastery, too, was taken over by Luther and filled with his family, students and transient male followers. Luther used this structure of close, communal living to enforce loyalty, to let students feel the privilege of proximity and to bolster his cultic standing, preserved for posterity in his table talk. He behaved like a type anthropologists call 'big man' and in ways a courtly culture could just about accommodate. His monastery was situated at one end of Wittenberg; the ducal castle on the other. This topography and the spaces in which Lutheranism could establish itself locally partly explain why it took the shape it did.[4] Calvin, by contrast, never had a university to draw on. He lived in a large urban community, dominated by merchants. He could never have behaved like a 'big man' and been tolerated by the magistrate. Calvin lived in a townhouse, which is now demolished, like a citizen. In Geneva, and perhaps in part *because* he found himself in Geneva, he ran his Compagnie des Pasteurs like a company: he selected personnel efficiently and so as to ensure consensual agreement and a proper social representation of what the company was about; he closely monitored the work and routine practices, gave mission statements, lobbied for greater political influence and invested in communication and publication networks to spread his influence. Before he died, he designated a successor. All of this fostered coherence and thus a notion of stability, order, civility and lived piety, which, as chapter 3 has argued, did much to make Calvinism convincing as a faith. It should also surprise us little that Calvin, in contrast to Luther, gradually came to defend aristocratic forms of government over monarchies or democracies. Geneva was a republic ruled by elites, and this had made Calvinism possible here; his Compagnie performed so well from 1546 onwards because so many of the pastors were highly educated French men from prominent or even aristocratic families who knew how to take responsibility, involve themselves in Genevan business life and embody civility. The most substantial stronghold of supporters he was in touch with from Geneva in

---

[4] I shall explore these connections more thoroughly in a future research project entitled 'Locating Luther'.

France, Italy and eastern Europe were male and female aristocrats, and they, likewise, could regard Geneva as a model for divinely sanctioned liberty from any overlord. In these different ways, for Luther as for Calvin, *place* seems to have mattered considerably for what they regarded as true and conforming to their religious ideals and which local resources helped them to make these ideas seem true to others.

I have furthermore suggested that masculinity deserves to be given its proper place as a category of historical analysis in Reformation studies. Contemporary notions of manliness were not only interlinked with the psychology of literary production, as the broadsheet about Frederick the Wise's dream intriguingly demonstrates. They also helped to explain why speeches were delivered in particular ways, why Italians could be regarded with scepticism, how reformers created leadership, why pastors wore long beards to gain authority, how racism against Muslims and Jews worked, why Cranach produced newly naturalistic nudes or sexualised monsters alongside pious portraits of the Luther couple and much more. Analysing manliness, above all, forces us to consider how men *thought* of themselves and what motivated their actions, their subjectivity, in short, which is crucial to understanding the age and its religious imagination.

A lot about the European experience of the Reformation remains to be discovered, too, and this is especially true if one turns to the history of Scandinavia and eastern Europe, or wishes to look at the intercultural ties and cultural exchange on which much of the European Reformation rested. Future historical writing about the Reformation, it is to be hoped, will move away from recreating separate national histories for an age in which nations in many ways had no solid political shape yet. It will attend to a period which was surprisingly often influenced by migrants, who, individually, could move from Naples to Gdansk, or, in huge numbers, reshape for periods of time the fate and fortune of cities like Emden or Geneva. We might also want to pay attention to unexplored microhistories of the confessional age and its aftermath, such as that of an 89-year-old educated German man, called Johann Heinrich Horstmann, who was condemned by the Inquisition of Valencia in 1752. Horstmann, a born Catholic, confessed to have been baptised twenty-one times as a Protestant or a Catholic during his life, persuading different authorities that he was converting to their faith! He even had been circumcised in Amsterdam and practised Judaism for eight months, and here, as elsewhere, partly supported himself with the gifts and hospitality he received. On his deathbed, he eventually chose to die as a Calvinist – refusing confession and the last rites of the church. Horstmann was burnt in effigy soon after.[5] Was this man mainly confused or an opportunist, or someone whose anthropological curiosity, perhaps, was more widespread among travellers of his time?

Horstmann's life, in any case, tells us that tolerance and pragmatic, legal ideas about truth finding took a long time to triumph over universalising theological truth claims after the Peace of Westphalia in 1648. For a start, Protestants and Catholics disagreed about time. Pope Gregory XIII had introduced a new calendar in 1582, which most Protestants refused to apply. Only in March 1700, when their calendars already diverged by ten days, could religious (*sic!*) arguments be found which supported the introduction of a unified calendar in the Holy Roman Empire, Denmark, the Dutch Republic and Protestant parts of northern Switzerland. England was the last European country to introduce the new calendar in 1751. For centuries to come there was no linear path towards secularisation of political and social life. The northern Ireland conflict shows that religious allegiance can still influence European politics today. At the very least, then, the Western battle with its Reformations and tolerance teaches us that other systems of belief are best analysed once we have revisited the peculiar history of the Christian imagination itself, its visions of hatred and its visions of forgiveness and love, and the cultural force they were given.

[5] Stephen Haliczer, *Inquisition and Society in the Kingdom of Valencia 1478–1834* (Berkeley, 1990), pp. 286f.

Further reading

I have sought to keep this bibliography short and to indicate further reading on selected mainline topics for students. More specialised readers can turn to my footnotes or will find bibliographies on specific subjects in most of the works listed below. They might also wish to consult the *Archive for Reformation History, Literature Review*, which for more than thirty years has been annually reviewing and indexing articles and monographs in the field.

General studies on Reformation Europe

Diarmaid MacCulloch, *Reformation: Europe's House Divided 1490–1700* (London, 2003) is a recent narrative synthesis on 832 pages and covers a long time span, whereas earlier generations of scholars usually focused on the sixteenth century and particularly on the early Protestant Reformation in Germany and the Swiss Confederation. MacCulloch is a historian of the church who is also interested in social history. James D. Tracy's *Europe's Reformations 1450–1650* (Oxford, 1999) is also engaging and innovative; it discusses war and politics during the period as well as everyday life and non-European Reformations. Andrew Pettegree (ed.), *The Reformation World* (London, 2000) contains a wide range of articles, many of them excellent; and so does the more recently published volume by Ronnie Po-Chia Hsia (ed.), *A Companion to the Reformation World* (London, 2003). Bob Scribner, Roy Porter and Mikuláš Teich (eds.), *The Reformation in National Context* (Cambridge, 1994) provides valuable discussions of different countries and a comparative overview, and can be read in tandem with Andrew Pettegree (ed.), *The Early Reformation in Europe* (Cambridge, 1992). Euan Cameron, *The European Reformation* (Oxford, 1991) now belongs to an older type of Reformation textbook, but is extremely good at presenting German research about the urban Reformation and Lutheranism up to 1555.

Religious thought since the Middle Ages

Steven Ozment, *The Age of Reform 1250–1550. An Intellectual and Religious History of Late Medieval and Reformation Europe* (New Haven, 1980) is a classic; Heiko A. Oberman, *The Dawn of the Reformation* (Edinburgh, 1986) presents the views of one of the most original historians of the Reformation, who died recently; Alistair McGrath, *The Intellectual Origins of the European Reformation* (Oxford, 1987) provides another clearly stated account of the medieval roots of Reformation thought and its new departures. Quentin Skinner, *The Foundations of Modern Political Thought*, vol. II, *The Age of the Reformation* (Cambridge, 1978) shows how religious thought interlinked with ideas about government and resistance.

Radicalism

Michael Baylor (ed.), *The Radical Reformation* (Cambridge, 1991) is an excellent sourcebook of radical thought in German-speaking lands; J. M. Stayer, *The German Peasants' War and Anabaptist Community of Goods* (Montreal, 1991) brilliantly relates part of the story of how these ideas were translated into practice.

Luther and Lutheranism in Germany

Many of the reformer's written or spoken words, including sermons and table talk, can be read in English in J. Pelikan and Hartmut Lehmann (eds.), *Luther's Works: American Edition*, 55 vols. (St Louis, Mo., and Philadelphia, 1955–). Martin Brecht, *Luther*, 3 vols., is the most detailed and factual biography yet; Heiko A. Oberman, *Luther: Man between God and the Devil* (New Haven and London, 1989) brings out well the extreme importance of the devil in Luther's thought. Scott Dixon, *The Reformation in Germany* (Oxford, 2002) is a reliable, up-to-date and wholly fluent recent synthesis. Essays by Robert William (Bob) Scribner show the achievements of the social history of Lutheranism and his pioneering work towards a cultural history of the Reformation, see R. W. Scribner, *Popular Culture and Popular Movements in Reformation Germany* (London, 1987) and *For the Sake of the Simple Folk. Popular Propaganda for the German Reformation* (Oxford, 1981), R. W. Scribner and Lyndal Roper (eds.), *Religion and Culture in Germany (1400–1800)* (Leiden, 2001). Lyndal Roper, *The Holy Household. Women and Morals in Reformation Augsburg* (Oxford, 1989) is a path-breaking book on the role of gender in the Lutheran urban Reformation; two essays in her *Oedipus and the Devil: Witchcraft, Sexuality and Religion in Early Modern Europe* (London, 1994) begin to tackle early modern masculinity and how it related to Reformed ideas.

Calvinism

Calvin's key work is available in a modern edition, John T. McNeill (ed.), *Institutes of Christian Religion*, 2 vols. (Philadelphia, 1960). William J. Bouwsma, *John Calvin: A Sixteenth-Century Portrait* (Oxford, 1988) presents an ambitious and interesting biography. Philip Benedict, *Christ's Churches Purely Reformed. A Social History of Calvinism* (New Haven, 2002) is a recent masterly and thorough synthesis by a social historian; Margo Todd, *The Culture of Protestantism in Early Modern Scotland* (New Haven, 2002) is a path-breaking analysis of Calvinism in everyday life following the approaches of a historical anthropology.

Protestant cultures

Apart from the works of Scribner, Roper, Benedict and Todd, listed above, I find the following monographs particularly pioneering and a great starting point for students interested in early modern religious mentalities: Natalie Zemon Davis, *Society and Culture in Early Modern France* (1965) and *Women on the Margins: Three Seventeenth Century Lives* (1995); Tessa Watt, *Cheap Print and Popular Piety, 1550–1640* (Cambridge, 1991); Alexandra Walsham, *Providence in Early Modern England* (Oxford, 1999); Lee Palmer Wandel, *Voracious Idols and Violent Hands. Iconoclasm in Reformation Zurich, Strasbourg and Basel* (Cambridge, 1994) and David Warren Sabean, *Power in the Blood. Popular Culture and Village Discourse in Early Modern Germany* (Cambridge, 1984). The material and visual culture of the Reformation in early modern everyday life is only slowly being investigated. Apart from Watt, *Cheap Print*, two recent book publications are Paul Corby Finney (ed.), *Seeing Beyond the Word. Visual Arts and the Calvinist Tradition* (Grand Rapids, 1999), which includes excellent illustrations and some interesting discussions, and David Gaimster and Roger Gilchrist (eds.), *The Archaeology of the Reformation 1480–1580* (Leeds, 2003) which shows what can be done.

Index

NEW APPROACHES TO EUROPEAN HISTORY